Felix Sawo

Nonlinear State and Parameter Estimation of Spatially Distributed Systems

Karlsruhe Series on Intelligent Sensor-Actuator-Systems

Volume 5

ISAS | Universität Karlsruhe (TH)
Intelligent Sensor-Actuator-Systems Laboratory

Edited by Prof. Dr.-Ing. Uwe D. Hanebeck

Nonlinear State and Parameter Estimation of Spatially Distributed Systems

von
Felix Sawo

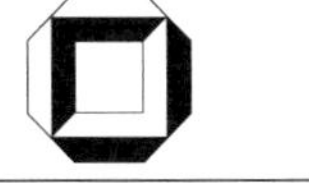

universitätsverlag karlsruhe

Dissertation, Universität Karlsruhe (TH)
Fakultät für Informatik, 2009

Impressum

Universitätsverlag Karlsruhe
c/o Universitätsbibliothek
Straße am Forum 2
D-76131 Karlsruhe
www.uvka.de

Universitätsverlag Karlsruhe 2009
Print on Demand

ISSN: 1867-3813
ISBN: 978-3-86644-370-9

Nonlinear State and Parameter Estimation of Spatially Distributed Systems

zur Erlangung des akademischen Grades eines

Doktors der Ingenieurwissenschaften

der Fakultät für Informatik
der Universität Fridericiana zu Karlsruhe (TH)

genehmigte

Dissertation

von

Felix Sawo

aus Erfurt

Tag der mündlichen Prüfung: 30. 01. 2009

Erster Gutachter: Prof. Dr.-Ing. Uwe D. Hanebeck

Zweiter Gutachter: Prof. Thomas C. Henderson

Acknowlegdements

The work on this thesis was performed during my time as a research assistant at the Intelligent Sensor-Actuator-Systems Laboratory (ISAS) of the Karlsruhe Universität (TH). Working there was a very rewarding experience, with many challenges and hard work, but also a lot fun. This work has benefited from many people over the past three years in various ways, and my gratitude is extended especially to those mentioned below.

First of all I would like to thank **Uwe D. Hanebeck**; he deserves special thanks for his guidance, valuable discussions, and support throughout my research. Without his never ending encouragements this thesis would probably not have been completed in such short time. I am also very grateful to **Thomas C. Henderson** for proof-reading the thesis, having so many fruitful discussions on sensor network issues and especially for inviting me to Utah. Thanks for the confidence he placed into my work and the opportunity to write a chapter in his book on computational sensor networks. It was a great honor to let him win all the basketball matches we had together. To his wife **Joëlle**, thanks for being such patient and strict ski instructor and the great mark in my final exam at "Doyle's Dive". Also I would like to thank **Mandi**, **Gerald**, **Chris**, their **cats** and **poorly behaved dogs** for giving me a lovely home during my research stay in Utah, for the nice trips and for shredding my wallet.

The team at the ISAS have made my time enjoyable and rewarding, in particular by showing interest for each other's problems and sharing ideas. Most of all, I must thank **Dietrich Brunn** for many hours of valuable discussions and endless bright ideas. The many evennings and nights in the laboratory where we wrote papers together, explored rare species such as *second order densities*, and the *lets-meet-in-Munich-and-write-on-our-thesis* trip are unforgetable memories. Special thanks go to **Frederik Beutler**, whose encouragement to help people goes far beyond what one could expect. His endless effort for the Research Training Group made the work for all participants and supervisors much easier, and supported me to complete this thesis in just three years. The chats with him and **Patrick Rößler** about daily occurences in the laboratory before the *sneak-preview nights* will always be a special memory. The development of the Sliced Gaussian Mixture Filter would not have been possible without the support of **Vesa Klumpp**. I am grateful both for many stimulating conversations about on-going research topics and for other entertaining dinner discussions. I also would like to thank **Marco Huber** for fruitful discussions about nonlinear estimation. To **Antonia Pérez Arias**, thanks for providing all of us with enough coffee and the natural happiness she spread in the laboratory. To the remaining PhD students of the ISAS, notably **Marcus Baum**, **Peter Krauthausen**, **Kathrin Roberts**, **Oliver Schrempf**, and **Florian Weißel**, thanks for your company and the enjoyable working conditions. Many thanks go to the students working together with me on several research projects, namely **Rene Gröne**, **Christian Herdtweck**, **Christian Hirsch**, **Julian Hörst**, **Achim Kuwertz**, **Daniel Ota**, **Daniel Seth** and **Eric Stiegeler**.

My life in Karlsruhe would not have been half as fun and many times a lot more difficult, if it had not been for all the friends I met along the way. Most of all, I am deeply in debted to **Dai-Yu Shiu** and **Wolfgang A. Mozart**, two great personalities who gave me so much strength and showed me that classical music is like research: *"difficult to compose, but so nice to listen."* Thanks for your support, distraction from work, and humor — you are an inspiration!

I would also like to take the chance and thank my parents **Uwe** and **Gerlinde**, my grandparents **Josef** and **Elsbeth**, remaining relatives, and friends for believing in me and my ambitions. Without all their constant support this thesis would not have been possible. This thesis is dedicated to my grandfather for his persistence in asking me "have you finished yet."

Karlsruhe, March 2009   Felix Sawo

*in memory of **Josef** (1922–2009)*

Contents

Conventions, Notations, and Glossary

General conventions

$x,\ \underline{x}$	deterministic variable/vector
$\boldsymbol{x},\ \underline{\boldsymbol{x}}$	random variable/vector
$\hat{x},\ \underline{\hat{x}}$	mean value of random variable/vector
$\tilde{x},\ \underline{\tilde{x}}$	realization of random variable/vector
$\mathbf{A}$	general matrix
$\mathbf{A}^T$	matrix transpose
$\mathbf{A}^{-1}$	matrix inverse
$\mathbf{A}^\dagger$	Moore-Penrose matrix inverse
$\mathbb{R},\ \mathbb{R}_+$	set of real numbers and non-negative real numbers
$\mathrm{E}\{\underline{x}\},\ \mathrm{Cov}\{\underline{x}\}$	mean and covariance of random vector $\underline{\boldsymbol{x}}$

Symbols for distributed-parameter system description

$\underline{r} := [x,\ y]^{\mathrm{T}}$	spatial coördinate in cartesian form
$p(\underline{r},t),\ s(\underline{r},t)$	space-time continuous state and input of the physical system
$\mathbb{L}(\cdot)$	linear operator
$\Psi_i(\cdot),\ \psi_i(\cdot)$	global and local shape function
N_x	number of shape functions (degree of freedom)
$\Omega,\ \Omega^e$	global and elemental solution domain
$\partial\Omega$	general boundary domain
$\Omega^D,\ \Omega^N$	domain with Dirichlet/Neumann boundary conditions
$g^D,\ g^N$	Dirichlet/Neumann boundary condition
$\mathbf{M}_G,\ \mathbf{N}_G,\ \mathbf{D}_G$	global mass, global advection, and global diffusion matrix
$M_{ij}^g,\ N_{ij}^g,\ D_{ij}^g$	individual entries of corresponding global matrices

Symbols for lumped-parameter system description

$\underline{a}_k(\cdot),\ \underline{h}_k(\cdot)$	nonlinear system function and nonlinear measurement function
$\mathbf{A}_k,\ \mathbf{B}_k,\ \mathbf{H}_k$	system matrix, input matrix, and measurement matrix for linear systems
$\underline{x}_k,\ \underline{u}_k,\ \underline{y}_k$	state vector, input vector, and measurement vector
$N_x,\ N_u,\ N_y$	dimension of state vector, input vector, and measurement vector
$\underline{\eta}_k^P,\ \underline{\eta}_k^M,\ \underline{\eta}_k^I$	vector containing parameters of system model, measurement model, and system input model
$P_p,\ P_m,\ P_i$	dimension of parameter vectors
$\underline{z}_k$	augmented vector containing state vector $\underline{x}_k$ and parameter vector $\underline{\eta}_k$
N_z	dimension of augmented state vector
$\underline{w}_k^x,\ \underline{w}_k^\eta,\ \underline{w}_k^z$	state noise vector, parameter noise vector, and augmented state noise vector
$\underline{v}_k$	measurement noise vector

Symbols for probability density functions

$f(\cdot)$	general probability density function
$\widetilde{f}(\cdot)$	true density function to be approximated
$f^L(\hat{\underline{y}}_k \vert \underline{z}_k)$	likelihood function
$f^T(\underline{z}_{k+1} \vert \underline{z}_k)$	transition density
$f^p(\underline{x}_{k+1})$	predicted density at time $k+1$
$f^e(\underline{x}_k)$	posterior density after measurement step at time k
$f_v(\underline{v}_k)$	probability density function of measurement noise $\underline{v}_k$
$f_w(\underline{w}_k)$	probability density function of system noise $\underline{w}_k$
$\delta(\cdot)$	Dirac delta function
$\mathcal{N}(\cdot, \underline{\mu}, \mathbf{C})$	Gaussian density with mean vector $\underline{\mu}$ and covariance matrix $\mathbf{C}$

Parameters for Sliced Gaussian Mixture Filter (SGMF)

α_k^i	total weight of i-th density slice
β_k^{ij}	weight of j-th component of i-th density slice
γ_k^{ij}	weight resulting from the measurement step
$\underline{\xi}_k^i$	position of i-th density slice
$\underline{\mu}_k^{ij}$	mean of j-th component of i-th density slice
$\mathbf{C}_k^{ij}$	covariance matrix of j-th component of i-th slice
$M_D,\ M_G^i$	number of density slices and Gaussian components for i-th slice

Parameters for Covariance Bounds Filter (CBF)

N_C	number of substate vectors
$\widetilde{\mathbf{C}}_k$	covariance matrix to be bounded
$\mathbf{C}_k^{\mathrm{B}}$	covariance bound for completely unknown correlations
$\mathbf{E}_k$	covariance bound for arbitrary correlation constraints
$\mathbf{U}_k,\ \mathbf{S}_k,\ \mathbf{A}_k$	matrices responsible for completely unknown correlation, symmetric constraints, and asymmetric constraints
β_k^{ij}	scaling parameter between individual components of covariance bound
$r_{\mathrm{avrg}}^{ij},\ r_{\mathrm{d}}^{ij}$	averaged and difference correlation coefficient
$\underline{\kappa}_k,\ \underline{\kappa}_k^*$	parameter vector for covariance bounds and its optimal selection
$\underline{\xi},\ \xi(r)$	parameter vector and function for the generalized correlation parameter

Constants and units of considered space-time continuous system (necessary for the used descriptive examples)

ρ	in	$\mathrm{kg\,m^{-3}}$	material density
c_p	in	$\mathrm{J\,kg^{-1}\,K^{-1}}$	heat capacity
k	in	$\mathrm{J\,m^{-1}\,s^{-1}\,K^{-1}}$	thermal conductivity
$p(\underline{r}, t)$	in	K or $^\circ\mathrm{C}$	continuous system state (here, a temperature distribution)
$s(\underline{r}, t)$	in	$\mathrm{J\,m^{-3}\,s^{-1}}$	continuous input driving the physical system
v	in	$\mathrm{m\,s^{-1}}$	velocity of convection field
$\alpha := \frac{k}{\rho\,c_p}$	in	$\mathrm{m^2\,s^{-1}}$	diffusion coefficient
$\gamma := \frac{1}{\rho\,c_p}$	in	$\mathrm{m^3\,K\,J^{-1}}$	system input coefficient

Glossary

SRI	simultaneous reconstruction and identification
SRL	simultaneous reconstruction and localization
SRSL	simultaneous reconstruction and source localization
SPLL	simultaneous probabilistic localization and learning
SGMF	Sliced Gaussian Mixture Filter
CBF	Covariance Bounds Filter
EKF	extended Kalman filter
UKF	unscented Kalman filter
PF	particle filter
MPF	marginalized particle filter

Zusammenfassung

Diese Arbeit entstand im Rahmen des DFG-Graduiertenkollegs 1194 "Selbstorganisierende Sensor-Aktor-Netzwerke" im Teilprojekt I1 "Dezentrale Rekonstruktion verteilter kontinuierlicher Phänomene aus orts- und zeitdiskreten Messungen". Eine der Hauptanwendungen von Sensornetzwerken ist die Beobachtung, Überwachung und Vermessung von dynamisch veränderlichen, räumlich verteilten physikalischen Phänomenen, wie beispielsweise einer Temperatur- oder Schadstoffverteilung. Dabei führen die in der Umwelt verteilten, miniaturisierten Sensorknoten zeit- und ortsdiskrete Messungen durch. Das Ziel dieser Forschungsarbeit ist es, aus den diskreten Messungen das *komplette verteilte Phänomen* zu rekonstruieren, also in physikalisch korrekter Weise zu interpolieren. Bei der Vermessung solcher verteilter Phänomene muss ein Kompromiss zwischen Genauigkeit und Realisierungsaufwand gefunden werden, wobei hierfür die Sensoranzahl sowie die Messrate entscheidende Größen darstellen. Die in dieser Arbeit entwickelten Verfahren und Methoden zeichnen sich durch die Einbeziehung von physikalischem Hintergrundwissen in Form von Systemmodellen aus und führen dadurch zu genauen Interpolationsergebnissen bei vertretbarem Messaufwand. Hierbei werden alle auftretenden Unsicherheiten, d.h. ausgehend von dem Modellierungsprozess bis hin zu den eigentlichen Messungen, in einer systematischen und integrierten Weise berücksichtigt.

Für die Rekonstruktion des zeitvarianten, räumlich verteilten physikalischen Phänomens aus den orts- und zeitdiskreten messbaren Daten wurden im Rahmen dieser Arbeit *probabilistische modellbasierte Interpolationsverfahren* entwickelt. Ein verteiltes Phänomen, also ein sogenanntes *verteilt-parametrisches System*, kann mittels *stochastischer partieller Differentialgleichungen* mathematisch beschrieben werden, die nicht nur die zeitliche Veränderung, sondern auch die räumlichen Ausbreitung berücksichtigen. Da eine direkte Verwendung solch einer Beschreibung für Rekonstruktionszwecke sehr komplex ist, ist eine Konversion des Modells inklusive dessen Unsicherheitsbeschreibung in ein entsprechend konzentriert-parametrisches System notwendig. Diese Darstellungsform dient als Grundlage für den Entwurf eines geeigneten Bayes'schen Zustandschätzers. Durch die probabilistische und modellbasierte Herangehensweise ist es möglich, die charakteristischen Größen, die das verteilte System an jedem Ort und zu jedem Zeitpunkt vollständig beschreiben, in einer physikalisch korrekten Weise zu bestimmen. Dadurch, dass auch Aussagen über das verteilte physikalische Phänomen an Nichtmesspunkten getroffen werden können, ist für eine gegebene Genauigkeit der Interpolation eine deutlich geringere Anzahl an Sensorknoten notwendig. Weiterhin kann das Ergebnis des modellbasierten Interpolationsalgorithmus als Eingang für die Generierung von optimalen Messparametern in Bezug auf Ort und Zeitpunkt verwendet werden.

Eine der Hauptschwierigkeiten bei der modellbasierten Rekonstruktion ist, dass Modellparameter sowohl des zu untersuchenden verteilten physikalischen Phänomens, als auch des verwendeten Messsystems (also des Sensornetzwerks) meist unbekannt oder nur durch aufwändige Methoden bestimmt werden können. Als weitere Schwierigkeit kommt hinzu, dass diese Modellparameter in den meisten Fällen als orts- und zeitvariant angenommen werden müssen. Um diese Unsicherheiten bei der Rekonstruktion des Zustands zu berücksichtigen und Informationen über das zu beobachtende verteilte physikalische Phänomen in Form von Modellparametern zu erhalten, wurden effiziente Verfahren zur *simultanen Rekonstruktion und Identifikation* entwickelt. Dieser simultane Ansatz führt selbst für ursprünglich lineare Modellgleichungen zu einem *hochdimensionalen nichtlinearen Schätzproblem*. Aus diesem Grund wurde im Rahmen dieser Forschungsarbeit ein spezielles Filter entwickelt, das sogenannte *S*liced *G*aussian *M*ixture *F*ilter (SGMF). Dieses Filter nutzt vorhandene lineare Unterstrukturen in nichtlinearen Schätzproblemen aus, um einen insgesamt effizienteren Schätzprozess zu ermöglichen. Durch das entwickelte Framework können die orts- und zeitdiskreten Messwerte des Sensornetzwerks für eine autonome Anpassung der Modellbeschreibung an das zu beobachtende physikalische Phänomen genutzt werden. Die dadurch erreichten Möglichkeiten werden anhand von folgenden Szenarien eindrücklich demonstriert: (a) Identifikation von Materialkennwerten in Form von Modellparametern, (b) Lokalisierung von Sensorknoten durch ausschließlich lokale Beobachtung eines verteilten Phänomens und (c) Quellen- und Senkenlokalisierung.

Bei *großen Sensornetzwerken* wird aus verschiedenen Gründen eine *dezentrale Verarbeitung* der Informationen in den einzelnen Sensorknoten einer Verarbeitung in einem zentralen Knoten vorgezogen. Die bei einer zentralen Informationsverarbeitung entstehenden stochastischen Abhängigkeiten zwischen den auf unterschiedlichen Knoten gespeicherten Teilschätzungen werden bei einer dezentralen Verarbeitung nicht gespeichert und gehen somit verloren. Allerdings ist bei der Fusion von zwei Teilschätzungen deren Abhängigkeitsstruktur, also im Allgemeinen die Verbundwahrscheinlichkeitsdichte, erforderlich. Für den Fall von *Gauß'schen Wahrscheinlichkeitsdichten* existieren besondere Verfahren, die es erlauben, die unbekannten stochastische Abhängigkeiten systematisch zu berücksichtigen. Um eine korrekte Verarbeitung von unsicheren Informationen zu gewährleisten, werden dabei alle möglichen Abhängigkeiten durch eine Beschreibung mit Hülldichten, den sogenannten *Kovarianzhüllen*, berücksichtigt. In dieser Arbeit wurde ein spezielles Filter entwickelt, das *C*ovariance *B*ounds *Filter (CBF)*, welches zusätzliches Hintergrundwissen über die stochastischen Abhängigkeiten in Form von (symmetrischen und asymmetrischen) Korrelationsbedingungen berücksichtigt. Dadurch werden konsistente und konservative Schätzergebnisse bei der dezentralen Rekonstruktion von sehr weiträumig verteilten physikalischen Phänomenen erreicht. Für den *nicht Gauß'schen* Fall wurden, unter gewissen strukturellen Annahmen, Möglichkeiten zur Parametrierung der unbekannten Verbundwahrscheinlichkeitsdichte durch sogenannte *verallgemeinerte Korrelationsparameter* hergeleitet. Durch eine entsprechende Verarbeitung der entstehenden parametrierten Dichtemenge und der Findung entsprechender Hülldichten, könnten Verfahren für *dezentrale nichtlineare Schätzprobleme* konzipiert werden. Hierfür legen die in dieser Arbeit entwickelten parametrierten Verbunddichten eine wichtige Grundlage.

Das Zusammenwirken der entwickelten Verfahren zur probabilistischen modellbasierten Rekonstruktion und Identifikation von räumlich verteilten physikalischen Phänomenen wird anhand von mehreren simulativen Fallstudien umfassend gezeigt und deren Leistungsfähigkeit evaluiert.

Abstract

This work was performed within the DFG Research Training Group 1194 "Self-organizing Sensor-Actuator Networks" in the subproject I1 "Decentralized Reconstruction of Continuous Phenomena based on Space-Time Discrete Measurements". One of the main applications for sensor networks is the observation, monitoring, and exploration of space-time continuous physical phenomena, such as temperature distributions or biochemical concentrations. In practical implementations, the individual miniaturized sensor nodes are widely deployed either inside the phenomenon or very close to it, and are gathering measurements. The main goal of this research work is the reconstruction and identification of the *complete continuous phenomena* using space-time discrete measurements. For the exploration by a sensor network, a trade-off between accuracy and cost needs to be found, where the number of used sensor nodes and their respective measurement rate can be regarded as deciding measures. The framework developed in this work is characterized by the rigorous exploitation of physical background knowledge in terms of a system model. This approach leads to more accurate interpolation results with justifiable measurement costs. The uncertainties inherently arising during the modelling process and existing in the measurements are systematically considered in an integrated fashion.

This research work is devoted to the development of *probabilistic model-based interpolation techniques* for the reconstruction of space-time continuous phenomena using discrete measurements. In general, space-time continuous phenomena, which are also called *distributed-parameter systems*, can be modelled by *stochastic partial differential equations* that describe not only the dynamic, but in particular the distributed properties. The derivation of reconstruction techniques that is directly based on such system description is a challenging task. For that reason, the model description including its uncertainty representation is converted into a corresponding lumped-parameter system. Based on this system description, an appropriate Bayesian estimator can be derived. Thanks to the probabilistic and model-based approach, the space-time continuous state vector describing the system in the entire area of interest can be reconstructed in a systematic and physically correct fashion. Due to the fact that the system is reconstructed even at non-measurement points, a lower number of sensor nodes is required for a given reconstruction accuracy. The results of the reconstruction can be used for several additional tasks concerning the observation of physical phenomena. For example, optimal placements and measurement time sequences for the individual measuring nodes can be derived.

In many cases, the underlying true physical phenomenon deviates from the nominal mathematical model, basically caused by neglecting particular physical effects or external disturbances. Hence, one of the main challenges for a model-based approach is that parameters of both the physical phenomenon being observed and the spatially distributed measurement system are usually imprecisely known or can be identified only with complex and expensive methods. In addition, these model parameters usually need to be regarded as varying over space and time. This research work is devoted to the development of efficient methods not only for reconstructing the space-time continuous system state, but also for identifying specific model parameters.

In general, the proposed simultaneous state and parameter estimation approach leads to a *nonlinear and high-dimensional estimation problem*, even when the original model equations are linear. To cope with such estimation problems, a special estimator is proposed, the so-called *S*liced *G*aussian *M*ixture *F*ilter (SGMF). This estimator exploits linear substructures in nonlinear estimation problems leading to an overall more efficient estimation process. The performance is presented by means of various simulation studies: (a) identification of process parameters, (b) localization of sensor nodes exclusively based on local observation of a space-time continuous phenomenon, and (c) localization of sources and leakages. Thanks to the proposed framework the space-time discrete measurements can be used for the autonomous adaptation of the system model to the physical phenomenon being observed.

In the case of *large sensor networks*, a *decentralized processing* of the information in the individual sensor nodes is prefered due to various reasons. The processing of information and the propagation through the network leads to stochastic dependencies between the individual estimates. Although local estimates are stored in each node, their dependencies are not stored in the sensor network. However, for processing local estimates, their stochastic dependencies, i.e., their joint statistics, are required. In the case of *Gaussian probability density functions*, methods are developed that allow the *decentralized reconstruction* of space-time continuous phenomena while systematically considering the imprecisely known stochastic dependencies. In order to ensure correct processing of the information, the estimator is required to systematically consider all possible dependencies. To cope with such estimation problems, a novel estimator is derived, the so-called *Covariance Bounds Filter (CBF)*. This special robust estimator allows the incorporation of additional background knowledge about the stochastic dependencies in order to obtain more accurate and consistent estimation results. In the *non-Gaussian case*, various types of parameterizations of the unknown joint probability density function are introduced. These density functions are parameterized by a so-called *generalized correlation parameter*. The processing of these density functions results in a set of corresponding probability density functions. By finding bounding densities that sufficiently represent the entire resulting set, approaches for *decentralized nonlinear estimation problems* can be derived. The parameterized joint densities that are proposed in this research work lay the foundation for these methods.

The performance of the methodology developed for the probabilistic model-based reconstruction and identification of space-time continuous systems is demonstrated by means of various simulation studies. These results clearly show the novel prospects for sensor network applications offered by the obtained methods.

CHAPTER 1

Introduction

In recent years, advances in science and technology have made it possible to build wireless sensor networks providing a smart interaction with the environment [39]. Networks consisting of a large number of such miniaturized and autonomous sensor nodes offer novel possibilities for industrial, medical, urban, and many other applications. An important application for such networks is the observation and the monitoring of natural physical phenomena, such as temperature distribution, biochemical concentration [67, 108, 155], fluid flow, deflection and vibration in buildings. More specific scenarios are the observation of the microclimate throughout the volume of redwood trees or entire forests, and the reconstruction of surface motion of a beating heart during minimally invasive surgery [10, 107].

For the observation of aforementioned space-time continuous phenomena, spatially distributed measurement systems can be exploited as huge information fields collecting readings over time across a volume of space. In practical implementations, the individual sensor nodes are widely deployed either inside the phenomenon or very close to it. Then, by distributing locally obtained measurements and estimates through the sensor network, significant information about internal variations can be coöperatively exhibited in an intelligent and autonomous manner. Thanks to the extended perception that provides useful information both to mobile agents and to humans, corresponding tasks can be accomplished more efficiently. Hence, dangerous situations, such as forest fires, seismic sea waves, or snow avalanches can be forcasted or even prevented. The distributed properties of the sensor network lead to a good spatial resolution, which can be adapted autonomously depending on the dynamics of the physical phenomenon being observed. Besides the observation task, the sensor nodes are able to interact with the physical phenomenon itself by integrated actuators [35, 48, 52, 104].

The large number of nodes significantly increases the fault tolerance and the robustness of the entire network, even for low reliability and availability of the individual nodes. However, these advantages are opposed by certain constraints that need to be considered in the design process of such spatially distributed measurement systems. For example, the energy constraints resulting from the required autonomy impose severe performance limits with respect to communication bandwidth and processing power. In addition, the intrinsic mobility, possible failure, and selective switch-off for energy reasons, leads to a regularly changing topology of the sensor network. It is often desirable to reduce communication activities to a minimum and to reduce the heavy computational burden. Moreover, for large sensor networks a decentralized approach is desirable implying that just parts of the information about the physical phenomenon are independently processed. Due to these constraints, novel requirements need to be tackled not only regarding the communication, but in particular regarding the techniques for information processing. In this thesis, the focus lies on the development of *efficient techniques*[1] for processing the information in a spatially distributed measurement system (e.g., sensor network) with the aim to observe a space-time continuous phenomenon.

---

1   Here, *efficient* means with a low computational load and in a decentralized fashion

1.1 Prospective Sensor Network Applications

This section is devoted to a more detailed description of prospective application scenarios where sensor networks, with the methodology proposed in this thesis, can provide novel possibilities. It is emphasized that the applications are not restricted to the following.

Snow avalanches and snowmelt For *snow monitoring scenarios*, there may exist two applications of special interest: (a) forcasting snow avalanches, and (b) predicting flood runoffs. *Snow avalanches* are a major hazard to people, equipment or facilities, such as buildings, ski slopes, roads, power lines, and railways, in mountainous regions throughout the world. Each year snow avalanches cause casualties and damages, not only in non-protected areas but also in popular cross-country skiing areas, e.g., Wasatch mountains in Utah. For supporting avalanche forecasting systems, useful information can be offered by intelligent and autonomous sensor networks [12, 89, 90, 114]. The individual sensor nodes that are deployed within the snowpack collect measurable information about the snow state, such as temperature, light intensity, pressure, or humidity. Based on these observations and after further processing, measures about the stability of the snowpack could be estimated, e.g., stress/strain distribution or location of so-called weak layers. Then, the sensor network may predict the possibility of avalanches [23, 45] and supports the optimization of defense structures in avalanche starting zones [134]. The methods proposed in this thesis can be conceptually used for example for the reconstruction of the space-time continuous snow state using just a low number of sensor nodes (see Chapter 2). Having a strong mathematical model about the temperature distribution in the snowpack, this model may be exploited for localizing sensor nodes that are deeply deployed in the snow by locally measuring the temperature, i.e., without depending on global positioning systems (see Section 4.4). An additional scenario where sensor networks could provide novel prospects is the accurate *evaluation of snowmelt*. By this means, water resources can be utilized more efficiently and flood runoffs can be forcast more accurately [86].

Ice condition in skating rinks A further scenario worth mentioning is the application of sensor networks for *monitoring* the condition and composition of ice in *skating rinks* [1]. For speed skaters to reach faster times, the optimal ice composition and especially the optimal temperature distribution of the ice is quite essential. For that reason, temperature nodes deployed at different locations within the icepack allow the estimation of the actual temperature distribution on the surface and eventually the environmental conditions that are necessary for achieving an optimal ice composition. In addition, the sensor nodes could be directly linked to ice making machines, so that they can be adjusted in order to compensate for changes in temperature, wind, or humidity [1]. The proposed methodology for the reconstruction and identification of space-time continuous phenomena can be used to identify the ice condition appearing as some parameters in the governing model equations, such as material properties, diffusion coefficient or viscosity (see Section 4.3).

Quality of groundwater Groundwater is an invaluable commodity endangered by various influences, such as the immoderate extraction [27] or the contamination by depositing nitrate concentration [2]. Spatially distributed measurement systems, such as sensor networks, offer the possibility to monitor and to observe the quality of the groundwater in certain areas. Using the measurements obtained from the individual sensor nodes, a map can be generated that describes the advective transport [5, 145] and the nitrate concentration [2]. Such maps about specific physical quantities visualize crucial influence factors as well as serve as an instrument for decisions and identification of nitrate contamination sources. In addition, optimal measurement

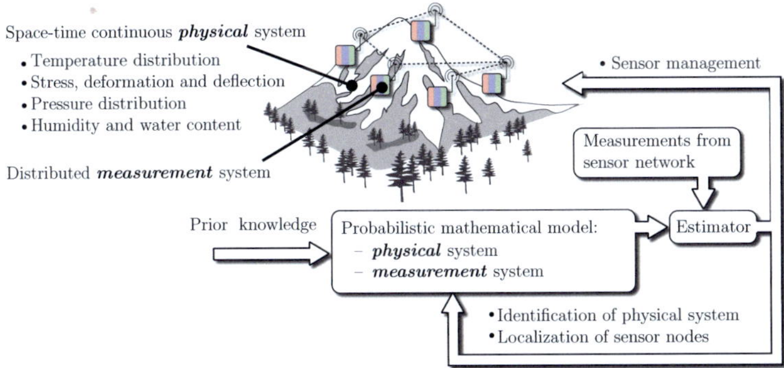

Figure 1.1: Visualization of the *model-based approach* for the estimation of distributed phenomena by means of a sensor network. Additional background knowledge in terms of mathematical models is exploited in order to obtain physically correct and more accurate estimation results. The result can be used to achieve additional tasks, e.g., identification of parameters, localization of sensor nodes, or planning of node locations and measurement sequences.

locations and sequences can be derived in order to perform the entire reconstruction and source localization process in a more efficient manner. The method for source localization proposed in this thesis can be used to localize sources of contamination, even in the case of imprecisely known distribution of the nitrate concentration or imprecisely known parameters in the governing model equations (see Section 4.5).

1.2 Mathematical Description of Dynamic Systems

In all aforementioned applications for sensor networks, the number of nodes and the measurement rates should be as low as possible due to economic and energetic reasons. It can be stated that the lower the measurement rate of the individual nodes, the higher their durability. Therefore, a trade-off between energy costs and accuracy has to be found. In addition, for obtaining measurements about the physical phenomenon being observed not all locations are directly accessible. Since measurements are available only at discrete locations, no direct information is available between the individual sensor nodes. In order to derive the desired continuous form with sufficient spatial and temporal accuracy, the measurements need to be interpolated between the node locations. In general, there are different approaches: (a) interpolation based on a mathematical model that describes the dynamic behavior and distribution of the underlying physical phenomenon, and (b) without using any physical background knowledge.

There are various reasons making a *model-based approach* for the interpolation[1] of the space-time continuous state of physical phenomena essential and inevitable. One of the major reasons is to give *noisy* measurements a physical meaning. Moreover, fusing space-time discrete measurements with respective information derived from physical background knowledge leads to a systematic and physically correct smoothing of the estimation results. Concerning space-time continuous phenomena, there is another reason calling for a model-based approach. Due to the distribution property, the individual sensor nodes are able to measure the physical quantity only

---

1   In this work, the interpolation based on a system model is also called *state reconstruction*.

at discrete locations, i.e., no direct information between nodes is available. By exploiting *additional background information* about the physical phenomenon being observed, more meaningful and more accurate information can be derived even at non-measurement points. Furthermore, additional information about the physical phenomenon in terms of model parameters can be obtained; see Figure 1.1.

There are several ways for classifying dynamic systems and its model description. In this research work, they are classified as (a) *lumped*-parameter models and (b) *distributed*-parameter models; main properties are visualized in Figure 1.2.

Lumped-parameter model The key characteristic of a *lumped-parameter system* is that the system state depends *only on time*. In general, such systems can be described by a system of *ordinary differential equations* according to

$$\mathbb{L}\left(\underline{x}(t),\, \underline{x}^{(1)}(t), \ldots, \underline{x}^{(i)}(t)\right) = \underline{s}(t) \ , \tag{1.1}$$

where $\underline{x}(t)$ denotes the time-continuous state vector, $\underline{x}^{(i)}(t)$ are their i-th derivatives, and $\underline{s}(t)$ represents the system input vector. Examples of systems that can be described by lumped-parameter models (1.1) are bird flocks or swarms of robots[1].

Accounting for the uncertainties arising in the modelling process and caused by external disturbances, the state and input vector are modelled as *random variables*[2] that are described by *probability density functions*. In the stochastic case, equation (1.1) is called *stochastic ordinary differential equation* that describes an underlying *random process* [46]. In comparison, a deterministic process deals with only one possible, exactly known realization of the physical system. In a random process, however, there is some indeterminacy in its future behavior. Roughly speaking, although initial conditions are precisely known, there are many possibilities on the state and input vector, and thus on how the process might behave.

Distributed-parameter model On the other hand, *space-time continuous phenomena* are usually described by distributed-parameter models. The space-time continuous state $p(\underline{r}, t)$ does not only depend on time but also on the spatial coördinate $\underline{r} \in \mathbb{R}^2$ or $\mathbb{R}^3$. Examples of systems that can be described by distributed-parameter models are temperature distributions, irrotational fluid flows, heat conductions, and wave propagations. Distributed-parameter models can be described by *partial differential equations*. In its most general form, the linear partial differential equation without cross-derivatives is given in implicit form by

$$\mathbb{L}\left(\boldsymbol{p}(\underline{r}, t),\, \boldsymbol{s}(\underline{r}, t),\, \frac{\partial \boldsymbol{p}(\underline{r}, t)}{\partial t}, \ldots, \frac{\partial^i \boldsymbol{p}(\underline{r}, t)}{\partial t^i},\, \nabla \boldsymbol{p}(\underline{r}, t), \ldots, \nabla^j \boldsymbol{p}(\underline{r}, t)\right) = 0 \ , \tag{1.2}$$

where $p(\underline{r}, t) : \mathbb{R}^3 \times \mathbb{R} \to \mathbb{R}$ and $\boldsymbol{s}(\underline{r}, t) : \mathbb{R}^3 \times \mathbb{R} \to \mathbb{R}$ denotes the system state and system input at time t and at spatial coördinate $\underline{r} := [x, y, z]^T \in \mathbb{R}^3$. The j-th derivative of the operator ∇ is defined as $\nabla^j = \frac{\partial^j}{\partial x^j} + \frac{\partial^j}{\partial y^j} + \frac{\partial^j}{\partial z^j}$. The system input $s(\cdot)$, the system state $p(\cdot)$, and its derivatives are related by means of a linear operator $\mathbb{L}(\cdot)$. In addition, the dynamic behavior and distributed properties strongly depend on specific parameters collected in the *process parameter vector* $\underline{\eta}_k^P$.

---

1 It is emphasized that in the case of lumped-parameter models the states and parameters are lumped at discrete points, however still can be spatially distributed, e.g., the position and velocity of the individual birds in a bird flock.

2 In this work, random variables are denoted bold face.

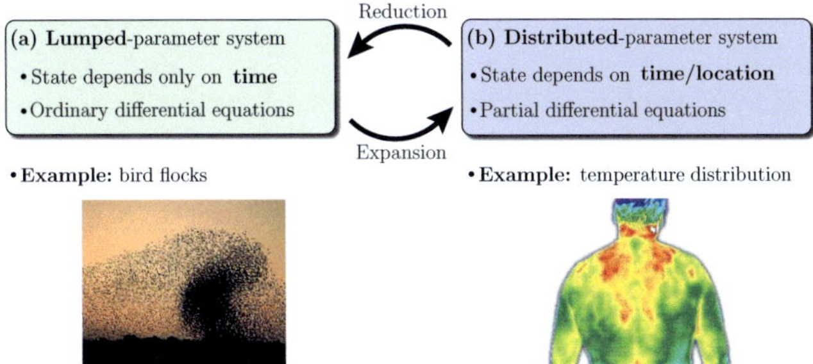

Figure 1.2: Classification of dynamic physical systems into **(a)** *lumped*-parameter systems (such as bird flocks) and **(b)** *distributed*-parameter systems (such as temperature distributions). The mathematical model describing the dynamic and distributed behavior can be converted from the distributed-parameter form into lumped-parameter form. In contrast, the model of certain lumped-parameter systems, such as a swarms of robots, can be expanded to a distributed-parameter form in order to derive a possibly simpler system description.

In the stochastic case, the equation (1.2) is called *stochastic partial differential equation* describing an underlying *random field*. Such fields are of great interest in studying natural processes with spatially varying properties. A random field can be regarded as a generalization of the aforementioned stochastic process such that the underlying process is spatially correlated, i.e., the covariance function contains a certain structure characterizing the spatial correlation. Roughly speaking, adjacent values do not differ as much as values that are farther apart. This structure is modelled in terms of the stochastic partial differential equation.

Conversion of system descriptions   At this point, it is worth mentioning that the mathematical model of a given space-time continuous system can be converted from the distributed-parameter form into a lumped-parameter form. Hence, the *partial differential equation* (1.2) can be expressed by a system of *coupled ordinary differential equations* (1.1) that still sufficiently characterizes the distributed properties by respective coupling terms. This can be achieved by the spatial decomposition of the solution domain (considered in this thesis).

In contrast, the mathematical model of certain lumped-parameter systems, such as swarms of robots, can be expanded to a distributed-parameter model for obtaining a possibly simpler system description. For example, the expanded form can be exploited to derive simple control algorithms for the individual robots that results in a self-organized and emergent behavior of the entire swarm [51, 52, 128, 129]. This expansion to distributed-parameter mathematical models is *not* considered in this work. However, it is imaginable to employ the proposed techniques, for example, to a swarm of robots in order to obtain the state and specific parameters of the dynamic and distributed behavior of the swarm.

Modelling of uncertainties   There are several sources of uncertainties to be systematically considered in the system description. The *first source* can be regarded as an inherent uncertainty in the physical phenomenon being observed. This arises from the general impossibility of an exhaustive deterministic description of the dynamic behavior and the distributed properties; for example, the irregularity contained within the *uncertainty principle* of quantum mechanics or the kinetic theory of gas. The *second source* can be related to a lack of knowledge about the processes involved. The derivation of a mathematical model describing *perfectly* the physical behavior of the distributed system is rather complex and due to the computational complexity

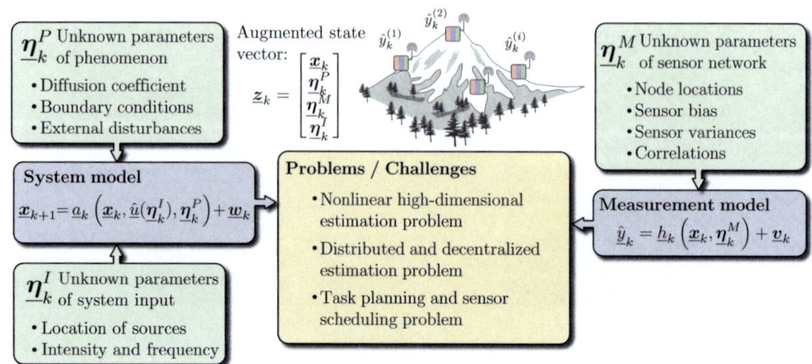

Figure 1.3: Overview and challenges of the simultaneous state and parameter estimation of distributed phenomena. Examples of unknown parameters to be estimated in the system model and the measurement model.

in most cases not desirable. This is in particular the case for sensor network applications associated with their constraints in computational load and storage capacity. Hence, an abstraction and reduction of the complex mathematical model description is necessary in order to derive a simpler model characterized by less parameters.

The simpler description is supposed to need less computational load and still be sufficiently accurate to describe the physical system and the measurement system. By using many more observations of the random process under consideration and by improving the measuring devices, the degree of these uncertainties can usually be reduced. However, for accurate and consistent observation results, the aforementioned types of uncertainties need to be systematically considered during the estimation process. In this research work, the space-time continuous system state $p(\underline{r}, t)$, system input $s(\underline{r}, t)$, and boundary conditions are represented as random variables[1]. The term *estimate* is understood to be a mathematical description, for example, of the system state with its associated uncertainties.

In the case of *stochastic uncertainty modelling*, the uncertainties of the reconstructed space-time continuous system (1.2) at time step k are described in terms of a conditional probability density function $f^e(p_k|\underline{r})$; conditioned on the spatial coördinate $\underline{r} \in \mathbb{R}^2$ or $\mathbb{R}^3$. Due to its property as a universal function approximator, the density function is modelled as a *Gaussian mixture density* [4], as follows

$$\boldsymbol{p}_k(\underline{r}) \sim f^e(p_k|\underline{r}) := \sum_{i=1}^{N} w_k^i(\underline{r}) \cdot \mathcal{N}\left(p_k - \hat{p}_k^{ei}(\underline{r}), C_k^{ei}(\underline{r})\right) \ , \tag{1.3}$$

where $\mathcal{N}(\cdot)$ denotes the Gaussian density function with space continuous mean $\hat{p}_k^{ei}(\cdot) : \mathbb{R}^3 \to \mathbb{R}$, space continuous variance $C_k^{ei}(\cdot) : \mathbb{R}^3 \to \mathbb{R}_+$ and weight $w_k^i(\cdot) : \mathbb{R}^3 \to \mathbb{R}_+$. This probability density function can be regarded as a Gaussian mixture density that is spatially distributed, i.e., parameters of the density function depend on the spatial coördinate. Throughout the entire estimation process, the uncertainties in the mathematical model (1.2) and the measurements are systematically considered. This consideration leads to physically correct and accurate reconstruction results in terms of the probability density function $f^e(p_k|\underline{r})$.

---

1   In this work, random variables $\underline{x}$ are denoted bold face and are associated with a probability density function $f(\underline{x})$.

1.3 Problem Formulation and Contributions

The main goal is to derive a framework including respective methods for the identification of space-time continuous phenomena and the reconstruction between the spatially distributed, however space-time discrete measurements. For most real world applications *additional background knowledge* about the physical system is available. For example, considering a heat distribution phenomenon the entire process can be mathematically described by a convection-diffusion equation. In order to obtain accurate estimation results that ensure physical correctness such available background knowledge needs to be exploited.

System model In general, space-time continuous phenomena, which are also called *distributed-parameter systems*, can be modelled by *stochastic partial differential equations* (1.2) that describe the distributed and dynamic properties. The formulation of the considered problem as a state and parameter estimation problem allows the application of *model-based Bayesian techniques* in a systematic manner. However, the reconstruction and identification based on a distributed-parameter model (1.2) is a challenging task. For sensor network applications efficient algorithms are of special interest arising from their constraints, such as low computational power and low storage capacity. For that reason, the system model (1.2) characterized by a space-time continuous system state $p(\underline{r}, t)$ is converted into a corresponding lumped-parameter form (1.1). For this concersion there are various techniques available, such as finite difference method, finite element method, or spectral element method.

The resulting *lumped-parameter model* is represented in discrete-time by a *finite-dimensional state vector* $\underline{x}_k \in \mathbb{R}^{N_x}$ that still sufficiently characterizes the distributed properties of the considered physical phenomenon. It is shown that the conversion leads to a *high-dimensional and nonlinear system model* with linear substructures. The nonlinearity is mainly caused by non-linear relationships between the system state $p(\underline{r}, t)$ and unknown parameters $\underline{\eta}_k$ characterizing the underlying process. Hence, the considered system model can be stated as follows

$$\underline{x}_{k+1} = \underline{a}_k\left(\underline{x}_k, \underline{\eta}_k^P, \hat{\underline{u}}_k(\underline{\eta}_k^I), \underline{w}_k^x\right) \ , \tag{1.4}$$

where $\underline{a}_k(\cdot) : \mathbb{R}^{N_x} \times \mathbb{R}^{P_p} \times \mathbb{R}^{N_u} \times \mathbb{R}^{P_i} \to \mathbb{R}^{N_x}$ denotes a system of nonlinear equations. The variables N_x, P_p, and N_u are the dimensions of the state vector, the process parameter vector, and the system input vector, respectively. The input vector $\underline{u}_k \in \mathbb{R}^{N_u}$ is a finite-dimensional vector describing the space-time continuous system input $s(\underline{r}, t)$ and $\underline{w}_k^x \in \mathbb{R}^{N_x}$ represents stochastic uncertainties in the system model. The *process parameter vector* $\underline{\eta}_k^P \in \mathbb{R}^{P_p}$ consists of all the *unknown parameters* to be identified, such as unpredictable variations of physical constants or material properties. The *system input vector* $\underline{\eta}_k^I \in \mathbb{R}^{P_i}$ contains parameters in the input model, such as location and intensity of spatially distributed sources and leakages.

Measurement model The physical properties of the spatially distributed measurement system is mathematically described by a measurement model. Basically, this model relates the measurements $\underline{y}_k \in \mathbb{R}^{N_y}$ to the finite-dimensional state vector $\underline{x}_k \in \mathbb{R}^{N_x}$, according to

$$\hat{\underline{y}}_k = \underline{h}_k\left(\underline{x}_k, \underline{\eta}_k^M, \underline{v}_k^y\right) \ , \tag{1.5}$$

where $\underline{h}_k(\cdot) : \mathbb{R}^{N_x} \times \mathbb{R}^{P_m} \to \mathbb{R}^{N_y}$ is a system of nonlinear equations. The variable N_y represents the dimension of the measurement vector and P_m is the dimension of the measurement parameter vector $\underline{\eta}_k^M$. The random vector $\underline{v}_k^y$ denotes a noise term that characterizes stochastic uncertainties in the measurements.

The *measurement parameter vector* $\underline{\eta}_k^M \in \mathbb{R}^{P_m}$ contains all the *unknown parameters* in the measurement model. Sensor bias and sensor variances, for example, could be included for the purpose of tracking wear of the sensor nodes. Furthermore, unknown locations of the individual sensor nodes could be collected; this case is of special interest in this research work.

Reconstruction of space-time continuous systems (Part I) The main goal is the reconstruction and interpolation of the not directly measurable space-time continuous system state $p(\underline{r}, t)$ that characterizes a given physical phenomenon (1.2) in the entire area of interest. In this thesis, methods are considered that allow the conversion of distributed-parameter systems into a description appropriate for a more efficient interpolation process; see Figure 1.4. In the case of *linear partial differential equations* (1.2), the resulting lumped-parameter system (1.4) is of a linear type and is represented by a high-dimensional state vector $\underline{x}_k \in \mathbb{R}^{N_x}$.

The lumped-parameter model (1.4) can be regarded as a *generic system model* that is required for deriving a corresponding *probabilistic model description*. The probabilistic form describes the dynamic behavior of the physical phenomenon including an uncertainty description in terms of a transition density function $f^T(\underline{x}_{k+1}|\underline{x}_k)$. Based on such system description, the Bayesian estimator allows the calculation of the probability density function $f^e(\underline{x}_k)$ representing the space-time discrete system state $\underline{x}_k$. In order to obtain an estimate of the space continuous system state $p_k(\underline{r})$, this density function needs to be converted into a space continuous form. The conversion results in a conditional probability density function $f^e(p_k|\underline{r})$; conditioned on the spatial coördinate $\underline{r} \in \mathbb{R}^3$. Roughly speaking, the resulting conditional density function can be regarded as a density function that is spatially distributed and thus, represents the space continuous state $p_k(\underline{r})$ of the physical phenomenon (1.2). Due to the fact that the physical phenomenon is reconstructed even at non-measurement points, a lower number of sensor nodes is required for a given accuracy. The results can be used for several additional tasks, such as optimal placements and measurement sequences for the individual sensor nodes, or localization and identification tasks.

Identification of space-time continuous systems (Part II) In many cases, the underlying true physical phenomenon deviates from the nominal mathematical model (1.2). This is basically caused by neglecting particular physical effects or external disturbances during the modelling process. Hence, one of the main challenges for model-based approaches is that model parameters $\underline{\eta}_k \in \mathbb{R}^P$ are usually imprecisely known or can be identified only with complex and expensive methods. For space-time continuos phenomena, the model parameters usually need to be regarded as varying over space and time. In such cases, *simultaneous approaches* are desired that reconstruct the space continuous system state $p_k(\underline{r})$ and simultaneously identify model parameters $\underline{\eta}_k$.

It is shown that for the parameter identification of space-time continuous phenomena, the mathematical model turns into a *nonlinear high-dimensional system model* according to (1.4); however, with linear substructures that can be exploited. In general, for the estimation of nonlinear systems, approximation methods are necessary due to its high computational demand and the resulting non-parametric density representation. The main goal, here, is the exploitation of linear substructures in nonlinear estimation problems in order to arrive at an overall more efficient estimation process. To cope with such combined linear/nonlinear estimation problems, a novel estimator is proposed, the so-called *Sliced Gaussian Mixture Filter (SGMF)*. Besides the exploitation of the linear substructure by decomposing the estimation problem, there are two key features leading to a significantly improved estimation result: (a) the definition of a

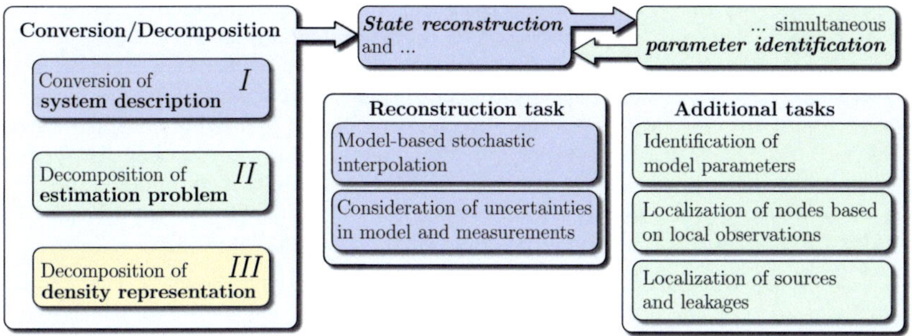

Figure 1.4: Visualization of *conversion and decomposition* methods for deriving a more efficient reconstruction and identification process of space-time continuous phenomena. The novelty of the *reconstruction task* is the interpolation of spatially distributed measurements by using physical background knowledge and the systematic consideration of uncertainties. Thanks to the simultaneous parameter estimation, *additional tasks* can be efficiently performed, such as identification and localization processes.

novel general-purpose density representation for the decomposition of the estimation problem into a linear and a nonlinear part, and (b) a systematic density approximation that is based on minimizing a certain distance measure.

Thanks to the developed framework for the efficient identification of space-time continuous phenomena, the spatially distributed measurements can be used for the autonomous adaptation of the mathematical models. Then, a unifying approach for *most important tasks* concerning the observation of physical phenomena by a sensor network can be obtained; see Figure 1.4.

- Identification of process parameters (SRI-method)

- Localization of individual sensor nodes based on local observations (SRL-method)

- Localization of spatially distributed sources and leakages (SRSL-method)

Decentralized observation of space-time continuous systems (Part III) For the observation of space-time continuous phenomena that are distributed over a wide area, sensor networks consisting of a higher number of nodes are necessary. In such cases, *decentralized processing* of the information in the individual sensor nodes is preferred due to various reasons, e.g., communication bandwidth, computational load, and storage capacity. The local processing of information and the propagation through the network leads to stochastic dependencies between the individual estimates that cannot be stored within the network. Thus, although local estimates are stored on each node, their stochastic dependencies are imprecisely known in the case of decentralized estimation approaches. The main challenge, here, is that for fusing individual local estimates, their stochastic dependencies and joint statistics are required. As a consequence, the joint probability density function needs to be reconstructed or an appropriate so-called bounding density needs to be derived. In this research work, methods for the *decentralized estimation of space-time continuous phenomena* are developed that systematically consider the imprecisely known stochastic dependencies during the estimation process.

In the case of *Gaussian densities*, the stochastic dependencies are sufficiently described by the *classical correlation coefficient*. In many research works dealing with decentralized estimation, it is usually assumed that the correlation coefficient between the considered random vectors are unconstrained and *completely unknown*, i.e., the maximum absolute correlation coefficient is less than or equal to one. Using just the natural bound of the coefficient would lead to quite conservative and usually not sufficient estimation results. In contrast, additional background knowledge about the correlation coefficient can be exploited to find tighter bounds. The constraints can be classified into three types, (a) completely unknown correlation, (b) symmetric correlation constraints, and (c) asymmetric correlation constraints. The proposed robust estimator *Covariance Bounds Filter (CBF)* allows the consideration of such knowledge about the correlation constraints and leads to correct and consistent estimation results.

In the case of *non-Gaussian densities*, the classical correlation coefficient is not a sufficient measure for describing the stochastic dependencies. Due to the universal approximation properties, it is assumed that the marginal densities (local estimates) and their joint densities can be represented by *Gaussian mixture* probability density functions. In this case, the joint density can be reconstructed and parameterized by so-called *generalized correlation parameters*. The processing of these parameterized joint densities leads to a set of corresponding estimation results. By finding bounding densities, the development of decentralized approaches for the nonlinear/non-Gaussian case might be possible. The proposed parameterization of the joint densities for given marginal densities lais the foundation for these methods.

1.4   Thesis Organization

The thesis is divided into *three main parts*, not accounting for the introduction and conclusions. Each part clarifies the attained methods, their respective contributions and performance by means of demonstrative examples and simulation studies. The structure of the thesis is illustrated in Figure 1.5. In the ***first part*** (Chapter 2), systematic methods for the *model-based interpolation* of spatially distributed measurements are derived that allow the *state reconstruction* of space-time continuous systems. The ***second part*** (Chapter 3 and Chapter 4) is devoted to nonlinear estimators that are necessary for the *parameter identification* of space-time continuous systems and their application to the most common tasks, such as identification and localization tasks. The ***third part*** (Chapter 5 and Chapter 6) consists of *decentralized approaches* for the efficient estimation of space-time continuous systems that are widely distributed by using a large sensor network. The chapters of the thesis are structured as follows:

Chapter 2   addresses the *state reconstruction* of space-time continuous physical systems based on space-time discrete measurements obtained from a spatially distributed measurement system. The novelty is the rigorous exploitation of additional background knowledge in terms of a model about the physics and the consideration of uncertainties. By this means, the physical system can be interpolated in a systematic and physically correct fashion, i.e., an estimate can be obtained at any desired location in the entire area of interest. The state reconstruction method lays the foundation for the methods introduced in the following chapters.

Chapter 3   introduces an efficient method for the estimation of special types of nonlinear dynamic systems containing a linear substructure. A special nonlinear estimator — *Sliced Gaussian Mixture Filter* (SGMF) — is proposed that allows the decomposition of the estimation problem into a (conditionally) linear and a nonlinear problem using a special density representation. The systematic approach for the density approximation necessary within the proposed framework is based on the minimization of a certain distance measure that allows the derivation of (close to) optimal and deterministic estimation results. Compared to an estimator working on the entire problem at once, this decomposition leads to an overall more efficient

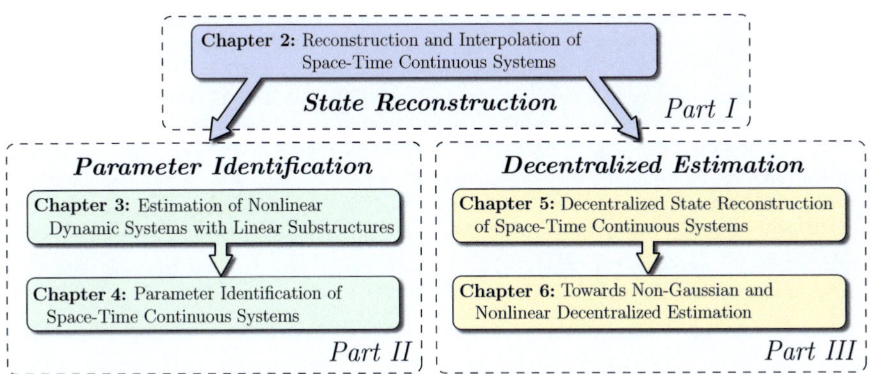

Figure 1.5: Structure and organization of the thesis.

process. This is beneficial for the parameter identification of space-time continuous systems; due to the high-dimensional linear substructure consisting in the nonlinear system description.

Chapter 4 presents a method for the simultaneous state and parameter estimation of space-time continuous physical systems monitored by a spatially distributed measurement system. The main challenge is that the parameter identification leads to a high-dimensional and nonlinear estimation problem. Thanks to the high-dimensional linear substructure contained in the augmented model description, the development of an overall more efficient estimation process is possible, e.g., by using the estimator derived in the preceding chapter. The proposed *simultaneous approach* provides novel prospects in sensor network applications. For example, the network is able to estimate the space-time continuous state of the physical phenomenon, identify *non-measurable* quantities, verify and validate the correctness of the estimation results, and eventually adapt its algorithms and behavior in an autonomous fashion. This is examined by various simulated case studies: (a) the identification of process parameters, (b) the sensor node localization based on local observations of a space-time continuous physical phenomenon, and (c) the localization of spatially distributed sources and leakages.

Chapter 5 addresses the problem of decentralized state reconstruction of space-time continuous systems observed by a sensor network. For decentralized reconstruction, a novel methodology consisting of three stages is proposed: (a) the *conversion* of the distributed-parameter system into a lumped-parameter system description, (b) the *decomposition* of the resulting system model into subsystems and the mapping to the individual sensor nodes, and (c) the *decomposition* of the probability density function leading to a decentralized estimation approach. The main problem of a decentralized approach is that due to the propagation of local information through the network unknown correlations are caused. This fact needs to be considered during the reconstruction process in order to obtain correct and consistent estimation results. Here, a special robust estimator — the *Covariance Bounds Filter* (CBF) — is developed for the local reconstruction update on each sensor node. This estimator allows the incorporation of *background knowledge about correlation constraints* (e.g., symmetric and asymmetric constraints) in order to derive tighter bounds, and thus more accurate estimation results. By this means, sensor nodes are able to reconstruct the *local substate* of the physical phenomenon using local estimates obtained and communicated by *adjacent nodes* only.

Chapter 6 discusses the challenges of processing random variables represented by *non-Gaussian density functions* with imprecisely known stochastic dependencies. To cope with such problems, various types of parameterizations of the unknown joint density function are introduced. These density functions are parameterized by so-called *generalized correlation parameters*. The processing of these density functions leads to a set of corresponding estimation results. By finding bounding densities that sufficiently represent the entire set of resulting densities (similar to the covariance bounds in the Gaussian case), the development of decentralized approaches for the nonlinear/non-Gaussian case may be possible. The parameterized joint densities proposed in this research work lay the foundation for such methods.

Chapter 7 presents conclusions and suggests future directions for the completion and extension of the methods introduced in this thesis.

CHAPTER 2

Reconstruction and Interpolation of Space-Time Continuous Systems

This chapter is devoted to the reconstruction of *space-time continuous systems*[1] using measurements that are obtained from a *spatially distributed measurement system*, such as a sensor network. The physical system being observed here can also be regarded as a huge spatially distributed *random field*. The main goal of the state reconstruction then, is to estimate the value of the space-time continuous state in the entire area of interest. For the derivation of accurate and physically correct estimates between the individual measurement points, systematic interpolation and extrapolation methods are necessary.

The *model-based reconstruction* approach proposed in this chapter is based on the rigorous exploitation of additional background knowledge in terms of mathematical models; in this research work *stochastic partial differential equations*. Such models describe the *dynamic behavior* as well as the *distributed properties* of the physical system being monitored. In order to derive more precise reconstruction results, basically, two different *sources of information* are exploited: (1) the measurements obtained from the sensor network and (2) a mathematical model of the physical system and the measurement system. Thanks to the mathematical model describing the physical behavior at any spatial coördinate, the space-time continuous physical system can be reconstructed not only at the actual measurement locations but also between the individual nodes. The novelty is the exploitation of a model about the physics and the integrated treatment of uncertainties occuring in the model description and arising from noisy measurements. This leads to an interpolation and extrapolation of space-time discrete measurements in a *systematic and physically correct manner*.

The results of the reconstruction process can be used for several additional tasks concerning the observation of physical systems by a spatially distributed measurement system. For example, optimal placements and measurement time sequences for the individual measuring nodes can be derived, as proposed in [167, 169]. In addition, the results can be exploited for the following tasks considered in this work: the identification of parameters characterizing the model of the physical system (see Section 4.3), the localization of several nodes of the spatially distributed measurement system based on local observations only (see Section 4.4), and the model-based source and leakage localization (see Section 4.5).

The model-based approach for the reconstruction and interpolation of space-time continuous systems that is described in this chapter is based on the puplications [167, 169, 182, 183]. However, here, explanations of the process are given for physical systems that are spatially distributed in two dimensions. Furthermore, the performance of the method, challenges, and novel prospects for sensor network applications are presented in a considerably extended form by means of various simulated case studies.

---

1   In the literature, this type of physical system is often called
    distributed-parameter system, see Section 1.2.

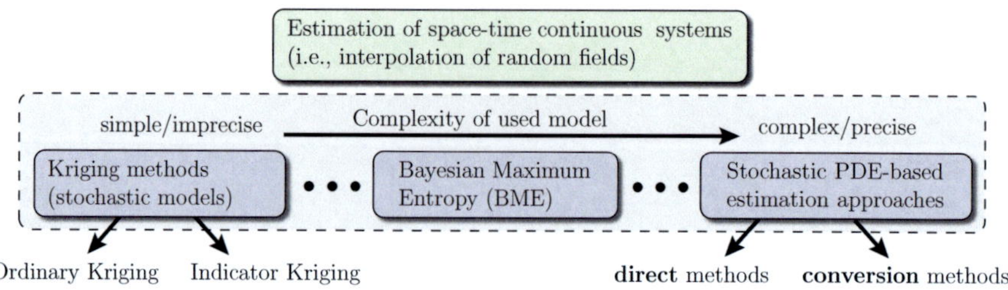

Figure 2.1: Overview of different approaches for the state and parameter estimation of space-time continuous, distributed-parameter systems (i.e., interpolation of random fields). The methods based on stochastic partial differential equations can be further classified into *direct methods* and *conversion methods*.

2.1 Related Work

There are various techniques for the interpolation and extrapolation of space-time continuous systems, also called random fields. An overview and a possible classification of different approaches being discussed in the remainder of this section is visualized in Figure 2.1. In general, the methods can be classified with respect to the type and the complexity of the underlying model description. The model complexity could range from simple toward more sophisticated, i.e., containing detailed descriptions about the physical behavior, for example in terms of stochastic partial differential equations.

The most common approach for interpolating a spatially distributed random field is the *Kriging interpolation* [38, 40, 60, 95, 144], which belongs to the family of linear least squares estimation algorithms. In the limited space of this thesis, it is not possible to give a comprehensive survey of all existing methods, such as simple Kriging, ordinary Kriging, indicator Kriging, and cokriging, to name just a few. Rather the key idea and main properties common to all of these types are stated. In the statistical community the very same approach is also known as *Gaussian process regression* [151, 152]. All these methods have in common that they obtain an estimate of the space-time continuous state by weighting individual measurements proximate to the desired location. Roughly speaking, the weights of closer measurements are higher since they are more likely to be similar to the value being estimated. The important point is that these approaches are based on a *stochastic model of spatial dependencies* in terms of either *variograms* or mean/variance functions. The variogram is a function relating the variance to spatial separations and provides a concise description of the spatial variability. A severe problem not easy to cope with is that the design of the variograms does not adapt locally to the character of *spatial variation* and especially not to the *dynamics of the physical system*. Possible ways to solve this problem are *non-stationary variogram models* [9], which are based on a segmentation of the considered area in separate segments. Then, after defining the size and location of each subregion the corresponding *local variograms* need to be derived. In addition, Kriging methods were primarily developed to account for exact measurements, and thus only realizations of the space-time continuous system (i.e., assumed to be precisely measured) can be considered for the interpolation. This means, existing uncertainties in the measurements cannot be sufficiently considered for the derivation of consistent and correct interpolation results. Another serious disadvantage is that additional background knowledge, for example about the physical behavior, cannot be exploited for more accurate and physically correct interpolation results.

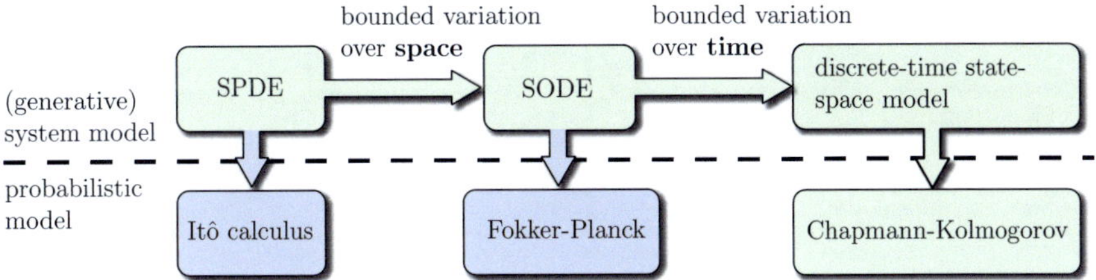

Figure 2.2: Visualiztion of the conversion of *generative system models* under the assumption of bounded variation over space-time. It is noted that the corresponding density representation is required to be converted in the same fashion as the system model. In this work, the stochastic partial differential equation (SPDE) is converted into a system of ordinary stochastic differential equation (SODE). Based on the resulting model, a *probabilistic description* in terms of a transition density can be derived that is required for solving the Chapmann-Kolmogorov equation.

In general, more accurate estimates can be derived by exploiting *additional background information,* for example about the *physical characteristic* of the space-time continuous system. This is especially the case for the region between the individual sensor nodes, where *direct* information can be derived only from such background knowledge. The method called **Bayesian Maximum Entropy (BME)** allows the incorporation of additional background information into the interpolation process [18, 33, 34, 41]. This includes a wide variety of data sources of various forms, like intervals of values, probability density functions or mathematical models about the physical system in terms of *ordinary differential equations.* The BME method can be regarded as a two-stage procedure. In the first stage (prior stage), general knowledge, such as physical laws, is incorporated and the most general prior distribution is derived by maximizing the entropy, which is a measure of the information content. In the second stage (posterior stage), specific knowledge in terms of hard and soft measurements is incorporated in order to obtain an improved interpolation result. However, for the consideration of partial differential equations (1.2), an additional and more complex **Space Transformation** (ST) for each discretization point is required [131]. By this transformation, for each point in the considered solution domain, the partial differential equation is transformed into a one-dimensional ordinary differential equation that can be implemented into the BME framework.

The most general approaches for the interpolation of a random field are those based on *stochastic partial differential equations* (1.2) representing the dynamic behavior and the distributed properties of the underlying physical system. In general, the methods can be classified into (a) direct methods and (b) conversion methods; see Figure 2.1. The *direct methods* are based on optimization techniques directly applied to the space-time continuous model. Basically, the analytic solution is used to obtain a large optimization problem. Solving this usually nonlinear problem, the model parameters, source locations, or node locations can be identified [68, 98, 108]. For direct approaches, assumptions and restrictions have to be made that are often inappropriate in order to obtain an analytic solution. In addition, the development of a Bayesian estimator is rather complex; in particular for the simultaneous approach, i.e., simultaneously estimate the state and parameters (see Chapter 4).

On the other hand, the *conversion methods* are based on converting the mathematical description into a finite-dimensional model; see Figure 2.2. This means, the stochastic partial differential equation (SPDE) is converted into ordinary differential equations, difference equations or algebraic equations. Based on the resulting space-time discrete model, a probabilistic description in terms of a transition density function can be derived that is necessary for solving

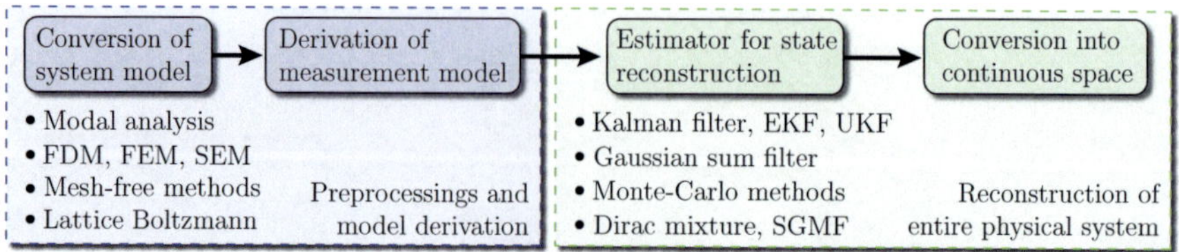

Figure 2.3: Overview of the *four main stages* for the *model-based reconstruction* of space-time continuous physical systems by means of a spatially distributed measurement system. The main stages can be further divided into the following: (a) the *preprocessing stage*, i.e., the model derivation stage, and (b) the *actual reconstruction stage*.

the Chapmann-Kolmogorov equation [109]. This methodology was proposed by various authors [3, 44, 80, 118, 139]. For all these methods, it is important to make the assumption of *bounded variation over space-time*. Roughly speaking, a continuous function is regarded to be of bounded variation, when the integral along the path has a finite value. When this assumption does not hold, then more sophisticated and complex methods are required for deriving the future behavior of the physical system, such as Itô calculus [91] or Fokker-Planck [111].

The state reconstruction and parameter identification method developed in this research work is based on the conversion of the stochastic partial differential equation (SPDE) into a system of ordinary stochastic differential equation (SODE). It is noted that the corresponding density representation is required to be converted in the same fashion as the system model. The main challenge is that the simultaneous state and parameter estimation of space-time continuous systems leads to a *high-dimensional strongly nonlinear* estimation problem. To cope with this difficulty, special estimators based on linearizations at consecutive state trajectories [97] or linearization of the system description [118] were employed in other research works. However, due to the estimation based on a linearized model, accurate results and convergence are not assured. Here, the high-dimensional linear substructure is exploited that naturally exists in the otherwise nonlinear estimation problem; this results in a more efficient reconstruction and identification process. In addition, linearization is not required, and thus convergence is assured. This novel approach is introduced in the *second part* of the thesis (Chapter 3 and Chapter 4).

2.2 Overview of the Reconstruction Process and Considered System

In this section, an overview of the proposed *model-based approach* for the state reconstruction of space-time continuous systems is given. The entire reconstruction process can be separated into *four main stages*, visualized in Figure 2.3. Before they are described in more detail, a brief description is given in the remainder of this section.

1) Conversion of the system model The state reconstruction of physical systems based on a distributed-parameter description is a challenging task. The main reason is that employing an estimator within the Bayesian framework requires a lumped-parameter system description. Hence, it is proposed by various authors [118, 139, 154] to convert the mathematical model from the distributed-parameter form into a lumped-parameter description. For this conversion

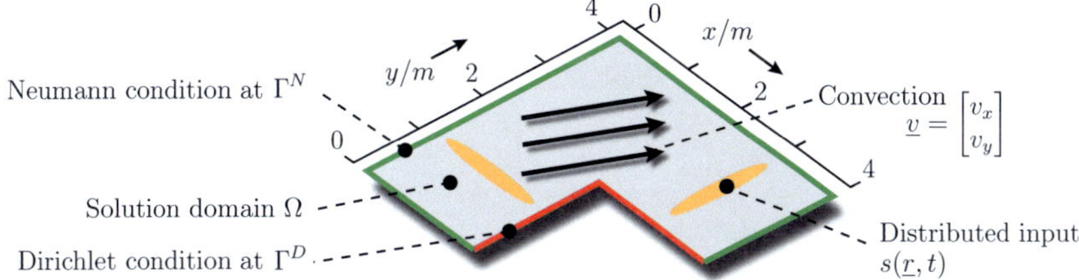

Figure 2.4: Visualization of the two-dimensional L-shaped solution domain $\Omega \in \mathbb{R}^2$ and assumed conditions at the boundary domains $\partial\Omega$ (Dirichlet condition at Γ^D and Neumann conditions at Γ^N). The physical system is driven by the space-time continuous input $\boldsymbol{s}(\underline{r}, t)$. The convection field $\underline{v} := [v_x, v_y]^\mathrm{T}$ and the material properties are assumed to be homogeneous in the entire domain Ω of interest, for simplicity reasons.

there exists various numerical methods. Based on the resulting *lumped-parameter system description*, the state of the space-time continuous system can be uniquely characterized by a *finite-dimensional* state vector. It is important to emphasize that the conversion of *stochastic partial differential equations* (1.2) does not only need to be performed on the actual model equations but especially on their associated *uncertainty representation*.

2) Derivation of measurement model For the estimation of physical systems using a spatially distributed measurement system, a special *measurement model* needs to be derived. This model considers the physical properties of the individual nodes as well as the *distributed characteristic* of the entire network, i.e., the topology. Basically, the derived model is responsible for mapping the readings received from the sensor nodes to the common global state vector characterizing the physical system.

3) Application of appropriate Bayesian estimator Based on the aforementioned lumped-parameter system and measurement model, the derivation of an appropriate Bayesian estimator is possible in a more efficient manner. In general, the structure of the estimator strongly depends on the structure of the obtained system description, i.e., being linear or nonlinear. Moreover, especially for sensor network applications, a *recursive estimation scheme* is essential. This means, although more and more measurements are obtained, the network only stores a density representation of a *fixed size*. Thanks to the probabilistic approach, uncertainties both in the measurements and the mathematical model (including uncertain model parameters and uncertain node locations) are considered.

4) Conversion into continuous space In order to reconstruct the space-time continuous state at *any desired spatial coördinate*, the estimated finite-dimensional state vector needs to be converted back into the continuous space. It is important to emphasize that within this processing step, in particular, the *probability density function* of the finite-dimensional state vector needs to be mapped. This results in a probability density function that represents the physical system at any location.

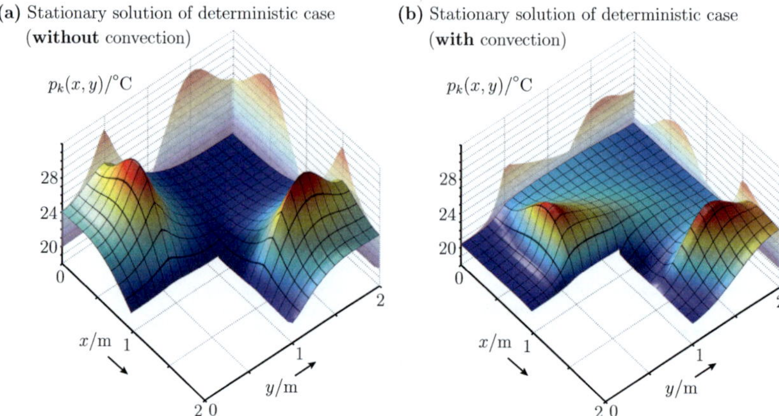

Figure 2.5: Stationary solution of the *deterministic space-time continuous system* in the considered L-shaped solution domain Ω with the assumed boundary conditions and system inputs. Solution of **(a)** the *diffusion* equation with a diffusion coefficient $\alpha = 0.8\,\mathrm{m^2\,h^{-1}}$ and **(b)** the *convection-diffusion* equation with velocity $\underline{v} = [8,\,8]^\mathrm{T}\,\mathrm{m\,h^{-1}}$.

Example 2.1: Considered space-time continuous physical system

The methods introduced in this chapter can be applied to the general case of linear partial differential equations (1.2). However, throughout the entire work, we consider a certain space-time continuous system occuring in many applications, the *convection-diffusion system*. The governing stochastic partial differential equation can be stated in the solution domain $\Omega \in \mathbb{R}^2$ as follows

$$\mathbb{L}(\boldsymbol{p}(\underline{r},t)) := \frac{\partial \boldsymbol{p}(\cdot)}{\partial t} - \alpha \underbrace{\left(\frac{\partial^2 \boldsymbol{p}(\cdot)}{\partial x^2} + \frac{\partial^2 \boldsymbol{p}(\cdot)}{\partial y^2} \right)}_{\text{diffusion term}} + \underbrace{\left(v_x \frac{\partial \boldsymbol{p}(\cdot)}{\partial x} + v_y \frac{\partial \boldsymbol{p}(\cdot)}{\partial y} \right)}_{\text{convection term}} - \gamma\,\boldsymbol{s}(\underline{r},t) \ , \qquad (2.1)$$

where $\underline{r} := [x,y]^\mathrm{T} \in \mathbb{R}^2$ denotes the spatial coördinate and $p(\underline{r},t)$ and $s(\underline{r},t)$ are the *space-time continuous system state* and the *space-time continuous system input*. The vector $\underline{v} := [v_x, v_y]^\mathrm{T} \in \mathbb{R}^2$ represents the homogeneous *convection field*. The *diffusion coefficient* $\alpha \in \mathbb{R}$ is characterized by specific material properties, such as the medium density ρ, the heat capacity c_p, and the thermal conductivity k, according to $\alpha := \kappa/(\rho\,c_p)$. The *system input coefficient* $\gamma \in \mathbb{R}$ that is here represented by $\gamma := 1/(\rho\,c_p)$ characterizes the influence of the system input $s(\cdot)$ on the physical system. In the case of *inhomogeneous systems*, all these material properties and the convection field depend on the spatial coördinate $\underline{r}$. In this work, only homogeneous physical systems are considered for simplicity; however the extension is conceptually straightforward.

For the estimation of the space-time continuous physical system (2.1), knowledge about the boundary conditions is necessary. There are several types of such conditions depending on the constraints at the boundaries of the solution domain Ω. In this thesis, the following conditions are assumed

$$\text{\textit{Dirichlet} boundary condition} \qquad \boldsymbol{p}(\underline{r},t) = \boldsymbol{g}^D(\underline{r},t) \ , \qquad \forall \underline{r} \in \Gamma^\mathrm{D} \ ,$$

$$\text{\textit{Neumann} boundary condition} \qquad \underline{n} \cdot \nabla \boldsymbol{p}(\underline{r},t) = -\boldsymbol{g}^N(\underline{r},t) \ , \qquad \forall \underline{r} \in \Gamma^\mathrm{N} \ ,$$

where $\boldsymbol{g}^N(\cdot)$ specifies a condition on the derivative, is referred to as a *Neumann* boundary condition and $\boldsymbol{g}^D(\cdot)$ is the so-called *Dirichlet* boundary condition. The solution domain Ω and the conditions at their respective boundary domains $\partial\Omega$ are visualized in Figure 2.4. ∎

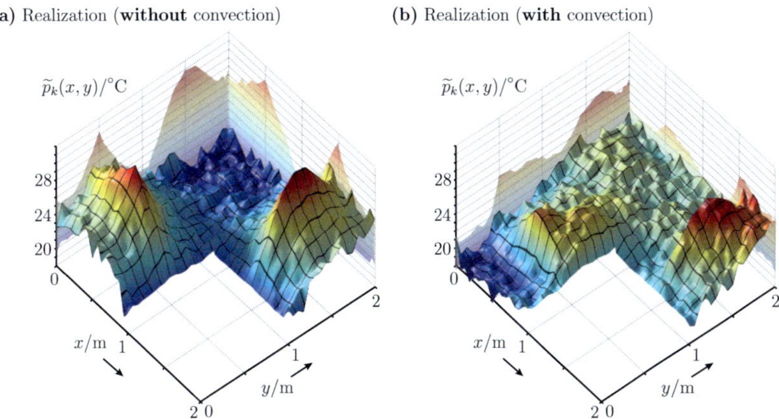

Figure 2.6: *Realization* of the space-time continuous system in the considered L-shaped solution domain Ω with assumed boundary conditions and system inputs: **(a)** *diffusion* equation (i.e., without convection) with a diffusion coefficient $\alpha = 0.8\,\mathrm{m^2\,h^{-1}}$ and **(b)** the *convection-diffusion* equation with velocity $\underline{v} = [8,\,8]^{\mathrm{T}}\,\mathrm{m\,h^{-1}}$.

The two-dimensional convection-diffusion equation (2.1) can be used as the governing equation for various physical phenomena arising in sensor network applications, such as the observation of temperature distributions or nitrate concentrations in the groundwater [5, 145]. The numerical solution of the physical system in the *deterministic case* is depicted in Figure 2.5 for specific initial and boundary conditions, *with* and *without* an underlying convection field. The assumed model parameters for the derivation of the solution are stated in more detail in Example 2.4. It can be clearly seen that the physical system is moving from the location of the spatially distributed inputs through the entire solution domain $\Omega \in \mathbb{R}^2$, driven by the *diffusion process* and the *convection field*. It is emphasized that the derivation of a *perfect* mathematical model can be rather complex and due to the computational complexity in most cases not desirable. A possible *realization* of the space-time continuous physical system (2.1) is depicted in Figure 2.6. The arising uncertainties associated with the abstraction and reduction process need to be systematically considered.

2.3 Conversion of Space-Time Continuous Systems

In general, the application of a Bayesian estimation approach for the state and parameter estimation based on a distributed-parameter system (1.2) is a challenging task. For that reason, in this research work, the stochastic partial differential equation (2.1) including its density representation is converted into a *finite*-dimensional *lumped*-parameter system (1.1). This system description can be derived by methods for solving partial differential equations; see Figure 2.3. An overview of different methods is given in the remainder of this section.

Spectral methods and grid/mesh-based methods The *modal analysis method* (also called *spectral method*) basically uses a set of *global* expansion functions for the approximation of the solution of the partial differential equation (1.2). This method just needs a few parameters to represent a smooth solution in the entire solution domain [43, 116]. It is generally understood that spectral methods use expansion functions[1] that have a nonzero definition throughout the *entire* solution domain [24]. However, such functions can be found only for simple problems with simple boundary conditions. Moreover, there are grid/mesh-based methods, such as the *finite-difference* method [36, 136], the *finite-element* method [11, 20, 28], and the *spectral-element* method [42, 79, 85]. These methods require a set of expansion functions that are only locally defined in finite sub-regions. The systematic decomposition of the solution domain into appropriate subdomains[2] involved in these methods allows the conversion of space-time continuous systems even for rather complex geometries, and thus complex boundary conditions. Since these techniques use expansion functions that are *locally defined* in a finite region, it is possible to derive a probabilistic system model sufficient for a *decentralized estimation approach*; see Chapter 5. This fact becomes especially important for physical systems that are distributed over a wide area and large sensor networks. All the aforementioned methods can be used with the same numerical methodology, the so-called *Galerkin formulation*. In this thesis, the conversion necessary for the state reconstruction is based on a predefined mesh.

Mesh-free methods In comparison, *mesh-free methods* were developed providing several advantages [15, 16, 37, 101]. These methods convert the distributed-parameter system (1.2) into a lumped-parameter form without requiring a predefined mesh; instead they are based on a set of nodes scattered within the considered solution domain. It is important to note that unlike the meshes, the scattered nodes do not contain any information about the relationship between the individual nodes. This means, it is not necessary to employ complex and computationally demanding re-meshing algorithms that are required for mesh-based methods in order to derive more precise results in the case of large deformations or strong discontinuities. The scattered nodes in mesh-free methods can be arbitrarily added and relocated without changing their relation to other nodes. A comprehensive overview on the theory and the description of various mesh-free methods with focus on mechanics of solids, beams, and plates is given in [94] and with focus on fluid dynamics and crack growths is given in [93]. The conversion process based on mesh-free methods results in a finite-dimensional system description that is similar to the mesh-based methods. Thus, the implementation of these methods in the proposed framework is conceptually straightforward.

Lattice Boltzmann modelling There are methods that *directly derive expressions* in explicit algebraic form, such as *lattice Boltzmann modelling* [148]. These methods are based on *directly modelling* the microscopic kinetic behavior on uniform grids with only *local interactions*, and thus allow parallelization and decentralization in a straightforward way. However, it is unclear how the uncertainties are consistently considered throughout the entire modelling process. In addition, the lattice Boltzmann method can be regarded as a finite difference discretization of the model equations. This means, there is a coupling of the grid size with the time step leading to the necessity of performing many time steps when refining the grid [135]. Moreover, the generalization of non-uniform grids is quite complex.

In the remainder of this section, the conversion of the system description and its underlying density representation is described based on: (a) the *spatial and temporal discretization* and (b) the *Galerkin formulation*. It is shown that the employment of such grid/mesh-based conversion methods to *linear* stochastic partial differential equations (1.2) always results in *linear* lumped-parameter systems in state-space form. Based on such a system description, probabilistic models can be derived that are necessary for the Bayesian estimator in order to reconstruct the space-time continuous state of the physical system.

---

1 In the case of modal analysis method the expansion functions
   consists of *trigonometric functions*.
2 For FDM and FEM/SEM they are respectively called *grid points* and *elements*.

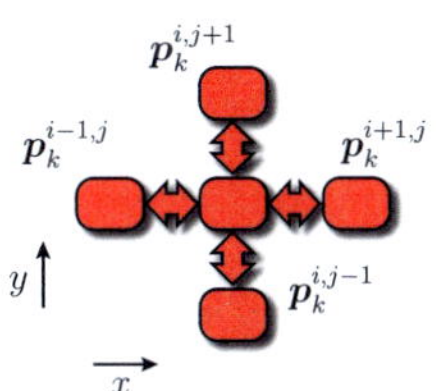

Figure 2.7: Schematic diagram of the spatial/temporal discretization using the finite-difference method. **(a)** Spatial discretization of the system description in the considered solution domain Ω. The nodes are classified into *software nodes* that are necessary only for describing the physical system and *hardware nodes* that are responsible for obtaining measurements. **(b)** Discretization of the distributed system using a *finite difference scheme*.

2.3.1 Spatial/temporal Discretization Methods

Finite-difference method The *finite-difference method* is undoubtedly the simplest method for the conversion of partial differential equations (1.2), however, suffers from computational inefficiency and possible discretization errors. In the first step, the solution domain $\Omega \in \mathbb{R}^2$ is spatially discretized into a grid consisting of so-called *software nodes*. Then, in the second step, the differential terms at these nodes are replaced by finite differences in the partial differential equation (1.2). In this research work, the space-time continuous physical system is converted, for simplicity, using the following *central finite difference scheme*

$$
\frac{\partial \boldsymbol{p}(\underline{r}, t)}{\partial t} \approx \frac{\boldsymbol{p}_{k+1}^{i,j} - \boldsymbol{p}_k^{i,j}}{\Delta t} \,,
$$

$$
\nabla \boldsymbol{p}(\underline{r}, t) \approx \frac{\boldsymbol{p}_k^{i+1,j} - \boldsymbol{p}_k^{i-1,j}}{2\Delta x} + \frac{\boldsymbol{p}_k^{i,j+1} - \boldsymbol{p}_k^{i,j-1}}{2\Delta y} \,,
$$

$$
\nabla^2 \boldsymbol{p}(\underline{r}, t) \approx \frac{\boldsymbol{p}_k^{i+1,j} - 2\boldsymbol{p}_k^{i,j} + \boldsymbol{p}_k^{i-1,j}}{\Delta x^2} + \frac{\boldsymbol{p}_k^{i,j+1} - 2\boldsymbol{p}_k^{i,j} + \boldsymbol{p}_k^{i,j-1}}{\Delta y^2} \,, \tag{2.2}
$$

where Δt is the sampling time and Δx and Δy denote the spatial sampling period in the respective directions. The superscript (i, j) and subscript k in $p_k^{i,j}$ denote the value of the physical system at the *software nodes* (i, j) and at the time step k.

Inserting the finite differences (2.2) into the partial differential equation (1.2) directly results in a system of difference equations, and thus the desired state-space model (1.4). The structure of the resulting equation is visualized in a schematic diagram focusing on one software node (i, j) in Figure 2.7. However, this so-called forward integration in time leads to poor numerical stability due to the limited accuracy of floating point arithmetic. In order to avoid such instabilities in case of forward integrations, *small step sizes* both in space and in time have to be chosen. This certainly results in many iterations that are necessary to calculate the propagation over time. Another way to overcome instabilities is to employ *implicit integration methods*, such as the Crank-Nicolson integration method [36, 182, 183]. A numerical integration method is called implicit, when after substituting the finite differences (2.2) into the equation being integrated, the value to be determined occurs on both sides of the equation. The Crank-Nicolson method is based on the central finite differences (2.2) in space, and a trapezoidal rule in time; thus, can be regarded as an implicit method.

Resulting lumped-parameter system It can be shown that employing any common finite difference scheme (i.e., explicit or implicit), any kind of *linear* stochastic partial differential equation (1.2) can be converted into a finite-dimensional system description in *linear form*

$$\underline{x}_{k+1} = \mathbf{A}_k\,\underline{x}_k + \mathbf{B}_k\left(\hat{\underline{u}}_k + \underline{w}_k^x\right) \ . \tag{2.3}$$

The system state vector $\underline{x}_k := [p_k^1, \ldots, p_k^{N_x}]^\mathrm{T} \in \mathbb{R}^{N_x}$ contains the values of the space-time continuous state $p(\cdot)$ at the corresponding N_x software nodes. The matrices $\mathbf{A}_k \in \mathbb{R}^{N_x \times N_x}$ and $\mathbf{B}_k \in \mathbb{R}^{N_x \times N_x}$ are the so-called system matrix and input matrix, respectively. The system input vector $\hat{\underline{u}}_k \in \mathbb{R}^{N_x}$ contains the values of the space-time continuous input $s(\cdot)$ at the respective software nodes, and $\underline{w}_k^x \in \mathbb{R}^{N_x}$ denotes its corresponding discretized process noise term.

Example 2.2: Spatial/temporal discretization for rectangular solution domains

In this example, the structure of the state-space model (2.3) resulting from the central finite-difference method is best envisioned for a rectangular solution domain Ω; see Figure 2.7. The extension to more complicated domains and the application to different types of linear partial differential equations (1.2) is straightforward.

The space-time discrete state vector is represented by $\underline{x}_k := [p_k^{1,1}, \ldots, p^{1,m}, \ldots, p_k^{m,m}]^\mathrm{T} \in \mathbb{R}^{m^2}$ containing the value of the physical system at the individual *software nodes* (i, j). The variable m denotes the total number of nodes used for the discretization in each dimension. The parameters are assumed to be inhomogeneous, which means they do depend on the spatial coördinates. Then, the conversion of the system (2.1) results in the following *system matrix* $\mathbf{A}_k \in \mathbb{R}^{m^2 \times m^2}$,

$$\mathbf{A}_k = \frac{\Delta t}{\Delta h^2}\begin{bmatrix} \widetilde{\mathbf{A}}_k^1 & \widetilde{\mathbf{B}}_k^1 & \mathbf{0} & \cdots & \mathbf{0} \\ \widetilde{\mathbf{C}}_k^2 & \widetilde{\mathbf{A}}_k^2 & \widetilde{\mathbf{B}}_k^2 & \cdots & \mathbf{0} \\ \vdots & \ddots & \ddots & \ddots & \vdots \\ \mathbf{0} & \cdots & \widetilde{\mathbf{C}}_k^{m-1} & \widetilde{\mathbf{A}}_k^{m-1} & \widetilde{\mathbf{B}}_k^{m-1} \\ \mathbf{0} & \cdots & \mathbf{0} & \widetilde{\mathbf{C}}_k^m & \widetilde{\mathbf{A}}_k^m \end{bmatrix} + \mathbf{I}_{m^2}\ ,$$

where $\mathbf{I}_{m^2} \in \mathbb{R}^{m^2 \times m^2}$ represents the identity matrix and the submatrices $\widetilde{\mathbf{A}}^i \in \mathbb{R}^{m \times m}$ are given by

$$\widetilde{\mathbf{A}}_k^i = \begin{bmatrix} -4\alpha_k^{i,1} & \alpha_k^{i,1} - \frac{\Delta h}{2}v_x^{i,1} & 0 & \cdots & 0 \\ \alpha_k^{i,2} + \frac{\Delta h}{2}v_x^{i,2} & -4\alpha_k^{i,2} & \alpha_k^{i,2} - \frac{\Delta h}{2}v_x^{i,2} & \cdots & 0 \\ \vdots & \ddots & \ddots & \ddots & \vdots \\ 0 & \cdots & \alpha_k^{i,m-1} + \frac{\Delta h}{2}v_x^{i,m-1} & -4\alpha_k^{i,m-1} & \alpha_k^{i,m-1} - \frac{\Delta h}{2}v_x^{i,m-1} \\ 0 & \cdots & 0 & \alpha_k^{i,m} + \frac{\Delta h}{2}v_x^{i,m} & -4\alpha_k^{i,m} \end{bmatrix},$$

and the submatrices $\widetilde{\mathbf{B}}_k^i \in \mathbb{R}^{m \times m}$ and $\widetilde{\mathbf{C}}_k^i \in \mathbb{R}^{m \times m}$ are respectively given by

$$\widetilde{\mathbf{B}}_k^i = \begin{bmatrix} \alpha_k^{i,1} - \frac{\Delta h}{2}v_y^{i,1} & \cdots & 0 \\ \vdots & \ddots & \vdots \\ 0 & \cdots & \alpha_k^{i,m} - \frac{\Delta h}{2}v_y^{i,m} \end{bmatrix}, \quad \widetilde{\mathbf{C}}_k^i = \begin{bmatrix} \alpha_k^{i,1} + \frac{\Delta h}{2}v_y^{i,1} & \cdots & 0 \\ \vdots & \ddots & \vdots \\ 0 & \cdots & \alpha_k^{i,m} + \frac{\Delta h}{2}v_y^{i,m} \end{bmatrix} .$$

For the conversion of the space-time continuous system, the input function $s(\underline{z}, t)$ needs to be discretized at the same *software nodes* (i, j) as the space-time continuous system state $p(\underline{z}, t)$. This leads to the *input vector* $\underline{u}_k := [s_k^{1,1}, \ldots, s^{1,m}, \ldots, s_k^{m,m}]^{\mathrm{T}} \in \mathbb{R}^{m^2}$. The *input matrix* $\mathbf{B}_k$ is given by a diagonal matrix with sampling time Δt and input parameters $\gamma_k^{i,j}$ on the diagonal entries,

$$\mathbf{B}_k = \mathrm{diag}\left\{\gamma_k^{1,1}\Delta t, \ \ldots \ , \gamma_k^{1,m}\Delta t, \ \ldots \ , \gamma_k^{m,m}\Delta t\right\} \ .$$

A detailed description of the boundary conditions, such as Dirichlet boundary condition and Neumann boundary condition, and how these conditions are considered throughout the conversion process is omitted in this thesis; instead the reader is refered to [36, 136]. ∎

2.3.2 Spatial Decomposition of System Description

The conversion of space-time continuous systems using mesh-based methods, such as the spectral method, finite-element method, or spectral-element method, may be used with the same numerical methodology, the so-called *Galerkin formulation*. Within this formulation, it is assumed that the exact solution of a partial differential equation (1.2) can be expanded as an infinite sum of shape functions $\Psi(\cdot)$. The approximated solution is then derived by truncating this expansion and projecting the resulting error onto the finite-dimensional subspace spanned by the shape functions. The lumped-parameter system model in discrete-time state-space form, can be derived in **three stages** (shown in Figure 2.8).

1. *Spatial decomposition* of the space-time continuous system description (see Section 2.3.2) and system input, including its uncertainty representation (see Section 2.3.3).

2. *Selection of appropriate shape functions* as a finite-dimensional set for representing the solution in the continuous-space domain of interest (see Section 2.3.4).

3. *Temporal discretization* of the resulting system of stochastic ordinary differential equations in order to arrive at a discrete-time system in state-space form (see Section 2.3.5).

Finite expansion of the solution domain　The purpose of the *spatial decomposition* is to convert the stochastic partial differential equation (1.2) into a system of stochastic ordinary differential equations (1.1). In a first step, the solution domain $\Omega \in \mathbb{R}^2$ is spatially decomposed into N_{el} non-overlapping subdomains Ω^e (the so-called *finite elements*). Then, an appropriate representation of the solution $p(\cdot)$ within each subdomain Ω^e needs to be defined. The Galerkin formulation assumes that the solution $p(\cdot)$ and the input $s(\cdot)$ in the entire domain Ω can be represented by a piecewise approximation, the *finite expansion*, according to

$$\boldsymbol{p}(\underline{r}, t) := \sum_{i=1}^{N_x} \Psi^i(\underline{r})\, \boldsymbol{x}^i(t) = \underline{\Psi}(\underline{r})^{\mathrm{T}} \cdot \underline{x}(t) \ , \quad \boldsymbol{s}(\underline{r}, t) := \sum_{i=1}^{N_x} \Psi^i(\underline{r})\, \boldsymbol{u}^i(t) = \underline{\Psi}(\underline{r})^{\mathrm{T}} \cdot \underline{u}(t)$$

where $\underline{\Psi}(\underline{r})^{\mathrm{T}} : \mathbb{R}^{N_x} \times \mathbb{R}^2 \to \mathbb{R}$ represents a linear mapping containing analytic functions $\Psi^i(\cdot)$ called *shape functions*; see Section 2.3.4. The vectors $\underline{x}(t) \in \mathbb{R}^{N_x}$ and $\underline{u}(t) \in \mathbb{R}^{N_x}$ are the vectors collecting their corresponding weighting coefficients. The variable N_x represents the number of shape functions used for approximating the solution in the domain of interest.

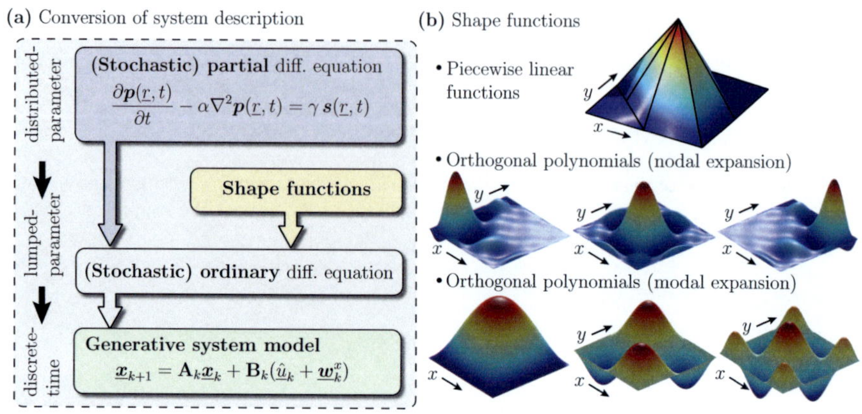

Figure 2.8: **(a)** Visualization of the individual stages for the conversion of *stochastic partial differential equations* into a time-discrete system model in state-space form. The process consists of a *spatial decomposition* leading to a system of *stochastic ordinary differential equation* and based on that a *temporal discretization*. **(b)** Examples of shape functions used for the spatial decomposition of the solution domain $\Omega \in \mathbb{R}^2$, piecewise linear functions and orthogonal polynomials in a nodal/modal expansion.

It is important to note that the individual shape functions $\Psi^i(\cdot)$ are usually defined to be non-zero only in a local finite region that are typically made up of non-overlapping subdomains. Truncating the series of shape functions (2.4) results in an approximate solution. It is obvious that concerning the finite expansion, the values of the individual shape functions $\Psi^i(\underline{r})$ depend only on the *spatial coördinate*, whereas the weighting coefficients $x^i(t)$ depend *only on time*. Because of that, this conversion method can be regarded as a *separation approach*, meaning that *spatial and temporal dependencies* in the space-time continuous system state $p(\cdot)$ are separated. The essence of aforementioned conversion methods lies in the choice of the shape functions $\Psi^i(\cdot)$, e.g., piecewise linear functions, orthogonal functions, or trigonometric functions.

Projection onto finite space (weak formulation) The approximated solution in terms of the finite expansion (2.4) cannot satisfy the infinite-dimensional description in terms of the stochastic partial differential equation (2.1). The consequence is that a *residual R_Ω* remains. To make this residual small in some sense a *weighted integral* over the solution domain $\Omega \in \mathbb{R}^2$ has to be minimized, according to

$$\int_\Omega \Psi^i(\underline{r}) \underbrace{\left[\frac{\partial \boldsymbol{p}(\underline{r},t)}{\partial t} - \alpha \nabla^2 \boldsymbol{p}(\underline{r},t) + \underline{v} \cdot \nabla \boldsymbol{p}(\underline{r},t) - \gamma \boldsymbol{s}(\underline{r},t)\right]}_{\text{SPDE to be converted}} \mathrm{d}\underline{r} = 0 \; , \tag{2.4}$$

which needs to be performed for all members of the finite expansion (i.e., $i = 1 \ldots N_x$). The minimization of the weighted integral automatically leads to the best numerical approximation of the solution $p(\cdot)$ governed by the convection-diffusion equation (2.1). The weighted integral (2.4) can also be regarded as a *projection* of the resulting approximation error *onto the finite-dimensional space* that is spanned by the shape functions $\Psi^i(\cdot)$.

In the following, the arguments in the shape functions $\Psi^i(\underline{r})$, in the solution $p(\underline{r}, t)$, and in the system input $\boldsymbol{s}(\underline{r}, t)$ are omitted for brevity reasons. The weighted integral (2.4) can be reformulated by using the rules of product differentiation, leading to

$$\int_\Omega \Psi^i \frac{\partial \boldsymbol{p}}{\partial t}\, \mathrm{d}\underline{r} - \alpha \underbrace{\int_\Omega \left[\nabla \cdot (\Psi^i \nabla \boldsymbol{p}) - \nabla \Psi^i \cdot \nabla \boldsymbol{p} \right]\, \mathrm{d}\underline{r}}_{=\int_\Omega \Psi^i \nabla^2 \boldsymbol{p}\, \mathrm{d}\underline{r}} + \int_\Omega \Psi^i\, \underline{v} \cdot \nabla \boldsymbol{p}\, \mathrm{d}\underline{r} - \gamma \int_\Omega \Psi^i \boldsymbol{s}\, \mathrm{d}\underline{r} = 0 \ , \quad (2.5)$$

which can be considered as the *weak formulation* of the partial differential equation (2.1). The second integral can be further manipulated using the *Gauss' divergence theorem* given as follows

$$\int_\Omega \nabla \cdot (\Psi^i \nabla \boldsymbol{p})\, \mathrm{d}\underline{r} = \oint_{\partial\Omega} \Psi^i\, \underbrace{\underline{n} \cdot \nabla \boldsymbol{p}}_{=:-\boldsymbol{g}^N}\, \mathrm{d}l \ ,$$

where $\underline{n}$ is the unit vector that is normal to the boundary domain $\partial\Omega$ *pointing outward*. The rough meaning of the theorem is that the areal integral of the divergence of any differentiable vector function over the domain $\Omega \in \mathbb{R}^2$ is equal to the flux across the boundary domain $\partial\Omega$. The term $\boldsymbol{g}^N$ is the so-called *Neumann boundary condition* specifying the flux at the boundary domain $\partial\Omega$ *into* the considered solution domain Ω.

Stochastic ordinary differential equation Replacing the solution function $p(\cdot)$ and the input function $s(\cdot)$ in the weak formulation (2.5) by the finite expansion (2.4), we arrive at following system of N_x linear *stochastic ordinary differential equations*

$$\sum_{i=1}^{N_x} M_{ij}^g \frac{\partial \boldsymbol{x}^i(t)}{\partial t} + \sum_{i=1}^{N_x} N_{ij}^g\, \boldsymbol{x}^i(t) + \alpha \sum_{i=1}^{N_x} D_{ij}^g\, \boldsymbol{x}^i(t) = \underbrace{\gamma \oint_{\partial\Omega} \Psi_i\, \underline{n} \cdot \nabla \boldsymbol{p}\, \mathrm{d}l}_{-:\underline{b}(t)} + \gamma \sum_{i=1}^{N_x} M_{ij}^g\, \boldsymbol{u}^i(t) \qquad (2.6)$$

where the terms M_{ij}^g, D_{ij}^g, and N_{ij}^g represent specific integrals of the shape functions $\Psi^i(\cdot)$ over the entire solution domain Ω to be evaluated. These integrals are given by

$$M_{ij}^g := \int_\Omega \Psi^i(\underline{r})\Psi^j(\underline{r})\, \mathrm{d}\underline{r} \ , \qquad D_{ij}^g := \int_\Omega \nabla\Psi^i(\underline{r}) \cdot \nabla\Psi^j(\underline{r})\, \mathrm{d}\underline{r} \ , \qquad N_{ij}^g := \int_\Omega \Psi^i\, \underline{v} \cdot \nabla\Psi^j\, \mathrm{d}\underline{r} \ ,$$
$$(2.7)$$

which makes obvious that they contain information about the structure of the decomposed solution domain $\Omega \in \mathbb{R}^2$ and merely depend upon the choice of the shape functions $\Psi^i(\cdot)$. This means, the solution of the integrals (2.7), and thus the structure of the stochastic ordinary differential equations (2.6) depends on the method used for the conversion of the space-time continuous system description, e.g., finite-element method or spectral-element method.

The individual integrals (2.7) can be assembled to the *global mass matrix* $\mathbf{M}_G$, the *global advection matrix* $\mathbf{N}_G$, and the *global diffusion matrix* $\mathbf{D}_G$, respectively. By this means, it is obvious that aforementioned conversion of *linear* partial differential equations (1.2) always results in a system of *linear* ordinary differential equations, according to

$$\underline{\dot{x}}(t) = \underbrace{-\mathbf{M}_G^{-1}(\mathbf{N}_G + \alpha\mathbf{D}_G)}_{=:\widetilde{\mathbf{A}}(t)}\, \underline{x}(t) + \gamma\, \underline{u}(t) + \mathbf{M}_G^{-1}\, \underline{b}(t) \ , \qquad (2.8)$$

where $\widetilde{\mathbf{A}}(t) \in \mathbb{R}^{N_x \times N_x}$ is the system matrix of the continuous-time system. The boundary conditions of the space-time continuous system to be monitored are collected in the so-called *boundary condition vector* $\underline{b}(t) \in \mathbb{R}^{N_x}$. The vector $\underline{x}(t) \in \mathbb{R}^{N_x}$ denotes the continuous-time state vector containing the weighting coefficients $x^i(t)$ of the finite expansion (2.4). A more detailed description on numerically solving the integrals (2.7) can be found [79].

2.3.3 Spatial Decomposition of Sytem Input and Process Noise

In the previous section, the *Galerkin formulation* for the conversion of a space-time continuous system (2.1) into a system of ordinary differential equations (2.8) was introduced. This section is devoted to the conversion of the *space-time continuous system input* $s(\underline{r}, t)$ and its underlying *probability density function* $f^s(s|\underline{r}, t)$ into a finite-dimensional lumped-parameter form in terms of the space-discrete time-continuous state vector $\underline{u}(t) \sim f^u(\underline{u}|t)$. This additional conversion is necessary for solving the system of stochastic ordinary differential equations (2.8).

Density representation of the space-time continuous system input   In this research work, the space-time continuous system input $s(\cdot)$ is modelled as a variable represented by following probability density function

$$\underbrace{s(\underline{r}, t)}_{=:\hat{s}(\cdot)+\boldsymbol{w}^s(\cdot)} \sim f^s(s|\underline{r}, t) := \mathcal{N}\left(\hat{s}(\underline{r}, t), C^s(\underline{r}, t)\right) , \tag{2.9}$$

where $\mathcal{N}(\cdot)$ is the Gaussian density function with respective mean and variance. In general, both the mean $\hat{s}(\cdot)$ and the variance $C^s(\cdot)$ of the system input $s(\cdot)$ are *space-variant*. Here, for simplicity reasons, it is assumed that the system input is *spatially and temporal mutually independent*. This means, the noise term $\boldsymbol{w}^s(\underline{r}, t)$ is represented by zero-mean white Gaussian process noise with following property

$$\mathrm{E}\left\{\boldsymbol{w}^s(\underline{r}_1, t) \cdot \boldsymbol{w}^s(\underline{r}_2, t)\right\} = \begin{cases} 0 & \text{for} \quad \underline{r}_1 \neq \underline{r}_2 \\ C^s(\underline{r}, t) & \text{for} \quad \underline{r}_1 = \underline{r}_2 = \underline{r} \end{cases} .$$

The main goal in this section is to derive a finite-dimensional input vector $\underline{u}(t) \sim f^u(\underline{u}|t)$ (including its *density representation*) for a given space-time continuous system input $s(\cdot)$. The finite-dimensional input $\underline{u}(t)$ then can be used for solving the stochastic ordinary differential equation (2.8) for the state vector $\underline{x}(t) \sim f^x(\underline{x}|t)$.

Projection onto finite space (projection problem)   In order to convert the space-time continuous input $s(\underline{r}, t) \sim f^e(s|\underline{r}, t)$ to the lumped-parameter input $\underline{u}(t) \sim f^u(\underline{u}|t)$, the infinite-dimensional description needs to be projected onto the finite-dimensional space represented by the shape functions $\Psi^i(\underline{r})$. This can be achieved in a similar way to the integral (2.4) by solving the following *projection problem*

$$\int_\Omega \Psi^i(\underline{r}) \underbrace{\sum_{j=1}^{N_x} \Psi^j(\underline{r})\boldsymbol{u}^j(t)}_{=\boldsymbol{s}(\underline{r},t)} \, \mathrm{d}\underline{r} = \int_\Omega \Psi^i(\underline{r})\boldsymbol{s}(\underline{r}, t)\mathrm{d}\underline{r} ,$$

which must hold for all shape functions $\Psi^i(\cdot)$ of the finite expansion (2.4), with $i = 1 \ldots N_x$. The definition of appropriate shape functions, and accordingly a lumped-parameter form of the space-time continuous system input $s(\cdot)$ leads to the following matrix problem to be solved

$$\underbrace{\begin{bmatrix} \int_\Omega \Psi^1(\underline{r})\Psi^1(\underline{r}) \, \mathrm{d}\underline{r} & \cdots & \int_\Omega \Psi^1(\underline{r})\Psi^{N_x}(\underline{r})\mathrm{d}\underline{r} \\ \vdots & \ddots & \vdots \\ \int_\Omega \Psi^{N_x}(\underline{r})\Psi^1(\underline{r}) \, \mathrm{d}\underline{r} & \cdots & \int_\Omega \Psi^{N_x}(\underline{r})\Psi^{N_x}(\underline{r}) \, \mathrm{d}\underline{r} \end{bmatrix}}_{=:\mathbf{M}_G} \underbrace{\begin{bmatrix} \boldsymbol{u}^1(t) \\ \vdots \\ \boldsymbol{u}^{N_x}(t) \end{bmatrix}}_{=:\underline{\boldsymbol{u}}(t)} = \underbrace{\begin{bmatrix} \int_\Omega \Psi^1(\underline{r})\boldsymbol{s}(\underline{r}, t) \, \mathrm{d}\underline{r} \\ \vdots \\ \int_\Omega \Psi^{N_x}(\underline{r})\boldsymbol{s}(\underline{r}, t) \, \mathrm{d}\underline{r} \end{bmatrix}}_{=:\underline{\boldsymbol{s}}(t)} . \tag{2.10}$$

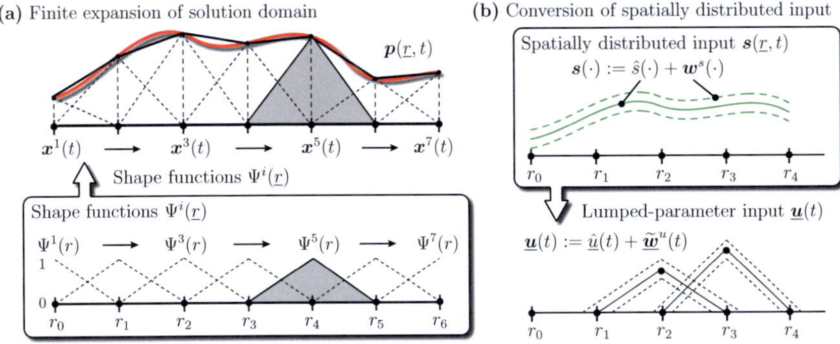

Figure 2.9: (a) Spatial decomposition of the solution $p(\underline{r},t)$ in the considered domain using finite expansions, which are represented by shape functions $\Psi^i(\underline{r})$ and corresponding weighting coefficients $x^i(t)$. (b) Conversion of the space-time continuous system input $s(\underline{r},t)$ including its density representation. This results in a lumped-parameter description $\underline{u}(t)$ represented by shape functions $\Psi^i(\underline{r})$ and weighting coefficients $\underline{u}^i(t)$.

The *global mass matrix* $\mathbf{M}_G \in \mathbb{R}^{N_x \times N_x}$ used in the matrix problem (2.10) is the same as the one used for the spatial decomposition of the stochastic partial differential equation (2.1). Since the mass matrix $\mathbf{M}_G$ is symmetric and square, the problem (2.10) can be solved for the lumped-parameter system input $\underline{u}(t) \in \mathbb{R}^{N_x}$ by simply using the inverse matrix $\mathbf{M}_G^{-1}$. This leads to following mapping for deriving the input vector $\underline{u}(t)$

$$\underline{u}(t) = \mathbf{M}_G^{-1} \cdot \widetilde{\underline{s}}(t) \ , \tag{2.11}$$

which can be regarded as the conversion of the system input (i.e., including its density representation) from space-time continuous form into the lumped-parameter space.

Integration of space-time continuous system input In the following, some remarks are given on the derivation of the random vector $\widetilde{\underline{s}}(t) \in \mathbb{R}^{N_x}$ required for solving the matrix problem (2.10). This vector contains the values that result from the areal integration of the space-time continuous system input $s(\underline{r},t)$ weighted with corresponding shape functions $\Psi^i(\underline{r},t)$. Using the notation proposed in (2.9), the integration can be achieved as follows

$$\widetilde{\underline{s}}^i(t) = \int_\Omega \Psi^i(\underline{r}) \left(\hat{s}(\underline{r},t) + w^s(\underline{r},t) \right) \mathrm{d}\underline{r} \ , \tag{2.12}$$

where $w^s(\cdot)$ denotes the process noise. In the special case of *space-invariant process noise* (i.e., the system at any spatial coördinate in the considered solution domain is disturbed by the same uncorrelated noise) the derivation of the random vector $\widetilde{\underline{s}}(t)$ can be significantly simplified to

$$\widetilde{\underline{s}}^i(t) = \underbrace{\int_\Omega \Psi^i(r)\hat{s}(r,t)\,\mathrm{d}\underline{r}}_{=:\hat{\widetilde{s}}^i(t)} + \underbrace{w^s(t) \int_\Omega \Psi^i(\underline{r})\,\mathrm{d}\underline{r}}_{=:\widetilde{w}^{si}(t)}$$

Assuming the noise term $w^s(\cdot)$ to be zero-mean Gaussian distributed according to $\mathcal{N}\left(0, C^s(t)\right)$, then the covariance matrix $\widetilde{\mathbf{C}}^s(t)$ of the integrated system input vector $\widetilde{\underline{s}}(t)$, i.e., the right-hand side of (2.10), can be derived as follows

$$\widetilde{\mathbf{C}}^s(t) = C^s(t)\,\mathrm{diag}\left\{ \int_\Omega \Psi^1(\underline{r})\mathrm{d}\underline{r},\ \dots,\ \int_\Omega \Psi^{N_x}(\underline{r})\mathrm{d}\underline{r} \right\} \ , \tag{2.13}$$

which consists only of diagonal entries. Eventually, the finite-dimensional input vector $\underline{u}(t)$ can be obtained by mapping the integrated system input $\widetilde{\underline{s}}(t)$ according to (2.11). Hence, in the Gaussian case, the mean $\hat{\underline{u}}(t)$ and the covariance matrix $\widetilde{\mathbf{C}}^u(t)$ of the desired system input $\underline{u}(t) \sim \mathcal{N}\left(\hat{\underline{u}}(t), \widetilde{\mathbf{C}}^u(t)\right)$ can be derived as follows

$$\hat{\underline{u}}(t) = \mathbf{M}_G^{-1}\hat{\underline{s}}(t) \quad , \quad \widetilde{\mathbf{C}}^u(t) = \mathbf{M}_G^{-1}\widetilde{\mathbf{C}}^s(t)\left(\mathbf{M}_G^{-1}\right)^{\mathrm{T}} \quad , \tag{2.14}$$

where $\mathbf{M}_G \in \mathbb{R}^{N_x \times N_x}$ is the precalculated global mass matrix. It is emphasized that these equations can be used for calculating the finite-dimensional input vector $\underline{u}(t)$ only when the assumption of *space-invariant* process noise $\boldsymbol{w}^s(\underline{r}, t)$ holds. In the case of space-variant process noise the integral (2.12) must be solved.

2.3.4 Selection of Shape Functions

In this section, the decomposition of the entire solution domain Ω into smaller subdomains Ω^e and the definition of shape functions $\Psi^i(r)$ in the respective subdomains Ω^e is described. For simplicity, the decomposition process is explained and visualized for the one-dimensional case. The functional description can be easily extended to the multi-dimensional case [79].

Definition of standard domain   The calculation of the individual entries of the mass matrix $\mathbf{M}_G$, the global advection matrix $\mathbf{N}_G$, and the global diffusion matrix $\mathbf{D}_G$ using *global shape functions* $\Psi^i(r)$ is uneconomical and numerically intractable, see (2.7). This is in particular the case when a large number of subdomains Ω^e, and thus a large number of different global shape functions $\Psi^i(r)$ is used for a sufficiently accurate approximation. Hence, it is reasonable to perform the calculation of the integrals (2.7) in a so-called *standard domain* $\Omega_{st} = \{\xi | -1 \leq \xi \leq 1\}$. The result can then be mapped to any desired *global domain* Ω^e using an isoparametric transformation $\chi^e(\xi)$ that expresses global coördinates r in terms of local ξ.

Types of polynomial expansions   In general, for a fixed mesh, the so-called *p-type expansions* achieve a higher accuracy of the solution by increasing the polynomial order *inside* the individual subdomains Ω^e. For the construction of p-type expansions, it is favorable to select a set of orthogonal functions, such as Legendre polynomials [79, 182], Chebyshev polynomials or trigonometric functions [24, 116]. The most commonly used polynomials that offer some numerical advantages compared to others are based on the *Legendre polynomials*. In the standard domain Ω_{st}, these polynomials are defined as follows

$$L_m(\xi) := \frac{1}{2^m\, m!}\frac{\mathrm{d}^m(\xi^2 - 1)^m}{\mathrm{d}\xi^m} \quad , \tag{2.15}$$

with m denoting the degree of the used polynomial. The Legendre polynomials (2.15) lay the foundation of different *elemental expansions* for the approximation of the solution in the subdomain Ω^e, namely *nodal* and *modal* polynomial expansions.

- *Nodal polynomial expansion:* Based on the Legendre polynomials (2.15) the *nodal* polynomial expansion is defined in the *standard domain* Ω_{st} as follows

$$\psi_p^e(\xi) := \frac{(1 - \xi^2)L_m'(\xi)}{m(m+1)L_m(\xi_p)(\xi_p - \xi)} \quad , \tag{2.16}$$

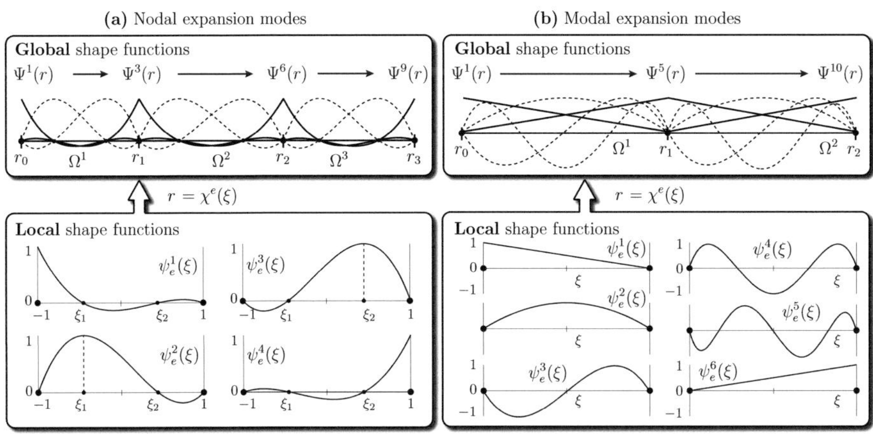

Figure 2.10: Examples of orthogonal polynomials as a representation for the shape functions. The solution $\boldsymbol{p}(r,t)$ is approximated in the respective subdomains Ω^e by means of following shape functions: **(a)** *nodal* polynomial expansion (for $m = 4$ refinement) and **(b)** *modal* polynomial expansion (for $m = 6$ refinement). The shape functions are depicted in the *global* bases and the *local* bases, and can be mapped by means of $r = \chi(\xi)$.

where L_m and L'_m is the Legendre polynomial of degree m and its derivative with respect to the argument, and ξ_p represents the p-th Gauss-Lobatto-Legendre quadrature points defined by the corresponding root of $(1 - \xi^2)L'_m(\xi) = 0$. The choice of these quadrature points plays an important role in the stability of the approximation. The nodal polynomial expansions $\psi_p^e(\xi)$ for $m = 4$ are shown in the standard domain Ω^e in Figure 2.10 **(a)**.

- *Modal polynomial expansion:* The *modal* polynomial expansion based on the Legendre polynomials (2.15) is represented in the *standard domain* Ω_{st} by

$$\psi_p^e(\xi) := \begin{cases} \frac{1-\xi}{2} & p = 1 \ , \\ (1 - \xi^2)L'_{p-1}(\xi) & 0 < p < m \ , \\ \frac{1+\xi}{2} & p = m \ . \end{cases} \tag{2.17}$$

The lowest expansion modes $\psi_1^e(\xi)$ and $\psi_m^e(\xi)$ are the same as the shape functions for the *finite-element method*. These modes are considered as boundary modes since they are the only modes that are nonzero at the boundaries of the respective subdomain Ω^e. The modal polynomial expansion $\psi_p^e(\xi)$ for $m = 6$ is visualized in Figure 2.10 **(b)**.

Calculation in elemental domain By means of the aforementioned *local* shape functions $\psi_p^e(\xi)$, the global matrices (2.7) can be derived more efficiently by the calculation on the standard domain Ω_{st} and then mapping the result to any desired global domain Ω^e by the isoparametric transformation $\chi^e(\xi)$. The entries of the *local matrices* M_{ij}^e and D_{ij}^e can be derived as

$$M_{ij}^e = \int_{-1}^{1} \psi_i^e(\xi)\psi_j^e(\xi)\mathrm{d}\xi \ , \qquad D_{ij}^e = \int_{-1}^{1} \frac{\mathrm{d}\psi_i^e(\xi)}{\mathrm{d}\xi} \frac{\mathrm{d}\psi_j^e(\xi)}{\mathrm{d}\xi}\mathrm{d}\xi \ .$$

Considering the conditions at the elemental boundary nodes, e.g., r_1 and r_2, the local matrices M_{ij}^e and D_{ij}^e can be easily transformed and assembled to the global matrices $\mathbf{M}_G$ and $\mathbf{D}_G$ [79].

2.3.5 Derivation of the Space-Time Discrete System Model

In the previous sections, it was demonstrated how the space-time continuous system in terms of the *stochastic partial differential equation* (2.1) is converted into a lumped-parameter system. This resulting description is characterized by a *system of stochastic ordinary differential equations* (2.8). For the derivation of an overall more efficient reconstruction process, a temporal discretization of the time-continuous differential equation including its density representation is required. The result of this discretization step is a *lumped-parameter system model* in *time-discrete* state-space form. This description is the foundation for designing a Bayesian estimator for reconstructing the entire spatially distributed physical system.

Uncertainty description for time-continuous case   In order to derive a probabilistic system model, the space-time continuous state $p(\underline{r}, t)$, the space-time continuous input $s(\underline{r}, t)$, and the boundary conditions $b(\underline{r})$ are modelled as random variables. Hence, the state vector, the input vector, and the boundary vector after the spatial decomposition are assumed to be given as

$$\underline{x}(t) := \underline{\hat{x}}(t) + \underline{\widetilde{w}}^{x}(t) \ , \qquad \underline{u}(t) := \underline{\hat{u}}(t) + \underline{\widetilde{w}}^{u}(t) \ , \qquad \underline{b}(t) := \underline{\hat{b}}(t) + \underline{\widetilde{w}}^{b}(t) \ ,$$

where the input uncertainties $\underline{\widetilde{w}}^{u}(t)$ and the boundary condition uncertainties $\underline{\widetilde{w}}^{b}(t)$ are assumed to be Gaussian zero-mean white noise. The joint covariance matrix is given as

$$\mathrm{Cov}\left\{\begin{bmatrix} \underline{\widetilde{w}}^{u}(t) \\ \underline{\widetilde{w}}^{b}(t) \end{bmatrix}\right\} := \begin{bmatrix} \widetilde{\mathbf{C}}^{u}(t) & \mathbf{0} \\ \mathbf{0} & \widetilde{\mathbf{C}}^{b}(t) \end{bmatrix} = \widetilde{\mathbf{C}}^{g}(t) \ ,$$

which further means that the input uncertainty $\underline{\widetilde{w}}^{u}(t)$ and the boundary uncertainty $\underline{\widetilde{w}}^{b}(t)$ are mutually independent. The lumped-parameter system state $\underline{x}(t)$ is assumed to be given by (2.4) and the system input $\underline{u}(t)$ can be derived using (2.12) and (2.11).

Density function for time-discrete case   In general, the time-discrete state vector $\underline{x}_{k}$ cannot be uniquely characterized by a Gaussian probability density function, rather turns out to be arbitrary. This is especially the case for the parameter identification of space-time continuous systems; see Chapter 4. For example, for the localization of individual sensor nodes by means of local observations (see Section 4.4) or the localization of sources and leakages (see Section 4.5), the density function could be multimodal and consists of a quite complex shape. Before the more involved case of arbitrary density functions is considered (nonlinear/non-Gaussian case), we restrict our attention to *Gaussian probability density*

$$\underline{x}_{k} \sim f^{x}(\underline{x}_{k}) := \mathcal{N}\left(\underline{x}_{k} - \underline{\hat{x}}_{k}, \mathbf{C}_{k}^{x}\right) \ ,$$

where $\underline{\hat{x}}_{k}$ and $\mathbf{C}_{k}^{x}$ respectively denote the mean vector and the covariance matrix. Due to the linear description of the stochastic partial differential equation (2.1), and the resulting linear stochastic ordinary differential equation (2.8), this assumption is sufficient for the *state reconstruction*, i.e., precisely known mathematical models.

Estimation based on time-continuous models   Modelling the state vector and the system inputs as random vectors, the lumped-parameter system (2.8) can be expanded to a stochastic system description in *time-continuous state-space form*, according to

$$\underline{\dot{x}}(t) = \underbrace{-\mathbf{M}_{G}^{-1}(\mathbf{N}_{G} + \alpha \mathbf{D}_{G})}_{\widetilde{\mathbf{A}}(t)} \underline{x}(t) + \underbrace{\begin{bmatrix} \gamma\mathbf{I} & \mathbf{M}_{G}^{-1} \end{bmatrix}}_{\widetilde{\mathbf{B}}^{g}(t)} \underbrace{\begin{bmatrix} \underline{\hat{u}}(t) + \underline{\widetilde{w}}^{u}(t) \\ \underline{\hat{b}}(t) + \underline{\widetilde{w}}^{b}(t) \end{bmatrix}}_{\underline{g}(t) := \underline{\hat{g}}(t) + \underline{\widetilde{w}}^{g}(t)} \ , \tag{2.18}$$

where $\widetilde{\mathbf{A}}(t) \in \mathbb{R}^{N_x \times N_x}$ represents the system matrix. The matrix $\widetilde{\mathbf{B}}^g(t) \in \mathbb{R}^{N_x \times 2N_x}$ and the vector $\widetilde{g}(t) \in \mathbb{R}^{2N_x}$ containing the input and boundary conditions are the so-called *augmented input matrix* and *augmented input vector*, respectively. Knowing the density function of the underlying state vector $\underline{x}_k$ at the present time and future distributed system inputs, then the values of all future states of system can be deduced.

Based on the aforementioned stochastic differential equation (2.18), a time-continuous estimator can be developed. The *Projection Filter* [14, 21, 81] converts the stochastic ordinary differential equation (2.18) into a deterministic partial differential equation; also called *Kolmogorov's forward equation* or *Fokker-Planck equation* [111]. This deterministic equation describes how the probability density function that represents the state vector $\underline{x}_k$ evolves over time. Using the Projection Filter for solving the high-dimensional stochastic differential equation (2.18) leads to a high-dimensional deterministic partial differential equation that needs lots of computational resources. Hence, in this work an additional *temporal discretization step* is performed in order to derive a time-discrete model (2.18). This discretization leads to a model beneficial for sensor network applications. The resulting model describes the propagation of the probability density function of a time-discrete state vector $\underline{x}_k$ to the next time step.

Temporal discretization   Here, we assume that the system input $\hat{\underline{u}}(t)$ and the boundary condition $\hat{\underline{b}}(t)$ change only at discrete time steps, i.e., $\hat{\underline{g}}(t) = \hat{\underline{g}}_k$ for $t \in [t_k, t_{k+1}]$. Then, the solution of the stochastic ordinary differential equation (2.18) is given at some arbitrary time instants t_{k+1} in terms of the system state $\underline{x}_{k+1} := \underline{x}(t_{k+1})$ as

$$\underline{x}_{k+1} = \underbrace{e^{\widetilde{\mathbf{A}}\Delta t}}_{=:\mathbf{A}_k}\underline{x}_k + \underbrace{\int_{t_k}^{t_{k+1}} e^{\widetilde{\mathbf{A}}(t_{k+1}-\tau)}\widetilde{\mathbf{B}}^g(\tau)\,\mathrm{d}\tau}_{=:\mathbf{B}_k^g}\,\hat{\underline{g}}_k + \int_{t_k}^{t_{k+1}} e^{\widetilde{\mathbf{A}}(t_{k+1}-\tau)}\widetilde{\mathbf{B}}^g(\tau)\underline{\widetilde{w}}^g(\tau)\,\mathrm{d}\tau \ ,$$

where $\Delta t := t_{k+1} - t_k$ is the sampling period. The system matrix $\mathbf{A}_k$ characterizing the transition of the state to the next time step $k+1$ can be derived by performing the exponential of the respective matrix. There are several ways to actually compute the exponential of a matrix; an overview is given in [100]. The most common way is to use the convergent power series according to

$$\mathbf{A}_k := e^{\widetilde{\mathbf{A}}\Delta t} = \sum_{i=0}^{\infty} \frac{(\widetilde{\mathbf{A}}\Delta t)^i}{i!} \approx \mathbf{I} - \mathbf{M}_G^{-1}\left(\mathbf{N}_G + \alpha\mathbf{D}_G\right)\Delta t \ , \tag{2.19}$$

which roughly speaking is analogous to the definition of the exponential of a scalar. For small values of the sampling time Δt the matrix exponential can be approximated as stated in (2.19). Using the same assumption of a small time step for computing the integral of the augmented input matrix $\mathbf{B}_k^g$ results in

$$\mathbf{B}_k^g := \int_{t_k}^{t_{k+1}} e^{\widetilde{\mathbf{A}}(t_{k+1}-\tau)}\widetilde{\mathbf{B}}^g(\tau)\,\mathrm{d}\tau \approx \left[\underbrace{\gamma\,\Delta t\,\mathbf{I}}_{\mathbf{B}_k^u} \quad \underbrace{\Delta t\,\mathbf{M}_G^{-1}}_{\mathbf{B}_k^b}\right] \ , \tag{2.20}$$

where the fact was exploited that the exponential of a matrix can be approximated by the identity matrix for small Δt. The resulting equation for the system matrix $\mathbf{A}_k$ and the input matrix $\mathbf{B}_k$ is similar to the result of performing a finite difference step (2.2) directly on the stochastic differential equation (2.18); see Section 2.3.1. When the assumption of small time steps Δt does not hold, then more components of the used power series of the matrix exponential (2.19) needs to be considered [76, 132].

Similar to the system state, the noise term is growing as time passes, both due to the actual integration and the injected noise term $\widetilde{\boldsymbol{w}}^g(t)$ itself. Hence, integrating the time-continuous system model (2.18) over a time interval Δt, the covariance matrix $\mathbf{C}_k^g$ affecting the system at time step k can be obtained as follows

$$
\mathbf{C}_k^g := \int_{t_k}^{t_{k+1}} e^{\widetilde{\mathbf{A}}(t_{k+1}-\tau)} \widetilde{\mathbf{B}}^g(\tau)\, \widetilde{\mathbf{C}}^g(\tau)\, \widetilde{\mathbf{B}}^g(\tau)\, e^{\widetilde{\mathbf{A}}^{\mathrm{T}}(t_{k+1}-\tau)}\, \mathrm{d}\tau
$$

$$
\approx \underbrace{\begin{bmatrix} \gamma\Delta t\mathbf{I} & \Delta t\mathbf{M}_G^{-1} \end{bmatrix}}_{\mathbf{B}_k^g} \underbrace{\begin{bmatrix} \frac{1}{\Delta t}\widetilde{\mathbf{C}}^u(t_k) & \mathbf{0} \\ \mathbf{0} & \frac{1}{\Delta t}\widetilde{\mathbf{C}}^b(t_k) \end{bmatrix}}_{=:\mathbf{C}_k^g} \begin{bmatrix} \gamma\Delta t\mathbf{I} \\ \Delta t\,(\mathbf{M}_G^{-1})^{\mathrm{T}} \end{bmatrix} , \tag{2.21}
$$

as described in [149]. In general, the calculation of this integral is quite difficult and computationally demanding for large system matrices. However, an approximation sufficiently accurate for small time steps Δt can be derived as stated in (2.21) [132].

Time-discrete state-space model The aforementioned methods for the spatial decomposition and the temporal discretization always result in a linear system model, in the case of *linear* partial differential equations (1.2). Hence, the mathematical model describing the dynamic and the distributed behavior of the physical system being observed can be stated as follows

$$
\underline{\boldsymbol{x}}_{k+1} = \mathbf{A}_k(\underline{\eta}_k^P)\, \underline{\boldsymbol{x}}_k + \mathbf{B}_k^u(\underline{\eta}_k^P)\,(\hat{\underline{u}}_k + \underline{\boldsymbol{w}}_k^u) + \mathbf{B}_k^b(\underline{\eta}_k^P)\,(\hat{\underline{b}}_k + \underline{\boldsymbol{w}}_k^b) . \tag{2.22}
$$

The system noise $\underline{\boldsymbol{w}}_k^u$ and the boundary noise $\underline{\boldsymbol{w}}_k^b$ are assumed to be zero-mean Gaussian and stochastically independent with following joint covariance matrix

$$
\mathrm{Cov}\left\{ \begin{bmatrix} \underline{\boldsymbol{w}}_k^u \\ \underline{\boldsymbol{w}}_k^b \end{bmatrix} \right\} = \begin{bmatrix} \frac{1}{\Delta t}\widetilde{\mathbf{C}}^u(t_k) & \mathbf{0} \\ \mathbf{0} & \frac{1}{\Delta t}\widetilde{\mathbf{C}}^b(t_k) \end{bmatrix} , \tag{2.23}
$$

where Δt is the sampling time. The matrix $\mathbf{A}_k \in \mathbb{R}^{N_x \times N_x}$ represents the system matrix, $\mathbf{B}_k^u \in \mathbb{R}^{N_x \times N_x}$ is the input matrix, and $\mathbf{B}_k^b \in \mathbb{R}^{N_x \times N_x}$ denotes the boundary matrix. These matrices, in general, strongly depend on parameters of the space-time continuous system (1.2) collected in the *process parameter vector* $\underline{\eta}_k^P \in \mathbb{R}^{P_p}$. In the case of the two-dimensional convection-diffusion equation (2.1), this vector may contain the following model parameters

$$
\underline{\eta}_k^P := \begin{bmatrix} \alpha & \gamma & v_x & v_y & \dots \end{bmatrix}^{\mathrm{T}} \in \mathbb{R}^{P_p} ,
$$

where α denotes the diffusion coefficient, γ is the system input coefficient, v_x and v_y is the velocity of the convection field. The parameters contained in the vector $\underline{\eta}_k^P$ are not restricted to the aforementioned parameters, rather can be easily extended depending on the structure of the space-time continuous system that is given in general form in (1.2).

Properties of spatial decomposition As a way of summary, the structure of the mathematical model resulting from the spatial decomposition is depicted in Figure 2.11. Their main properties are stated as follows:

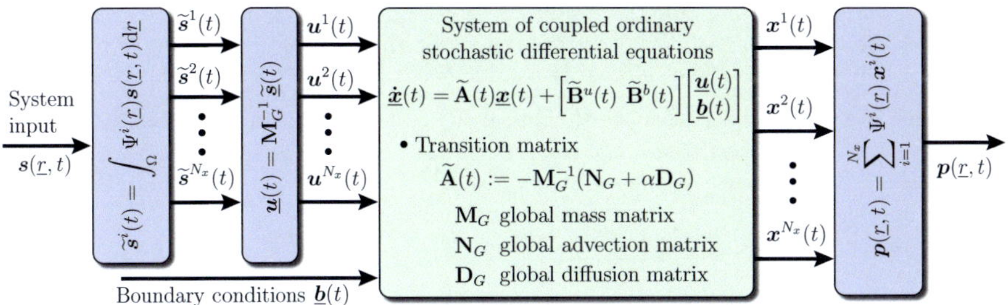

Figure 2.11: By means of the *spatial* decomposition the mathematical description of the space-time continuous physical system is converted into a system of *coupled ordinary* differential equations. In the given example, the dynamic and distributed behavior is characterized by the mass matrix $\mathbf{M}_G$, the convection matrix $\mathbf{N}_G$, and the diffusion matrix $\mathbf{D}_G$. The physical system is defined in the *entire solution domain* Ω by the shape functions $\Psi^i(\underline{r})$ and their respective weighting coefficients $x^i(t)$; in general, an infinite number of components, i.e., $N_x \to \infty$

- By means of the spatial decomposition, the space-time continuous system (characterized by a stochastic partial differential equation) can be converted into a generally *infinite* number of *coupled* lumped-parameter systems (characterized by a system of stochastic ordinary differential equations). Due to computational reasons, however, just a finite number are used for the approximation of the solution.

- The state of the physical system is uniquely characterized by the underlying shape functions $\Psi^i(\underline{r})$ (used as a domain representation) and their corresponding weighting coefficients $x^i(t)$. This fact can be regarded as a decomposition into a *spatial dependent part* and a *temporal dependent part*, i.e., the shape functions depend only on the spatial coördinate and the weighting coefficients only on the time [169, 182].

- The specific structure of all the matrices consisting in the resulting system of coupled differential equations (2.8) merely depend on the choice of shape functions. Especially, by selecting special shape functions, the *coupled* system of equations can be *entirely decoupled*. This is the case for modal analysis methods (spectral methods) using trigonometric functions and using just one single element [10, 116].

The system model (2.22) can be used for the *stochastic simulation* of the space-time continuous system by simply propagating the finite-dimensional state vector $\underline{x}_k$ in terms of the density function over time. Based on this propagation, the space-continuous state $\underline{p}_k(\underline{r})$ of the underlying system is directly derived using the finite expansion (2.4) for given initial conditions and boundary conditions. By this means, several realizations of the physical system can be generated. However, for the state reconstruction, the aim is not just the simulation of the system behavior. Instead, the goal is the *reconstruction of the entire space-time continuous state* $\underline{p}_k(\underline{r})$ using space-time discrete, spatially distributed measurements.

2.4 Derivation of the Measurement Model

In order to incorporate measurements obtained from a *spatially distributed measurement system* into the reconstruction process, it is necessary to derive a special *mathematical model* characterizing the properties of the entire measurement system. For spatially distributed systems, such as sensor networks, not only the *physical properties* need to be modelled but especially the *distributed properties*. In particular, the dependency on the locations, and thus the topology of the sensor network needs to be sufficiently considered.

The vector containing the spatial coördinates of the i-th sensor node is represented as $\underline{r}_k^{si} :=$ $[r_k^{sx}, r_k^{sy}]^\mathrm{T} \in \mathbb{R}^2$ in the two-dimensional case. Then, the node coördinates of the entire network can be collected in the *node location vector* $\underline{r}_k^M \in \mathbb{R}^{2 \cdot M}$

$$\underline{r}_k^M := \left[(\underline{r}_k^{s1})^\mathrm{T} \quad (\underline{r}_k^{s2})^\mathrm{T} \quad \cdots \quad (\underline{r}_k^{sM})^\mathrm{T} \right]^\mathrm{T} \in \mathbb{R}^{2 \cdot M} \ , \tag{2.24}$$

where M is the number of considered nodes in the network. The mathematical model of spatially distributed measurement system consists of **two parts**, (a) the *measurement equation* and (b) the *output equation*, described in the remainder of this section.

Measurement equation The measurement equation describes the *physical* properties of the individual nodes in the network. This equation relates the nominal value of measurements $\hat{y}_k^i$ at their respective node locations $\underline{r}_k^{si}$ to the value of the physical system $\boldsymbol{p}_k(\cdot)$, according to

$$\hat{y}_k^{si} = h_k^{si} \left(\boldsymbol{p}_k(\underline{r}_k^{si}) \right) + \boldsymbol{v}_k^{si} \ , \tag{2.25}$$

where the uncertainties $\boldsymbol{v}_k^{si} \sim \mathcal{N}(\cdot)$ are assumed to be zero-mean white Gaussian. The uncertainties of the individual sensor nodes are possibly correlated with other nodes. This arises for example from spatially distributed disturbances that affects more than one sensor node. The covariance matrix $\mathbf{C}_k^v \in \mathbb{R}^{M \times M}$ of the measurement noise $\underline{v}_k$ is given as follows

$$\mathrm{Cov}\left\{ \begin{bmatrix} \boldsymbol{v}_k^{s1} \\ \vdots \\ \boldsymbol{v}_k^{sM} \end{bmatrix} \right\} := \begin{bmatrix} C^{s11} & \cdots & C^{s1M} \\ \vdots & \ddots & \vdots \\ C^{sM1} & \cdots & C^{sMM} \end{bmatrix} \ ,$$

where M denotes the number of nodes contained in the sensor network. In general, the mapping $h_k^{si}(\cdot) : \mathbb{R} \to \mathbb{R}$ in the aforementioned measurement equation consists of nonlinear functions characterizing the physical principle of the actual sensor nodes.

Output equation For the reconstruction of space-time continuous systems, it is essential to characterize the *distribution* properties of the measurement system $\mathcal{M}$, such as the location of the individual nodes (topology of the network). This is described by means of the output equation. The output equation relates the system state $\boldsymbol{p}_k(\cdot)$ at the measurement points directly to the finite-dimensional state vector $\underline{x}_k \in \mathbb{R}^{N_x}$, according to

$$\boldsymbol{p}_k(\underline{r}_k^{si}) = \sum_{j=1}^{N_x} \Psi^j(\underline{r}_k^{si}) \, \boldsymbol{x}_k^j \ , \tag{2.26}$$

where $\Psi^i(\cdot) : \mathbb{R}^2 \to \mathbb{R}$ represents the value of the *shape functions* at the location $\underline{r}_k^{si}$ of the i-th sensor node. It is noted that the shape functions $\Psi^i(\cdot)$ used here needs to be identical to the functions in the finite expansion (2.4) used for the *spatial decomposition*.

Complete measurement model The complete measurement model for the reconstruction of the space-time continuous system can be derived by plugging the output equation (2.26) into the measurement equation (2.25). For simplicity and brevity, we assume that the individual

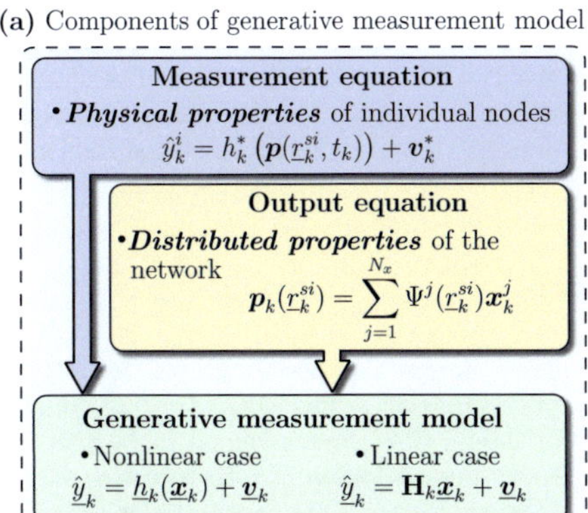

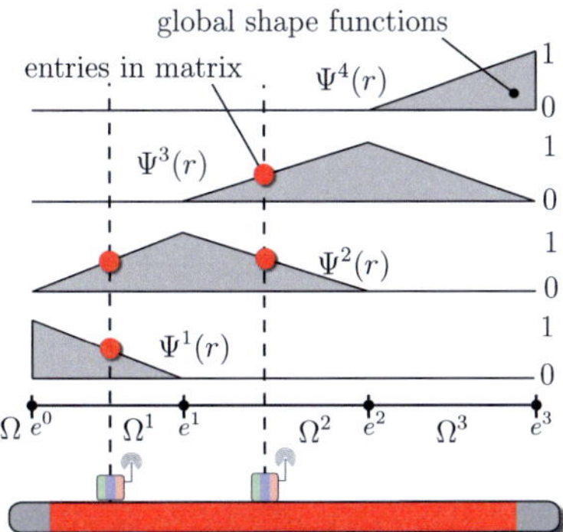

Figure 2.12: **(a)** Components of the generative model of spatially distributed measurement systems for the estimation of physical systems. The *measurement equation* relates the measurements $\hat{y}_k^i$ to the space-time continuous state $\boldsymbol{p}(\underline{r}_k^{si}, t_k)$, which is then related to the finite-dimensional state vector $\underline{x}_k$ by the *output equation*. **(b)** Construction of the measurement matrix $\mathbf{H}_k$ depending on the shape functions and the location of the individual sensor nodes.

sensor nodes directly measure the space-time continuous system $\boldsymbol{p}_k(\underline{r}_k^{si})$ at their respective locations $\underline{r}_k^{si}$. In this case, the measurement matrix $\mathbf{H}_k \in \mathbb{R}^{M \times N_x}$ for the entire network is assembled by simply evaluating the individual shape functions $\Psi^i(\cdot)$ at the node locations $\underline{r}_k^{si}$. This leads to following linear *measurement model*

$$\underline{\hat{y}}_k = \underbrace{\begin{bmatrix} \Psi^1(\underline{r}_k^{s1}) & \cdots & \Psi^{N_x}(\underline{r}_k^{s1}) \\ \vdots & \ddots & \vdots \\ \Psi^1(\underline{r}_k^{sM}) & \cdots & \Psi^{N_x}(\underline{r}_k^{sM}) \end{bmatrix}}_{=: \mathbf{H}_k(\underline{r}_k^M)} \underline{x}_k + \underline{v}_k \, , \tag{2.27}$$

where $\underline{v}_k$ denotes the measurement noise and M represents the number of sensor nodes used in the network. The measurement model (2.27) directly relates the nominal values $\underline{\hat{y}}_k \in \mathbb{R}^M$ of the measurements to the state vector $\underline{x}_k \in \mathbb{R}^{N_x}$. It is obvious that the measurement matrix $\mathbf{H}_k$ merely depends on the location vector $\underline{r}_k^M$ containing the individual node locations. For illustration purposes, the structure of the measurement matrix $\mathbf{H}_k$ and in particular its dependency on the node locations is illustrated in the following example.

Example 2.3: Structure of the measurement model

In this example, we clarify the structure of the measurement matrix $\mathbf{H}_k$ subject to *piecewise linear shape functions*, for simplicity purposes only for the one-dimensional case. The entire solution domain $\Omega \in \mathbb{R}$ is decomposed into 3 subdomains and appropriate piecewise linear shape functions $\Psi^i(\cdot) : \mathbb{R} \to \mathbb{R}$ are defined on each subdomain Ω^i. Assuming a network consisting of two nodes that are located at r_k^{s1} and r_k^{s2}, then the measurement model is given as follows

$$\begin{bmatrix} \hat{y}_k^{s1} \\ \hat{y}_k^{s2} \end{bmatrix} = \begin{bmatrix} \overbrace{c_1^1 + c_2^1 \hat{r}_k^{s1}}^{\Psi^1(\hat{r}_k^{s1})} & \overbrace{c_3^1 + c_4^1 \hat{r}_k^{s1}}^{\Psi^1(\hat{r}_k^{s1})} & 0 & 0 \\ 0 & \underbrace{c_1^2 + c_2^2 \hat{r}_k^{s2}}_{\Psi^2(\hat{r}_k^{s1})} & \underbrace{c_3^2 + c_4^2 \hat{r}_k^{s2}}_{\Psi^2(\hat{r}_k^{s2})} & 0 \end{bmatrix} \begin{bmatrix} \boldsymbol{x}_k^1 \\ \boldsymbol{x}_k^2 \\ \boldsymbol{x}_k^3 \\ \boldsymbol{x}_k^4 \end{bmatrix} + \underline{v}_k \, .$$

The constants c_i^j arise from the definition of the piecewise linear shape functions in each subdomain, i.e., the geometry of the applied grid for the finite elements. The construction of the measurement matrix $\mathbf{H}_k$ is shown in Figure 2.12 **(b)**. Basically, the shape functions $\Psi^i(r)$ are evaluated at the locations r_k^{si} and define respective entries in the measurement matrix. The extension to orthogonal polynomials [182] and trigonometric functions [116] can be derived in a straightforward fashion. ∎

2.5 Process of State Reconstruction

This section is devoted to a detailed description of the *state reconstruction process* for physical systems that are observed by spatially distributed measurement systems. Here, the parameters in the system model (2.22) and the measurement model (2.27) are assumed to be precisely known. The introduced reconstruction process allows the derivation of estimates not only at the actual measurement points but also at *non-measurement points*, i.e., between the individual nodes in the sensor network. It is shown that assuming a precise mathematical model, the space-time continuous system can be extrapolated and interpolated between the measurements in a *systematic* and *physically correct manner*.

In general, depending on the structure of the model description, i.e., being linear or nonlinear, an appropriate estimator has to be chosen. For the *state reconstruction* based on linear partial differential equations (1.2), the system model (2.22) and the measurement model (2.27) are linear in terms of the random state vector $\underline{x}_k \in \mathbb{R}^{N_x}$. Thus, it is sufficient to use linear estimators, such as the Kalman filter, in order to obtain the best possible estimate, and eventually reconstruct the entire physical system. In the case of a *nonlinear system model* and/or a *nonlinear measurement model*, the employment of *nonlinear estimators* is necessary[1]. In the next chapter, an efficient nonlinear estimator is introduced exploiting linear substructures in the mathematical model (2.22) for such cases. For a detailed description of state-of-the-art of nonlinear estimation approaches refer to Section 3.1.

Based on the (linear) system and the (linear) measurement model, the actual *state reconstruction* process consists of **three steps**: (1) the prediction step, (2) the measurement step, and (3) the conversion back into the continuous space. These steps are alternately performed.

2.5.1 Prediction Step

The purpose of the prediction step is to propagate the current estimate of the finite-dimensional state vector $\underline{x}_k \sim f^e(\underline{x}_k)$ through the system equation (2.22) to the next time step $k+1$. This leads to an estimate for the predicted state vector $\underline{x}_{k+1} \sim f^p(\underline{x}_{k+1})$ in terms of the predicted density function. For the state reconstruction, we assume a precise mathematical model (2.22) of the underlying space-time continuous system, i.e., precisely known parameter vector η_k^P. For linear dynamic systems characterized by *Gaussian densities*, the stochastic nature of the random vector $\underline{x}_k$ is uniquely characterized by the mean and covariance matrix. Hence, the predicted probability density function $\underline{x}_{k+1} \sim \mathcal{N}\left(\underline{x}_{k+1} - \hat{\underline{x}}_{k+1}^p, \mathbf{C}_{k+1}^p\right)$ can be calculated by

$$\hat{\underline{x}}_{k+1}^p = \mathbf{A}_k(\underline{\eta}_k^P)\,\hat{\underline{x}}_k^e + \mathbf{B}_k^u(\underline{\eta}_k^P)\,\hat{\underline{u}}_k + \mathbf{B}_k^b(\underline{\eta}_k^P)\,\hat{\underline{b}}_k \;,$$

$$\mathbf{C}_{k+1}^p = \mathbf{A}_k(\underline{\eta}_k^P)\,\mathbf{C}_k^e\left(\mathbf{A}_k(\underline{\eta}_k^P)\right)^{\mathrm{T}} + \mathbf{B}_k^u(\underline{\eta}_k^P)\,\mathbf{C}_k^u\left(\mathbf{B}_k^u(\underline{\eta}_k^P)\right)^{\mathrm{T}} + \mathbf{B}_k^b(\underline{\eta}_k^P)\,\mathbf{C}_k^b\left(\mathbf{B}_k^b(\underline{\eta}_k^P)\right)^{\mathrm{T}} \;, \quad (2.28)$$

---

[1] This is the case for the simultaneous state reconstruction and parameter identification of space-time continuous systems, see Chapter 4.

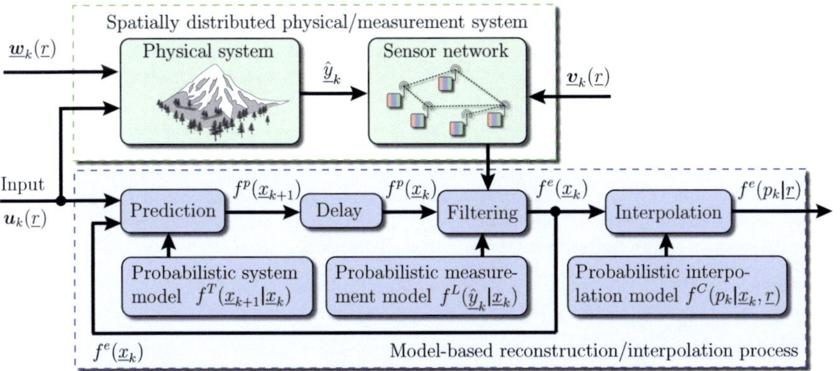

Figure 2.13: Overview of the model-based reconstruction process for space-time continuous physical systems. The process consists of the *prediction step*, the *measurement step* (filtering), and a so-called *interpolation step*. Thanks to the model-based approach, the extrapolation and the interpolation between the actual measurement points can be achieved in a systematic and physically correct fashion.

where $\hat{\underline{x}}_k^e \in \mathbb{R}^{N_x}$ and $\mathbf{C}_k^e \in \mathbb{R}^{N_x \times N_x}$ are the mean and the covariance matrix of the estimated state vector $\underline{x}_k$ from the previous processing step. The covariance matrix of the system input vector $\underline{u}_k$ and the boundary vector $\underline{b}_k$ are given by $\mathbf{C}_k^u := \frac{1}{\Delta t}\widetilde{\mathbf{C}}^u(t_k)$ and $\mathbf{C}_k^b := \frac{1}{\Delta t}\widetilde{\mathbf{C}}^b(t_k)$, respectively; see Section 2.3.5.

There are several features to note about the prediction step (2.28) that is necessary for the state reconstruction of space-time continuous systems. It is obvious that the structure of the system matrix $\mathbf{A}_k(\underline{\eta}_k^P)$ and the input matrix $\mathbf{B}_k(\underline{\eta}_k^P)$ merely depends on the process parameter vector $\underline{\eta}_k^P$ containing the parameters in the partial differential equation (2.1). This means, for the accurate reconstruction by means of a sensor network, parameters characterizing the behavior of the physical system need to be precisely known. Due to such dependencies, the deviation of the model description from the true behavior leads to poor estimation results; see Section 2.6.2. On the other hand, thanks to the dependency of the model description on such parameters, the identification problem can be stated as a *simultaneous state and parameter estimation problem*. Hence, the space-time continuous system can be reconstructed and unknown parameters can be identified in a simultaneous fashion. The method for the *simultaneous reconstruction and parameter identification* (SRI method) is introduced in Section 4.3.

2.5.2 Measurement Step (Filtering)

For the purpose of improving the estimate of the space-time continuous system, measurements are incorporated into the reconstruction process. The distributed measurements $\hat{\underline{y}}_k \in \mathbb{R}^{N_y}$ are related to the state vector $\underline{x}_k \in \mathbb{R}^{N_x}$ via the measurement model (2.27) derived in the previous section. Assuming a precise measurement matrix $\mathbf{H}(\underline{\eta}_k^S)$, i.e., precisely known node locations and sensor characteristics, the mean $\hat{\underline{x}}_k^e$ and covariance matrix $\mathbf{C}_k^e$ of the estimated finite-dimensional state vector $\underline{x}_k \sim \mathcal{N}\left(\underline{x}_k - \hat{\underline{x}}_k^e, \mathbf{C}_k^e\right)$ can be derived by

$$\hat{\underline{x}}_k^e = \hat{\underline{x}}_k^p + \mathbf{C}_k^p \left(\mathbf{H}_k(\underline{\eta}_k^S)\right)^{\mathrm{T}} \left(\mathbf{C}_v + \mathbf{H}_k(\underline{\eta}_k^S)\mathbf{C}_k^p \left(\mathbf{H}_k(\underline{\eta}_k^S)\right)^{\mathrm{T}}\right)^{-1} \left(\hat{\underline{y}}_k - \mathbf{H}_k(\underline{\eta}_k^S)\hat{\underline{x}}_k^p\right) \, ,$$

$$\mathbf{C}_k^e = \mathbf{C}_k^p - \mathbf{C}_k^p \left(\mathbf{H}_k(\underline{\eta}_k^S)\right)^{\mathrm{T}} \left(\mathbf{C}_v + \mathbf{H}_k(\underline{\eta}_k^S)\mathbf{C}_k^p \left(\mathbf{H}_k(\underline{\eta}_k^S)\right)^{\mathrm{T}}\right)^{-1} \mathbf{H}_k(\underline{\eta}_k^S)\mathbf{C}_k^p \, , \tag{2.29}$$

where $\hat{\underline{x}}_k^p \in \mathbb{R}^{N_x}$ and $\mathbf{C}_k^p \in \mathbb{R}^{N_x \times N_x}$ are respectively the predicted mean and the predicted co-variance matrix of the preceding prediction step. The matrix $\mathbf{C}_v$ denotes the possibly correlated covariance matrix of the individual nodes in the entire sensor network.

There are several properties of the measurement step (2.29) essential for the estimation of space-time continuous systems. The structure of the measurement matrix $\mathbf{H}_k(\underline{\eta}_k^S)$ merely depends on the location $\underline{\eta}_k^S$ of the individual sensor nodes. This means, for the accurate state reconstruction of the physical system, the node locations are required to be precisely known. Due to this dependency, deviations of true locations from the modeled ones lead to poor estimation results. On the other hand, thanks to the dependency of the measurement matrix $\mathbf{H}_k(\underline{\eta}_k^S)$ on the node locations, the localization problem can be reformulated as a *simulatneous state and parameter estimation problem*. By this means, the distributed physical system can be reconstructed and the sensor nodes can be localized in a simultaneous fashion. The method for the *simultaneous reconstruction and node localization* (SRL method) is introduced in Section 4.4.

By means of the prediction step (2.28), the finite-dimensional state vector $\underline{x}_k$ characterizing the space-time continuous state $\underline{p}(\underline{r}, t)$ is spatially correlated in a natural way based on the physical model. In the measurement step (2.29) these correlations are exploited to obtain an improved estimate of the space-time continuous system not only at the measurement points but also between the individual nodes. This means, the individual measurements are interpolated in a systematic and physically correct manner. Compared to classical interpolation methods (such as Kriging methods), this fact is certainly a novelty and leads to physically correct interpolation results while considering uncertainties in the model and the measurements.

2.5.3 Conversion into Continuous Space

The prediction step propagates the finite-dimensional state vector $\underline{x}_k \sim f^e(\underline{x}_k)$ over time while exploiting a mathematical model of the space-time continuous system. Then, the measurement step incorporates the measurements received from the sensor network. In order to obtain an estimate of the distributed state $\underline{p}_k(\underline{r}) \sim f^e(p_k|\underline{r})$ at any desired spatial coördinate, the state vector $\underline{x}_k$ needs to be converted back into the continuous-space. This conversion can also be regarded as a so-called *interpolation step* deriving estimation results between the locally defined estimated states $\underline{x}_k^i$. This step eventually results in the density function $f^e(p_k|\underline{r})$, which can be seen as a conditional probability density function conditioned on the spatial coördinate $\underline{r}$. Hence, the space continuous state $\underline{p}_k$ is characterized in the *entire domain*. The conversion can be achieved as follows

$$\underline{p}_k = \sum_{i=1}^{N_x} \Psi^i(\underline{r})\, \underline{x}_k^i = \underline{\Psi}(\underline{r})^{\mathrm{T}} \cdot \underline{x}_k \, , \tag{2.30}$$

where $\Psi^i(\underline{r}) : \mathbb{R}^2 \to \mathbb{R}$ denote the same shape functions used for the conversion of the space-time continuous system. It is emphasized that the *mapping* (2.30) consists of a system of *linear equations* merely depending on the shape functions $\Psi^i(\cdot)$ used during the spatial decomposition and the spatial coördinate $\underline{r}$ in the continuous space.

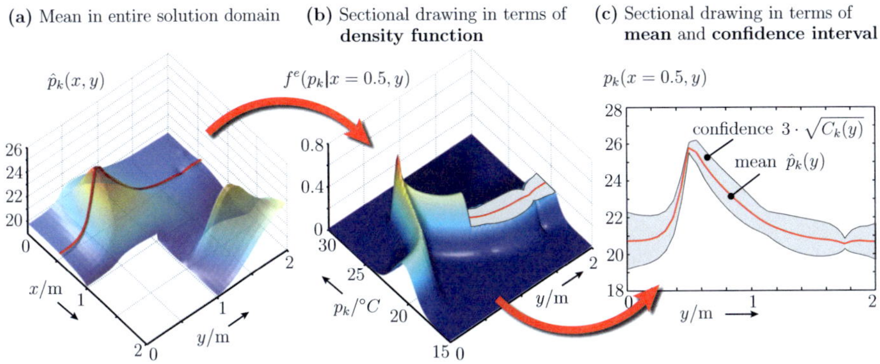

(a) Mean in entire solution domain   **(b)** Sectional drawing in terms of **density function**   **(c)** Sectional drawing in terms of **mean** and **confidence interval**

Figure 2.14: The conversion of the random state vector $\underline{x}_k$ into the continuous space results in a description of the distributed state $\underline{p}_k(\underline{r})$ in terms of the density function $f^e(p_k|\underline{r})$ (in this thesis only Gaussian density and Gaussian mixture density are considered). Visualization of an example for the estimation result of the model-based reconstruction process: **(a)** distributed mean $\hat{p}_k^e(\underline{r})$ in the entire solution domain, sectional drawing at $x = 0.5$ in terms of **(b)** density function and **(c)** mean and confidence interval ($3\,\sigma$-bound).

Based on the linear mapping (2.30) the density function characterizing the space-continuous state $\underline{p}_k$ can be derived according to

$$f^e(p_k|\underline{r}) = \int_{\mathbb{R}^{N_x}} \underbrace{f^C\left(p_k - \underline{\Psi}(\underline{r})^\mathrm{T}\underline{x}_k\right) f^e(\underline{x}_k)\,\mathrm{d}\underline{x}_k}_{f^C(p_k|\underline{x}_k,\underline{r})}\,, \tag{2.31}$$

where $f^C(\cdot)$ denotes the transition density for the conversion process. In Figure 2.14 the density function $f^e(p_k|\underline{r})$ resulting from the conversion is visualized, and respective sectional drawings of the density are shown. The remainder of this section is devoted to the actual derivation of the density function (2.31) for different types of prior density function $f^e(\underline{x}_k)$ characterizing the state vector $\underline{x}_k$. In this work, *Gaussian densities* (for the state reconstruction) and *Gaussian mixture densities* (for the state and the parameter estimation) are of special interest.

Gaussian density   In the case of the *state reconstruction* with precisely known model parameters the estimated finite-dimensional state vector $\underline{x}_k$ is uniquely characterized by a Gaussian density. The density function $f^e(p_k|\underline{r})$ can be derived in the entire domain as follows

$$\underline{p}_k \sim f^e(p_k|\underline{r}) = \mathcal{N}\left(p_k - \hat{p}_k^e(\underline{r}), C_k^e(\underline{r})\right)\,,$$

where $\mathcal{N}(\cdot)$ denotes the Gaussian density with respective mean and variance conditioned on the spatial coördinate $\underline{r} \in \mathbb{R}^2$. Thanks to the linear characteristic of the mapping (2.31), the mean $\hat{p}_k^e(\cdot)$ and the variance $C_k^e(\cdot)$ are given by

$$\hat{p}_k^e(\underline{r}) = \underline{\Psi}(\underline{r})^\mathrm{T}\hat{\underline{x}}_k^e\,,$$
$$C_k^e(\underline{r}) = \underline{\Psi}(\underline{r})^\mathrm{T}\,\mathbf{C}_k^e\,\underline{\Psi}(\underline{r})\,,$$

which uniquely represent the stochastic of the underlying physical system. It is obvious that $\hat{p}_k^e(\cdot)$ and $C_k^e(\cdot)$ depend on the spatial coördinate $\underline{r}$, and thus characterize the distributed mean and distributed variance of the entire random field in the area of interest.

Gaussian mixture density For the *state and parameter estimation* of space-time continuous systems, the density function $f^e(\underline{x}_k)$ representing the finite-dimensional state vector $\boldsymbol{x}_k$ turns out to be a non-Gaussian density function; see Chapter 4. In this work, this density is modelled as a Gaussian mixture density due to its properties as a universal approximator,

$$f^e(\underline{x}_k) = \sum_{i=1}^{N} w_k^i \, \mathcal{N}\left(\underline{x}_k - \hat{\underline{x}}_k^{ei}, \mathbf{C}_k^{ei}\right) \; ,$$

where w_k^i, $\hat{\underline{x}}_k^{ei}$, and $\mathbf{C}_k^{ei}$ respectively are the weights, the mean, and the covariance matrix of the individual Gaussian components. The variable N denotes the number of used components. Then, the density function $f^e(p_k|\underline{r})$ is a *Gaussian mixture density* according to

$$\boldsymbol{p}_k(\underline{r}) \sim f^e(p_k|\underline{r}) = \sum_{i=1}^{N} w_k^i \, \mathcal{N}\left(p_k - \hat{p}_k^{ei}(\underline{r}), C_k^{ei}(\underline{r})\right) \; , \tag{2.32}$$

where the mean $\hat{p}_k^{ei}(\cdot)$ and variance $C_k^{ei}(\cdot)$ of the individual components are given by

$$\hat{p}_k^{ei}(\underline{r}) = \underline{\Psi}(\underline{r})^{\mathrm{T}} \, \hat{\underline{x}}_k^{ei} \; ,$$
$$C_k^{ei}(\underline{r}) = \underline{\Psi}(\underline{r})^{\mathrm{T}} \, \mathbf{C}_k^{ei} \, \underline{\Psi}(\underline{r}) \; . \tag{2.33}$$

This equation can be used to derive the stochastic properties in terms of the density function for the space-time continuous system in the entire solution domain $\underline{r} \in \Omega$.

2.6 Simulation Results

In this section, the performance of the proposed *model-based state reconstruction* is demonstrated based on the convection-diffusion system (2.1). This is achieved by the rigorous investigation of different simulated case studies interesting for sensor network applications. The purpose is to emphasize the clear advantage of a model-based approach compared to interpolation methods not using any physical background knowledge and to show the novel prospects for sensor network applications. In particular, the following case studies are investigated:

1. The first simulation study shows the performance of the *state reconstruction* in the case of a *precisely known* model description. To be more specific, all the parameters in the stochastic partial differential equation (2.1), the location of the individual measurement points, and the parameters of the space-time continuous input are precisely known.

2. In the second case study, the degradation of the reconstruction performance caused by *parameter deviations* in the mathematical model (2.1) are demonstrated. The purpose is the motivation for simultaneous state reconstruction and parameter identification methods (see Chapter 4) in order to obtain *accurate interpolation results*.

3. The third simulated case study is devoted to the investigation of the *effect of the node locations* on the reconstruction error. This clearly shows the necessity for more sophisticated planning algorithms in order to find optimal measurement locations leading to optimal reconstruction and identification results. The derivation of such techniques is not considered in this thesis, rather see [22, 167, 169].

2.6.1 Simulated Case Study 1: Precise System Description

In this case study, the performance of the reconstruction method using physical background knowledge is demonstrated in the case of a precisely known mathematical model. The underlying space-time continuous physical system is described in the following.

Example 2.4: State reconstruction of space-time continuous physical systems
Throughout this section, we assume the underlying physical system to be governed by the two-dimensional convection-diffusion equation (2.1), introduced in Example 2.1. The process parameters of the respective stochastic partial differential equation are given by:

Dirichlet/Neumann boundary conditions $\quad g_D = 20\,^\circ\text{C} \; , \quad g_N = 0\,^\circ\text{C}\,\text{m}^{-1}$

Model parameters of physical system $\quad \alpha_{\text{true}} = 0.8\,\text{m}^2\,\text{h}^{-1} \; , \quad \gamma_{\text{true}} = 1\,\text{m}^3\,^\circ\text{C}\,\text{cal}^{-1}$

Homogenous convection field $\quad \underline{v}(\underline{r}, t) = \begin{bmatrix} 8 & , & 8 \end{bmatrix}^{\text{T}}\,\text{m}\,\text{h}^{-1}$

Space-time continuous system input $\quad \hat{s}(\underline{r}, t) = 10^3 \left(e^{-\frac{(0.5-\hat{x})^2}{0.1} - \frac{(0.5-\hat{y})^2}{0.0005}} + e^{-\frac{(1.5-x)^2}{0.0005} - \frac{(1.5-y)^2}{0.1}} \right)$

$$C^s(\underline{r}, t) = 0.5\,\text{cal}^2\,\text{m}^{-6}\,\text{h}^{-2}$$

The two-dimensional L-shaped solution domain $\Omega \in \mathbb{R}^2$, boundary conditions, and the location of the system input $s(\underline{r}, t)$ are depicted in Figure 2.4. The individual sensor nodes in the spatially distributed measurement system are randomly deployed in the considered solution domain Ω. The stochastic partial differential equation (2.1) including its density representation is converted into a lumped-parameter time-discrete system (2.22) based on *piecewise linear* shape functions, i.e., using the finite-element method. The parameters of the conversion process are assumed to be given by $N_x = 833$, $N_{el} = 1536$ (spatial decomposition) and $\Delta t = 0.001\,\text{h}$ (time discretization constant). Similar to the conversion of the stochastic partial differential equation (2.1), the corresponding noise term of the system input $s(\underline{r}, t)$ represented by the mutually independent spatially distributed variance $C^s(\underline{r}, t)$ needs to be converted. In the homogeneous case, this conversion can be specifically achieved by using (2.13), (2.14) and (2.23). The covariance matrix of the boundary condition noise is assumed to be $\widetilde{\mathbf{C}}^b(t_k) = 0.05 \cdot \mathbf{I}_{N_x}\,\text{cal}^2\,\text{m}^{-6}\,\text{h}^{-2}$ and the covariance matrix of the spatially distributed measurement system is given by $\mathbf{C}_v = 0.5 \cdot \mathbf{I}_{N_y}\,\text{K}^2$. $\blacksquare$

By means of the resulting generative system model (2.22) and the generative measurement model (2.27) with aforementioned parameters, it is possible to design the state reconstruction process based on a linear Bayesian estimator, such as the Kalman filter. The numerical solution of the physical system (2.1) in the *deterministic case*, i.e., without process noises, is visualized for different time steps in Figure 2.15. Compared to this deterministic case, typical realizations of the *stochastic case* with aforementioned process noise parameters are shown in Figure 2.16.

The goal is the reconstruction of the space-time continuous system state $\underline{p}(\underline{r}, t)$ using both a mathematical model describing the physical characteristic and measurements obtained from a sensor network. It is important to emphasize that the novelty of the proposed approach is to consider remaining uncertainties arising from noisy measurements and occuring in the mathematical model. For the *pure reconstruction* of the entire distributed system using a sensor network, we assume the model parameters to be precisely known. The simulation results are depicted in Figure 2.17 and in Figure 2.18.

(a) Numeric solution at $k = 10$ **(b)** Numeric solution at $k = 50$ **(c)** Numeric solution at $k = 200$

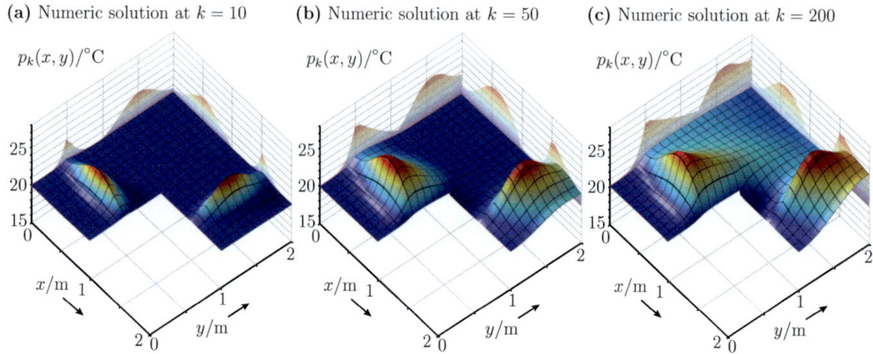

Figure 2.15: *Simulation setup*: Numerical solution of the *deterministic physical system* considered for the verification of the reconstruction process. The solution $p(x, y)$ of the physical system is visualized in the entire L-shaped solution domain for different time steps: **(a)** $k = 10$, **(b)** $k = 50$, and **(c)** $k = 200$.

(a) Realization at $k = 10$ **(b)** Realization at $k = 50$ **(c)** Realization at $k = 200$

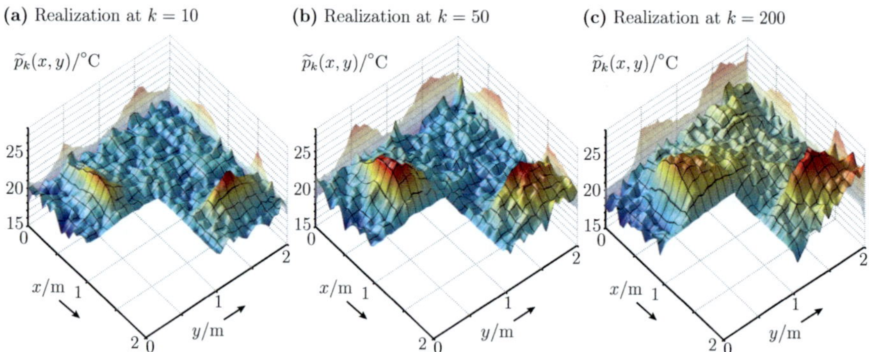

Figure 2.16: *Simulation setup*: *Realization* of the space-time continuous system considered for the verification of the reconstruction process. The solution $p(x, y)$ of the physical system is visualized in the entire L-shaped solution domain for different time steps: **(a)** $k = 10$, **(b)** $k = 50$, and **(c)** $k = 200$.

2.6.2 Simulated Case Study 2: Incorrect Process Parameters

In the previous case study, the parameters of the stochastic partial differential equation (2.1) exploited for the state reconstruction were assumed to be precisely known. Hence, the entire physical system can be accurately reconstructed, even at non-measurement points thanks to the model-based and systematic interpolation approach.

In many cases, however, the underlying true physical system deviates from the nominal mathematical model, basically caused by neglecting particular physical effects or external disturbances. Furthermore, respective model parameters could vary over time without knowing the exact dynamic behavior of such variations. In addition, due to the distributed characteristic of the physical system, not only the states are distributed and inhomogeneous, but also the parameters decribing the dynamic behavior. Considering all these issues in the mathematical model quickly increases the complexity of the model description, and thus the computational load. On the other hand, neglecting these physical effects leads to a deviation of the mathematical model and causes a degradation of the reconstruction performance. This means, for practical applications a trade-off between accuracy and computational load needs to be found. In particular, the equations (2.28) and (2.29) used for the reconstruction process requires a rather precise model of the underlying physical system and a precisely known uncertainty description.

If any of the aforementioned assumptions are violated, then the performance of the model-based reconstruction process can quickly degrade. In this simulated case study, degradations of the performance caused by assuming parameters in the stochastic partial differential equation (2.1) that deviate from the true parameters are described by means of an example; in particular the severe effect to the accuracy of the estimation result is shown. The degradation of the results undoubtedly justifies the *simultaneous approach* for the state reconstruction and the identification of possibly deviating parameters (introduced in Chapter 4).

Example 2.5: Reconstruction with incorrect process parameters
In this example, we consider a physical system that is represented by the two-dimensional convection-diffusion equation (2.1) with respective model parameters as described in Example 2.4. The state reconstruction is performed on the basis of the prediction step (2.28) and the measurement step (2.29) with the nominal parameter set for the diffusion coefficient α_{model} according to

$$\alpha_{\mathrm{model}} \in \{0.5,\, 0.6,\, \ldots,\, 1.5\}\ \mathrm{m^2\,h^{-1}}\ ,$$

where the true parameter is assumed to be given by $\alpha_{\mathrm{true}} = 0.8\,\mathrm{m^2\,h^{-1}}$. The distributed measurement system consists of different number of nodes randomly deployed in the domain of interest,

$$S \in \{2,3,4,5,6,8,10,15,20,25,30,40,50,60,80,100\}\ .$$

The reconstruction process is performed for a simulation time of $N_t = 200$ time steps ($t_{\mathrm{sim}} = 20\,\mathrm{min}$). For each combination of the modelled diffusion coefficient α_{model} and the number S of randomly deployed nodes, 50 independent Monte Carlo simulation runs have been performed. This results in $N_{\mathrm{MC}} = 50$ true realizations $\widetilde{x}_k^i$ of the state vector characterizing the distributed state $p_k(r)$. ∎

Based on the reconstruction process described in Section 2.5 the entire space-time continuous system can be reconstructed using the nominal mathematical model descriptions. The estimated finite-dimensional state vector $\underline{x}_k$ can be directly derived from (2.28) and (2.29). The mean $\hat{e}_k^x$ and variance C_x^{rmse} of the root mean square error e_k^x (rmse) of the state vector $\underline{x}_k$, and

(a) Simulation setup and location of sensor nodes

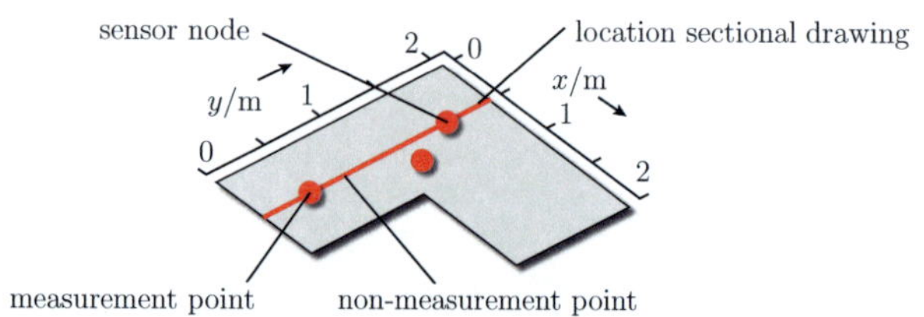

(b) Mean and variance of space-time continuous state

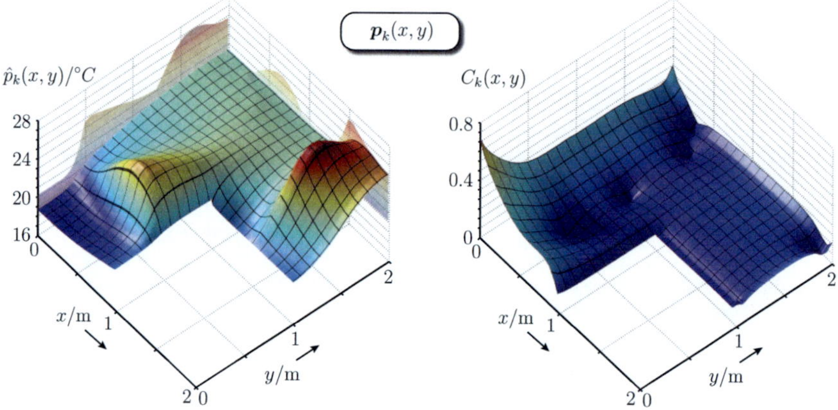

(c) Sectional drawing of space-time continuous state over time

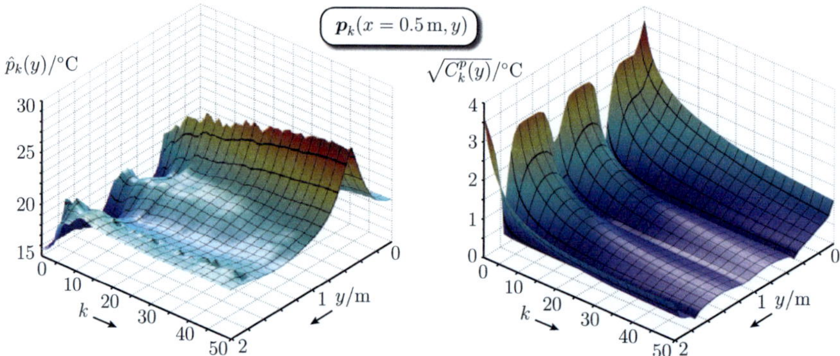

Figure 2.17: *Simulated case study 1* (precise model): **(a)** Location of sensor nodes for the depicted simulation results and location of the profile for the sectional drawings. **(b)** Typical results of the reconstruction process at time step $k = 200$; spatially distributed mean $\hat{p}_k(x, y)$ and spatially distributed variance $C_k(x, y)$ in the entire solution domain Ω. **(c)** Sectional drawing of the reconstruction result at $x = 0.5\,\mathrm{m}$ over time.

(a) Measurement and non-measurement point

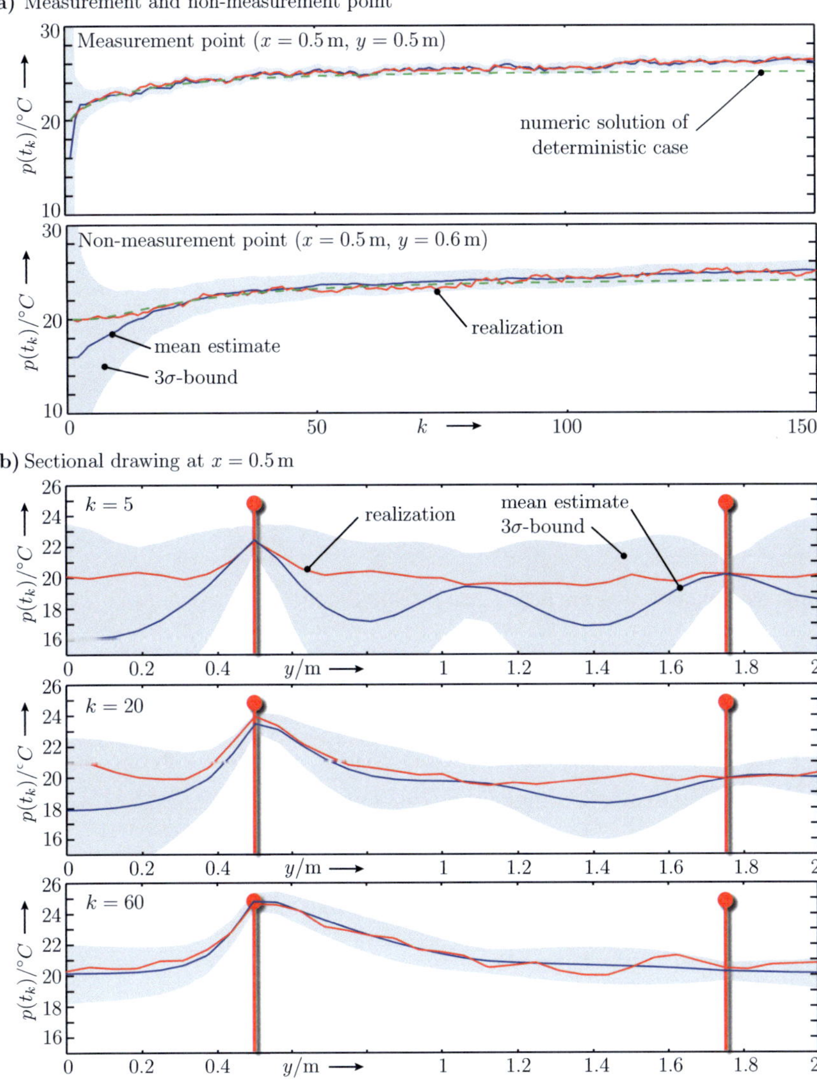

(b) Sectional drawing at $x = 0.5$ m

Figure 2.18: *Simulated case study 1* (precise model): **(a)** Estimation results at a measurement point ($x = 0.5$ m, $y = 0.5$ m) and at a non-measurement point ($x = 0.5$ m, $y = 0.6$ m); depicted are a realization (red), the solution of the deterministic case (green dotted), the mean estimate (blue), and the 3σ-bound (gray shaded). **(b)** Sectional drawing of the estimation result at $x = 0.5$ m for different time steps $k = 5, 20, 60$. It is obvious that the reconstruction results (interpolation) between the individual sensor nodes improves over the time, thanks to the exploitation of the physical model and the measurements obtained from the network.

(a) State vector rmse averaged over time
(node number vs. model parameter)

(b) State vector rmse averaged over time

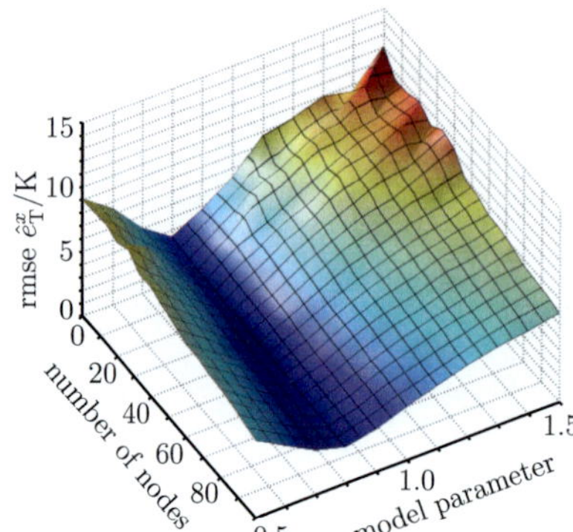

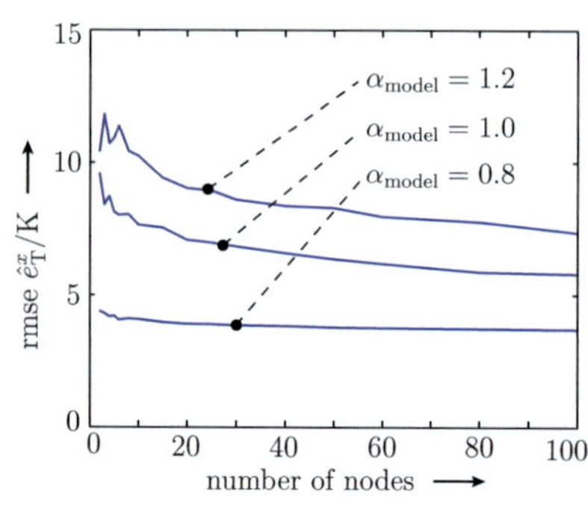

Figure 2.19: *Simulated case study 2* (deviating model): Reconstruction results for using a mathematical model deviating from the true physical system, e.g., the modeled diffusion coefficient α_{model} deviates from the true coefficient α_{true}. **(a)** Mean of root means square error $\hat{e}_T^x$ (rmse) averaged over time versus the diffusion coefficient α_{model} and the number S of sensor nodes. **(b)** Detailed figure of the rmse for $\alpha_{\mathrm{model}} \in \{0.8, 1.1, 1.4\}\ \mathrm{m}^2\,\mathrm{h}^{-1}$.

the error averaged over time are approximated by calculating according to

$$
\hat{e}_k^x = \sqrt{\frac{1}{N_{\mathrm{MC}}} \sum_{i=1}^{N_{\mathrm{MC}}} \|\widetilde{x}_k^i - \hat{x}_k^{ei}\|}\ , \qquad
C_x^{\mathrm{rmse}} = \frac{1}{N_{\mathrm{MC}}-1} \sum_{i=1}^{N_{\mathrm{MC}}} (e_k^{xi} - \hat{e}_k^x)^2\ , \qquad
\hat{e}_T^x = \frac{1}{N_t} \sum_{k=1}^{N_t} \hat{e}_k^x\ ,
$$

$$(2.34)$$

where $\hat{x}_k^{ei}$ denotes the mean of the estimated state vector and $\widetilde{x}_k^i$ is a specific realization. The simulation results for the state reconstruction with incorrect model parameters is shown in Figure 2.19. It can be clearly seen that the more the nominal parameter α_{model} deviates from the true parameter α_{true}, the more the performance of the estimation results degrades. Roughly speaking, the physical system is less accurately interpolated between the individual measurement points in the case of incorrect model parameters. Using a higher number of sensor nodes also can improve the reconstruction result in the case of deviating model description to a certain degree. Due to a higher number of sensor nodes (i.e., denser sensor network), the distance between the individual measurement points automatically decreases, and thus basically, a shorter distance needs to be interpolated. An additional explanation of the simulation result is that the more information obtained from the measurement system, the less the reconstruction result depends on the (possibly deviating) mathematical model description. However, in this simulated case study, where the sensor network consists of more than $S = 100$ nodes, the reconstruction error still turns out to be quite high in the case of a deviating model description. This certainly shows the necessity of simultaneous approaches for the interpolation (i.e., state reconstruction) and the identification of possibly deviating model parameters. In particular, this leads to an improved performance of the reconstruction process while using a decreased number of sensor nodes; see Section 4.3.

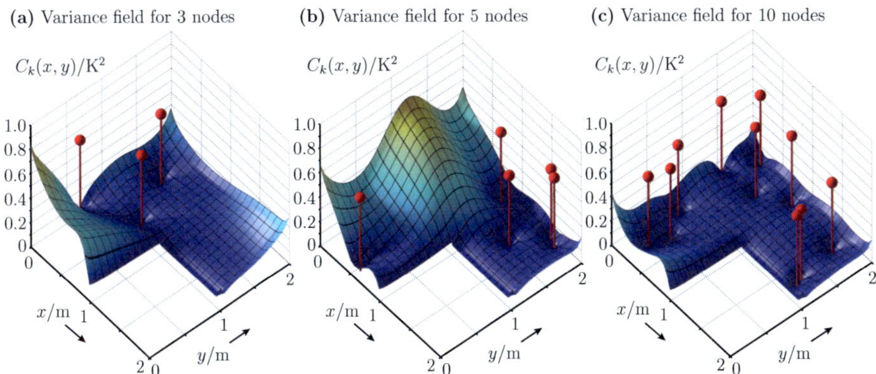

Figure 2.20: *Simulated case study 3* (effect of node locations): Visualization of the variance field $C_k(x,y)$ at time step $k = 300$ for a sensor network consisting of **(a)** 3 nodes, **(b)** 5 nodes, and **(c)** 10 nodes. The variance in the close surrounding to the sensor nodes is much lower than further away. In addition, it is obvious that besides the number of used sensor nodes, their optimal placement plays an important role in deriving a precise estimation result (low variance) of the entire space-time continuous system.

2.6.3 Simulated Case Study 3: Effect of Sensor Locations

This simulated case study is devoted to an investigation of the effect of measurement locations on the accuracy of the reconstruction result. In the sense of space-time continuous systems, methods for optimal sensor placement make it possible to derive optimal sequences and locations. Then, the costs of measurements can be minimized for a given reconstruction error. The relationship between such planning methods and the model-based reconstruction method proposed in this research work is schematically visualized in Figure 1.1. The aim of such techniques, as introduced in [22, 169], is to derive the best possible measurement parameters for performing future measurements. The term best possible here means: maximum information gain under certain constraints, such as limited energy or number of nodes, leading to accurate reconstruction results [112, 167]. It is obvious from Figure 2.20 that not only increasing the number of used sensor nodes but especially selecting appropriate locations leads to more accurate results, i.e., estimates with a lower variance in the entire area of interest. Here, the clear advantage of model-based reconstruction methods using physical background knowledge becomes obvious, because only then the necessity of gathering information at non-measurement points can be evaluated in a systematic and physically correct fashion.

Example 2.6: Effect of sensor locations

In this example, the effects of sensor locations on the accuracy of the state reconstruction is investigated and the benefits of optimum locations is demonstrated. As the underlying physical system, the system described in Example 2.4 is chosen, and the simulation is performed for $N_t = 80$ ($t_{\mathrm{sim}} = 8\,\mathrm{min}$) time steps. The initial state vector for the reconstruction process is assumed to be deviated from the realization, i.e., given by $\hat{\underline{x}}_0 = \underline{0}$. As potential sensor locations, all individual points on a regular grid (with a grid size of $\Delta x = 0.05\,\mathrm{m}$ and $\Delta y = 0.5\,\mathrm{m}$) were tested by performing for each assumed location $N_{\mathrm{MC}} = 20$ state reconstruction experiments. ∎

In Figure 2.21, the root mean square error (rmse) according to (2.34) of the state reconstruction versus the assumed node location is depicted. As predicted, the best possible location of one

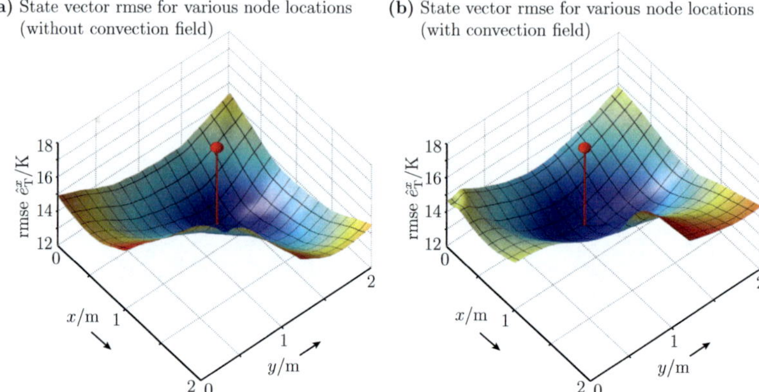

Figure 2.21: *Simulated case study 3* (effect of node locations): Visualization of the mean of the state vector root mean square error (rmse) averaged over time versus the node location. **(a)** The physical system is driven *only* by a *diffusion process*. In this case the node location $r^s_{\mathrm{opt}} = [0.6\,,\,1.35]^T$ m results in the best reconstruction results with the least error. **(b)** The system is driven by *diffusion process and convection field*. Here, the best location turns out to be $r^s_{\mathrm{opt}} = [0.6\,,\,1.1]^T$ m.

single sensor node for taking measurements is simply the center of the area of interest Ω. Also note that the accuracy of the estimates is almost twice as great for the optimal point as for the outermost tested locations. That indicates even sophisticated and more involved methods of sensor placement can be worthwhile for the observation of space-time continuous physical systems, especially when precise reconstruction results are of interest. In the simulated case study the effect of only one sensor node was considered. The investigation of effects in the case of more than one sensor node and the derivation of methods for optimal placements and sequences is out of the scope of this thesis, and thus not considered here. Rather see publications on this particular topic, such as [87, 112, 138, 167, 169].

2.7 Summary and Discussion

This chapter introduces the methodology for the systematic state reconstruction of space-time continuous systems; considered are systems that are governed by *stochastic partial differential equations*. In particular, it is described how finite-dimensional probabilistic models are derived characterizing the dynamic and the distributed properties of the physical system as well of the measurement system. Then, based on the finite-dimensional system description, a Bayesian estimator is designed for reconstructing the physical system in the entire area of interest, even at non-measurement points. Here, it is emphasized that the conversion of *linear* stochastic partial differential equations always results in a *linear* lumped-parameter system. The distributed properties of the physical system is then described by respective coupling terms. The entire reconstruction process is presented by means of a specific physical phenomenon that is governed by convection-diffusion system. However, the extension to higher dimensions and to physical systems governed by more sophisticated linear stochastic partial differential equations is conceptually straigthforward.

Compared to classical interpolation techniques, the *novelty of the proposed method* is the rigorous exploitation of additional background knowledge in terms of mathematical models, for example about the physical behavior. Based on such an approach, the interpolation and also extrapolation of spatially distributed measurements is achieved in a systematic and physically correct fashion. Moreover, throughout the entire process the uncertainties arising in the modelling process and inherently existing in the measurements are systematically considered. By this means, a measure of the reconstruction result is obtained in terms of a *space-continuous probability density function* representing the system state including its uncertainty description. The application of such model-based reconstruction provides novel prospects for several additional tasks in various sensor network applications, such as optimal sensor placement, parameter and system identification in order to improve the knowledge about the physical system being monitored. Especially tackling the problem of system identification is essential for self-organized and autonomous behavior in a completely unknown surrounding. The methods proposed in this chapter lays the foundation for such *additional tasks* in sensor network applications.

The drawback of the derived technique is the necessity of a model description with sufficiently precise model parameters. It is shown by a simulation study that deviations in the mathematical model leads to degradations of the reconstruction result. This makes sophisticated identification methods necessary. Due to the fact that for space-time continuous systems the proposed parameter identification process leads to a high-dimensional and nonlinear estimation problem, effficient estimation methods are necessary. For that reason, a novel estimator that is based on the decomposition of the nonlinear estimation problem into a linear part and a nonlinear part is introduced in Chapter 3. By this means, the high-dimensional linear substructure naturally existing in the model of space-time continuous systems can be exploited for the identification of such systems; see Chapter 4. By using methods for the identification of an appropriate mathematical model, as introduced in Section 4.3, it would be possible for the sensor nodes to identify, observe, and reconstruct unknown distributed physical systems. In addition, it is possible to derive novel *passive localization* techniques based on the local observation of physical systems, and thus without the necessity of additional infrastructure (such as a global positioning systems); see Section 4.4.

CHAPTER 3

Estimation of Nonlinear Dynamic Systems with Linear Substructures

This chapter addresses the framework for an efficient estimator for nonlinear systems with linear substructures, so-called mixed linear/nonlinear dynamic systems. Based on a novel density representation — *sliced Gaussian mixture density* — the decomposition into a (conditionally) linear and nonlinear estimation problem is derived. The proposed *Sliced Gaussian Mixture Filter* (SGMF) consists of a systematic approximation procedure that minimizes a certain distance measure, and thus allows the derivation of (close to) optimal and deterministic estimation results. This leads to high-quality representations of the probability density function of the system states. Compared to an estimator performing on the entire estimation problem at once, the decomposition results in an overall more efficient estimation process.

The methods for the efficient state estimation by exploiting linear substructures in nonlinear systems presented in this chapter were published at [170, 172, 181]. However, explanations and the derivation of the estimator equations are stated in a considerably extended way and further simulation results clarify the advantages compared to other estimators.

3.1 Related Work

Linear state estimation   The estimation of the state that represents a dynamic system from noisy measurements is a common task in many applications. The exact solution to this problem can be found only in some special cases. For *linear systems* with Gaussian noise, the *Kalman filter* [77] provides optimal estimation results in an analytic form. This is the case for the state reconstruction of space-time continuous systems governed by linear partial differential equations (1.2); see Section 2.5. However, since most systems cannot be truly regarded as linear, *linear estimators* do not apply directly to most physical systems. For *nonlinear systems* with non-Gaussian noise an analytic solution of the estimation problem cannot be derived and exactly solving the problem within a Bayesian framework becomes computationally demanding. Hence, approximation methods as described in the following are inevitable.

Estimation based on linearizations   There exist a vast variety of approaches for the state estimation of nonlinear systems. The well-known *extended Kalman filter* (EKF) [133] is based on a local linearization of the nonlinear equations and the application of the standard Kalman filter to the resulting linearized equations. This filter was employed for various application scenarios, such as localization and tracking, and the parameter identification of space-time continuous physical systems [118, 154]. Due to the linearization of the nonlinear

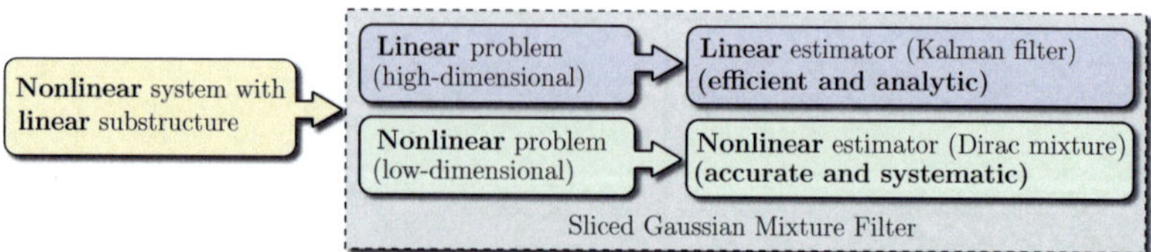

Figure 3.1: Visualization of decomposing a nonlinear system with a linear substructure by means of the *Sliced Gaussian Mixture Filter* (SGMF). The nonlinear estimation problem is decomposed into a *linear part* (application of analytic estimator such as *Kalman filter*) and into a *nonlinear part* (application of accurate and systematic nonlinear estimator such as *Dirac mixture filter*).

system, such estimators result in analytic equations that can be implemented in a straightforward and efficient fashion. However, for strongly nonlinear systems the errors occuring during the linearization process lead to a divergence of the estimation results. Some properties of the EKF can be found in [8, 132]. The so-called *Gaussian Filters*, such as the *unscented Kalman filter* (UKF) [72, 74, 142] or the extended approach proposed in [64], use deterministic samplings of the true probability density function that characterizes the system state. Compared to the extended Kalman filter, this offers an increased higher-order accuracy. The methods based on a *system approximation* (EKF) and a *density approximation* (UKF) result in a single Gaussian density. This type is often not sufficient for representing the underlying true density function.

Particle filter and Dirac mixture filter   One possibility for increasing the performance of the estimation result is to use a kind of sample representation for the probability density function, like in particle filters (PF) [6, 8, 19]. In this filter framework, the density is represented by a set of realizations, the so-called particles. This allows the point-wise analytic calculation of the estimation problem. Due to complexity reasons, the samples are usually not drawn from the underlying density function, instead so-called *proposal densities* are used. The main drawbacks of particle filters are sample degenerations and impoverishments mainly caused by positioning the individual particles at unfavorable locations with less support for approximating the underlying density function. Furthermore, in most applications, a high number of particles is necessary to achieve sufficiently accurate estimation results. A more involved and sophisticated way for increasing the performance using discrete density representations is the so-called *Dirac mixture filter* (DMF) [59, 126]. This estimator is based on the systematic positioning of the individual Diracs while minimizing a certain distance measure. By means of this systematic and deterministic approach, the underlying probability density function can be usually represented with less parameters and yields more accurate results with respect to the selected distance measure.

Marginalized particle filter   In many applications, the *nonlinear equations* of the mathematical model contain *linear substructures*. For example, in navigation, localization [178], tracking, robot mapping and localization, and parameter identification of space-time continuous physical systems [181]. The performance of nonlinear estimators can be significantly improved with respect to accuracy and implementation effort, when the linear substructure in such systems is rigorously exploited during the estimation process. This can be achieved by the *decomposition* of the entire estimation problem into a *linear problem* and a *nonlinear problem*. One possibility for exploiting linear substructures is the marginalized (or Rao-Blackwellized) particle filter (MPF) [6, 25, 31, 92, 49]. Herein, the dimensionality of the estimation problem is reduced by a marginalization over the linear subspace. Then, the remaining density is subsequently represented by particles. By this means, the standard particle filter is adopted to cope

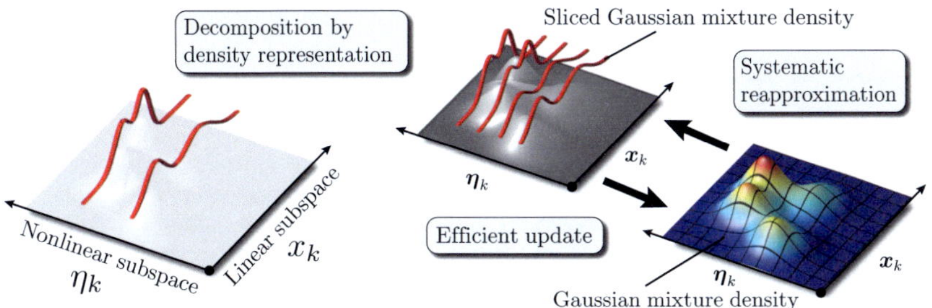

Figure 3.2: Visualization of the ***three stages*** of the *Sliced Gaussian Mixture Filter* (SGMF): (a) Decomposition of the estimation problem by means of a special density representation, (b) the efficient procedure of the prediction step and measurement step, and (c) the systematic reapproximation of the resulting *Gaussian mixture* density by a *sliced Gaussian mixture* density.

with the reduced nonlinear estimation problem, whereas the Kalman filter is used to find the optimal estimate for the linear subspace associated with each particle. In [78] the complexity of the marginalized particle filter (MPF) is analyzed and a method for actually performing this analysis is given. A comprehensive overview and references to the state-of-the-art about theory, analysis, and various applications can be found in [50].

Drawbacks of PF and MPF   Thanks to the exploitation of linear substructures during the overall estimation process, the marginalized particle filter (MPF) undoubtedly improves the performance in comparison to the standard particle filter (PF). However, the most severe drawbacks still remain within this estimator framework. Similar to the standard particle filter, special algorithms have to be achieved in order to avoid effects like sample degeneration and impoverishment. In addition, the filter does not provide measures on how well the estimated joint density actually represents the true density to be estimated. This means, for determining which number of particles are high enough for a sufficient performance, there appears to be no other way than actually simulating the entire estimation process. Another drawback is that the framework of the marginalized particle filter as introduced in [78, 124, 123] is restricted to single Gaussian densities in the linear subspace. This means, for the representation of multimodal densities several particles would be necessary. It is well known that the particle filters are often incapable of maintaining multimodality during the entire estimation process. Then, the degeneration of single particles results in a loss of entire (possibly important) modes under unfavorable circumstances. A possible solution to tackle this problem for the standard particle filter are offered by mixture tracking methods that rely on clustering algorithms in order to reposition the particles of a completely discrete density representation [143]. However, it is not clear how such an operation translates into the mixed representation of the marginalized particle filter. As it stands, there is no other interaction between the individual particles of the marginalized particle filter than stemming from the resampling step after the measurement update. In its standard implementation, this boils down to duplicating some samples while discarding others.

The estimator – ***S***liced ***G***aussian ***M***ixture ***F***ilter (SGMF) – proposed in this research work leads to more accurate estimation results by combining the key idea of the Rao-Blackwellization [25] with the systematic approach of the Dirac mixture filter [59, 126]; see Figure 3.1.

3.2 Overview of the Sliced Gaussian Mixture Filter (SGMF)

In this chapter, a novel approach for the efficient recursive estimation of nonlinear systems with linear substructures is introduced. Besides the exploitation of the linear substructure by decomposing the estimation problem (as in the marginalized particle filter), there are two key features leading to a significantly improved estimation result: (a) the definition of a novel general-purpose density representation for the decomposition of the estimation problem and approximation purposes, and (b) a systematic and deterministic (nonrandom) density approximation for a recursive estimation process. Basically, within this framework, sliced Gaussian mixture densities are used as density representations. The resulting *S*liced *G*aussian *M*ixture *F*ilter consists of ***three stages***. In the remainder of this section, the stages and the *novelties* are briefly described; see also Figure 3.2 for the visualization of the individual stages.

1) Decomposition: In the first stage, the general nonlinear estimation problem is decomposed into a conditionally *linear* problem (usually high-dimensional state estimation) and a *nonlinear* problem (usually lower-dimensional parameter identification). The decomposition during the estimation process can be achieved by means of a novel density representation, the *sliced Gaussian mixture densities*. Basically, this density consists of a discrete representation (*Dirac mixture*) in the nonlinear subspace and a continuous representation (*Gaussian mixture*) in the linear subspace; see Figure 3.2.

2) Decomposed estimation step: Based on the previous decompostion into a conditionally linear and nonlinear estimation problem, both the prediction step and the measurement step can be performed with an overall more efficient performance. This means, once the slices with the Gaussian mixture components have been positioned, the predicted and estimated density in the linear subspace can be computed in an efficient and analytic fashion (using a set of Kalman filters). The estimation in the nonlinear subspace is performed using nonlinear estimators, such as the Dirac mixture filter (DMF) [59, 126]. The posterior density function turns out to be a Gaussian mixture density that is continuous both in the linear and in the nonlinear subspace. Thus, the subsequent reapproximation procedure can take full advantage of the complete knowledge about the joint density being approximated.

3) Systematic reapproximation: The estimation based on the *sliced Gaussian mixture densities* leads to a density representation consisting of *Gaussian mixtures* in all subspaces. In order to bound the complexity, the resulting continuous probability density needs to be reapproximated by means of density slices. The positioning of the slices is performed in a systematic and determinstic (nonrandom) fashion that minimizes a specific distance measure between the true probability density function and the density to be approximated. Besides providing a measure for the evaluation of the approximation performance, this results in less parameters that are necessary for a sufficient density representation. Roughly speaking, the density slices are positioned exactly at the locations with most support for the approximated density function. Less density slices, in addition, means that the application of fewer Kalman filters is required for the linear subspace, which is of special interest for high-dimensional state vectors (e.g., space-time continuous physical systems). Furthermore, the final positions of the density slices are not independent, and therefore, a kind of interaction between them is enforced in a natural way. There are different approaches for the actual derivation of an (exactly or almost) optimal solution to the approximation problem.

Example 3.1: Considered model structure for the SGMF
The key idea of decomposing the estimation problem by sliced Gaussian mixture densities and the deterministic reapproximation can be applied to general dynamic systems occuring in various application scenarios. However, in order to show the novelties of the estimation approach, a specific system structure is considered similar to the structure of the state and parameter estimation of space-time continuous systems. In particular, it is similar to the identification of process parameters, the localization of individual nodes based on local measurements, and the localization of sources and leakages; compare the structure given in Section 4.1. The following nonlinear dynamic system with a linear substructure is considered,

$$\underline{x}_{k+1} = \mathbf{A}_k(\underline{\eta}_k)\,\underline{x}_k + \mathbf{B}_k(\underline{\eta}_k)\,(\hat{\underline{u}}_k + \underline{w}_k^x)\ ,$$
$$\underline{\eta}_{k+1} = \underline{a}_k(\underline{\eta}_k) + \underline{w}_k^\eta\ , \tag{3.1}$$

where $\underline{x}_k \in \mathbb{R}^{N_x}$ and $\underline{\eta}_k \in \mathbb{R}^{N_\eta}$ denote the linear and nonlinear substate vectors being decomposed by the *sliced Gaussian mixture density*. For simplicity reasons, the noise terms $\underline{w}_k^x$ and $\underline{w}_k^\eta$ are assumed to be zero-mean white Gaussian with following covariance matrix

$$\text{Cov}\left\{\begin{bmatrix}\underline{w}_k^x\\\underline{w}_k^\eta\end{bmatrix}\right\} = \begin{bmatrix}\mathbf{C}_w^x & 0\\0 & \mathbf{C}_w^\eta\end{bmatrix} = \mathbf{C}_w\ , \tag{3.2}$$

which means that the process noises in linear and nonlinear subspace are mutually independent. Furthermore, the structure of the measurement model is given by

$$\hat{\underline{y}}_k = \mathbf{H}_k(\underline{\eta}_k)\underline{x}_k + \underline{h}_k(\underline{\eta}_k) + \underline{v}_k\ . \tag{3.3}$$

where the noise term $\underline{v}_k$ is assumed to be zero-mean white Gaussian noise with covariance matrix $\mathbf{C}_v$. The structure of the considered system description is shown in Figure 3.1 (a). This model structure is quite often referred to as a *conditionally linear dynamic model* [31], which means, given the trajectory of the nonlinear state vector $\underline{\eta}_k$, the system can be regarded as linear. ∎

3.3 Density Representation

Joint probability density function   By employing a special density representation, the estimation problem based on the nonlinear system description (3.1) and (3.3) can be decomposed into a (conditionaly) linear and nonlinear problem. This density function consists of a discrete function in the *nonlinear* subspace $\underline{\eta}_k \in \mathbb{R}^{N_\eta}$ (*parameter space*) and a continuous function in the *linear* subspace $\underline{x}_k \in \mathbb{R}^{N_x}$ (*state space*). To be more specific, the *sliced Gaussian mixture density* is represented as follows

$$f(\underline{x}_k, \underline{\eta}_k) := \sum_{i=1}^{M_D} \alpha_k^i \underbrace{\delta(\underline{\eta}_k - \underline{\xi}_k^i)}_{\text{Dirac mixture}}\ \underbrace{f(\underline{x}_k|\underline{\xi}_k^i)}_{\text{Gaussian mixture}}\ , \tag{3.4}$$

where $\delta(\cdot)$ denotes Diracs' delta distribution and $\alpha_k^i \in \mathbb{R}_+$ are their corresponding weighting coefficients. The variable M_D denotes the number of density slices used for representing the system state and parameters. The notation and the structure of the density (3.4) is visualized in Figure 3.3. The density parameters $\underline{\xi}_k^i \in \mathbb{R}^{P_\eta}$ can be regarded as the positions of the individual density slices and M_D denotes their number.

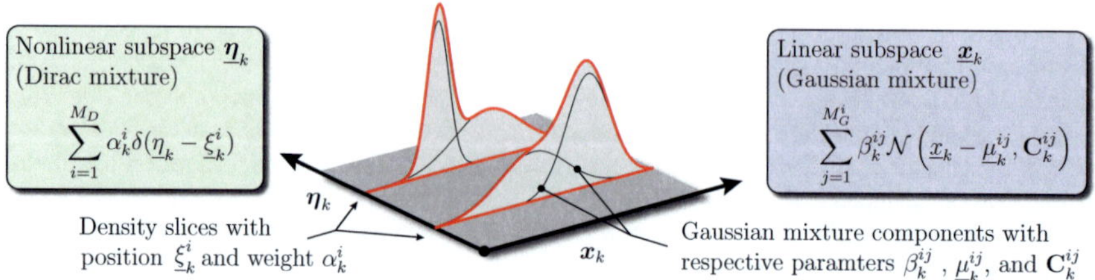

Figure 3.3: Notations and visualization of sliced Gaussian mixture densities consisting of *Dirac mixtures* in nonlinear subspace $\underline{\eta}_k$ and *Gaussian mixtures* in linear subspace $\underline{x}_k$.

Discrete marginal density (nonlinear subspace)   The marginal density function characterizing the random vector $\underline{\eta}_k \sim f(\underline{\eta}_k)$ in the nonlinear subspace is given by the following *Dirac mixture representation*

$$f(\underline{\eta}_k) = \sum_{i=1}^{M_D} \alpha_k^i \delta(\underline{\eta}_k - \underline{\xi}_k^i) \ , \qquad \sum_{i=1}^{M_D} \alpha_k^i = 1 \ , \qquad \alpha_k^i \geq 0 \ , \qquad (3.5)$$

where $\alpha_k^i \in \mathbb{R}_+$ and $\underline{\xi}_k^i$ represent the weights and positions of the Dirac function $\delta(\cdot)$, respectively. The Dirac mixture function (3.5) can be used to represent arbitrary continuous density functions and can be exploited for deriving an efficient process for the prediction and measurement step of general nonlinear systems [59, 126]. Basically, the discrete property of the density representation (3.5) is responsible for decomposing the estimation problem. Roughly speaking, by fixing the value of the parameter vector $\underline{\eta}_k$ for the nonlinear subspace, the estimation problem of the system structure (3.1) and (3.3) turns out to be a linear problem. This means, for a set of discrete values for $\underline{\eta}_k$, which is equal to the Dirac mixture density representation, the estimation problem can be solved by a set of linear estimators; as shown in Section 3.4.

Continuous marginal density (linear subspace)   In general, the density along the individual slices, i.e., in the *nonlinear subspace* $\underline{\eta}_k$, can be represented by any continuous density function. In this thesis, Gaussian mixture densities are employed due to their properties as a universal approximator for arbitrary density functions [4]. Then, the density function for the (conditional) linear subspace $\underline{x}_k \sim f(\underline{x}_k | \underline{\xi}_k^i)$ is given by

$$f(\underline{x}_k | \underline{\xi}_k^i) = \sum_{j=1}^{M_G^i} \beta_k^{ij} \mathcal{N}\left(\underline{x}_k - \underline{\mu}_k^{ij}, \mathbf{C}_k^{ij}\right) \ , \qquad \sum_{j=1}^{M_G^i} \beta_k^{ij} = 1 \ , \qquad \beta_k^{ij} \geq 0 \ , \qquad (3.6)$$

with weights $\beta_k^{ij} \in \mathbb{R}_+$, means $\underline{\mu}_k^{ij} \in \mathbb{R}^{N_x}$, and covariance matrices $\mathbf{C}_k^{ij} \in \mathbb{R}^{N_x \times N_x}$ of the j-th component of the Gaussian mixture contained in the i-th density slice. The variable M_G^i is the number of Gaussian mixture components used for representing the respective density slices. Here, it is important to emphasize that the density parameters β_k^{ij}, $\underline{\mu}_k^{ij}$, and $\mathbf{C}_k^{ij}$ of the individual mixture components are conditioned on the nonlinear subspace $\underline{\eta}_k$, and thus are conditioned on the location $\underline{\xi}_k^i$ of the density slices.

Application to mixed linear/nonlinear systems The sliced Gaussian mixture densities as given in (3.4) can be used for the approximation of arbitrary density functions arising in estimators for nonlinear dynamic systems. However, the full advantages of such density representation can be exploited in the case of system structures that allow a decomposition of the estimation problem into a *linear* and a *nonlinear* part. This is the case for so-called *mixed linear/nonlinear systems*. For example, having the system structure (3.1) and (3.3) with a *known fixed* parameter vector $\underline{\eta}_k$, then the system description should turn out to be linear. Since only in this case, the system can be regarded as a linear description along the individual density slices, where it is sufficient to employ analytic and linear estimators such as the Kalman filter. In the following section, it is shown how the density representation (3.4) can be exploited for deriving a more efficient estimation process for systems with linear substructures.

3.4 Decomposed Estimation Step

The aim of the Bayesian estimator is to calculate the density function representing the system state as precisely as possible. Due to its high computational demand and the resulting non-parametric density representation, approximation methods are necessary for nonlinear dynamic systems. In general, the Bayesian estimator consists of two steps being performed alternately: (a) the *prediction step* and (b) the *measurement step*; visualized in Figure 3.4 **(b)**. This section is devoted to the Bayesian estimation based on the *sliced Gaussian mixture densities* (3.4). It is shown, how this density representation can be exploited for decomposing the general-purpose prediction step and the general-purpose measurement step into a *linear* and *nonlinear part*.

3.4.1 Prediction Step

The purpose of the prediction step is to determine the predicted density function $f^p(\underline{z}_{k+1})$ characterizing the random vector $\underline{z}_{k+1}$ for the next discrete time step $k+1$ based on a given prior density function $f^e(\underline{z}_k)$ for $\underline{z}_k$. This can be achieved by evaluating the well-known Chapman-Kolmogorov equation [109]

$$f^p(\underline{z}_{k+1}) = \int_{\mathbb{R}^{N_z}} \underbrace{f^T(\underline{z}_{k+1}|\underline{z}_k)}_{\text{Transition density}} f^e(\underline{z}_k)\, \mathrm{d}\underline{z}_k \ , \tag{3.7}$$

where $f^T(\underline{z}_{k+1}|\underline{z}_k)$ is the so-called *transition density* containing the information of the considered dynamic system in terms of a *probabilistic system model*. It is noted that for brevity reasons the state vector is denoted as $\underline{z}_k := [\underline{x}_k^{\mathrm{T}}, \underline{\eta}_k^{\mathrm{T}}]^{\mathrm{T}}$. For the derivation of (3.7), it was assumed that the underlying physical process is a Markov process of first order. This means, the state $\underline{z}_{k+1}$ for the next time step depends only on the current state $\underline{z}_k$ and the current system input $\underline{u}_k$, however, *does not depend* on the states and system inputs further in the past. The additive noise term $\underline{w}_k^z$ subject to the considered system model, similar to (3.1), is assumed to be zero-mean white Gaussian with following density function

$$\underline{w}_k^z \sim f_k^w(\underline{w}_k^z) := \mathcal{N}\left(\underline{w}_k^z - \underline{\mu}_k^w, \mathbf{C}_k^w\right) \ , \tag{3.8}$$

where $\underline{\mu}_k^w := 0$ is the mean vector and $\mathbf{C}_k^w$ is the system covariance matrix. Assuming the process noise $\underline{w}_k^z$ to be given by (3.8), the transition density $f^T(\cdot)$ can be derived according to

$$f^T(\underline{z}_{k+1}|\underline{z}_k) = \mathcal{N}\left(\underline{z}_{k+1} - \underline{a}_k(\underline{z}_k, \hat{\underline{u}}_k), \mathbf{C}_k^w\right) \ , \tag{3.9}$$

where $\underline{a}_k(\cdot)$ is the nonlinear system model. Thus, the transition density (3.9) characterizes the probability of the transition of the state $\underline{z}_k$ to the next time step; and its structure strongly depends on the actual structure of the underlying system model.

(a) Dynamic system with linear substructure (b) Bayesian estimator

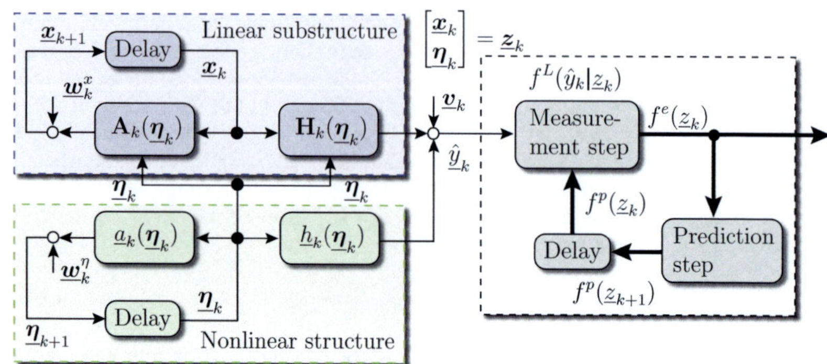

Figure 3.4: (a) Visualization of the considered dynamic system with a linear substructure. The system and the measurement matrix are characterized by the nonlinear substate $\underline{\eta}_k$. For simplicity, the input $\hat{\underline{u}}_k$ is omitted here. **(b)** Structure of the model-based Bayesian estimation process consisting of a prediction and measurement step.

Efficient SGMF prediction step In the case of a system structure as given in Example 3.1, the existing linear substructure can be exploited for deriving a more efficient prediction step. The prior density function $f^e(\underline{x}_k, \underline{\eta}_k)$ is assumed to be given by a *sliced Gaussian mixture* representation (3.4). By means of such representation, and thanks to the *conditionally linear* system model, the solution of the Chapman-Kolmogorov equation (3.7) can be derived by solving a linear and nonlinear estimation problem.

The true predicted density $\widetilde{f}^p(\underline{x}_{k+1}, \underline{\eta}_{k+1})$ for the next discrete time step can be determined by substituting the prior density into the Chapman-Kolmogorov equation (3.7), leading to

$$\widetilde{f}^p(\underline{x}_{k+1}, \underline{\eta}_{k+1}) = \int_{\mathbb{R}^{N_x}} \int_{\mathbb{R}^{N_\eta}} \underbrace{f^T(\underline{x}_{k+1}, \underline{\eta}_{k+1}|\underline{x}_k, \underline{\eta}_k)}_{\text{Transition density}} \underbrace{\sum_{i=1}^{M_D} \alpha_k^i \delta(\underline{\eta}_k - \underline{\xi}_k^i) f^e(\underline{x}_k|\underline{\xi}_k^{ei})}_{\text{Prior SGM density}} \, \mathrm{d}\underline{x}_k \, \mathrm{d}\underline{\eta} \ ,$$

which cannot be solved analytically for general nonlinear systems and arbitrary representations of the prior density $f^e(\underline{x}_k|\underline{\xi}_k^{ei})$. However, in view of the system model (3.1), the transition density $f^T(\cdot)$ can be stated as follows

$$f^T(\cdot) = \mathcal{N}\left(\begin{bmatrix}\underline{x}_{k+1} - \mathbf{A}_k(\underline{\eta}_k)\, \underline{x}_k - \mathbf{B}_k(\underline{\eta}_k)\, \hat{\underline{u}}_k \\ \underline{\eta}_{k+1} - a_k(\underline{\eta}_k)\end{bmatrix}, \mathbf{C}_w\right) \ ,$$

with uncorrelated process noise between the linear and nonlinear subspace, i.e., the covariance matrix $\mathbf{C}_w$ is structured according to (3.2). In this case, the transition density $f^T(\cdot)$ can be written simply as a product of two density functions; one for the nonlinear subsystem and one for the conditionally linear subsystem. By this kind of decomposition of the transition density, we arrive at the following equation for the prediction step,

$$\widetilde{f}^p(\underline{x}_{k+1}, \underline{\eta}_{k+1}) = \int_{\mathbb{R}^{N_x}} \int_{\mathbb{R}^{N_\eta}} \overbrace{\mathcal{N}\left(\underline{\eta}_{k+1} - \underline{a}_k(\underline{\eta}_k), \mathbf{C}_w^\eta\right)}^{\text{Nonlinear subsystem}}$$

$$\cdot \underbrace{\mathcal{N}\left(\underline{x}_{k+1} - \mathbf{A}_k(\underline{\eta}_k)\,\underline{x}_k - \mathbf{B}_k(\underline{\eta}_k)\,\hat{\underline{u}}_k, \mathbf{C}_w^x\right)}_{\text{Conditionally linear subsystem}} \sum_{i=1}^{M} \alpha_k^i \delta(\underline{\eta}_k - \underline{\xi}_k^{ei}) f^e(\underline{x}_k | \underline{\xi}_k^{ei})\, \mathrm{d}\underline{x}_k\, \mathrm{d}\underline{\eta}_k \ ,$$

which already makes the key idea for the decomposition into a linear and a nonlinear estimation problem obvious. Applying the sifting property of Diracs' delta distribution and rearranging the individual terms leads to

$$\widetilde{f}^p(\underline{x}_{k+1}, \underline{\eta}_{k+1}) = \sum_{i=1}^{M_D} \alpha_k^i \, \mathcal{N}\left(\underline{\eta}_{k+1} - \underline{a}_k(\underline{\xi}_k^{ei}), \mathbf{C}_w^\eta\right)$$

$$\cdot \int_{\mathbb{R}^{N_x}} \mathcal{N}\left(\underline{x}_{k+1} - \mathbf{A}_k(\underline{\xi}_k^{ei})\,\underline{x}_k - \mathbf{B}_k(\underline{\xi}_k^{ei})\,\hat{\underline{u}}_k, \mathbf{C}_w^x\right) f^e(\underline{x}_k | \underline{\xi}_k^{ei})\, \mathrm{d}\underline{x}_k \ , \tag{3.10}$$

where the estimated density $f^e(\underline{x}_k | \underline{\xi}_k^{ei})$ is stated as a Gaussian mixture density (3.6). It can be clearly seen that in the case of *conditionally linear dynamic models* (3.1), the integral term can be solved analytically using a linear prediction step for Gaussian mixtures [4]. To be more specific the integral term in (3.10) yields

$$\int_{\mathbb{R}^r} \mathcal{N}\left(\underline{x}_{k+1} - \mathbf{A}_k(\underline{\xi}_k^{ei})\,\underline{x}_k - \mathbf{B}_k(\underline{\xi}_k^{ei})\,\hat{\underline{u}}_k, \mathbf{C}_w^x\right) \sum_{j=1}^{M_G^i} \beta_k^{ij} \mathcal{N}\left(\underline{x}_k - \underline{\mu}_k^{ij}, \mathbf{C}_k^{ij}\right)\, \mathrm{d}\underline{x}_k$$

$$= \sum_{j=1}^{M_G^i} \beta_k^{ij} \mathcal{N}\left(\mathbf{A}_k(\underline{\xi}_k^{ei})\underline{\mu}_k^{eij} + \mathbf{B}_k(\underline{\xi}_k^{ei})\hat{\underline{u}}_k, \ \mathbf{A}_k(\underline{\xi}_k^{ei})\mathbf{C}_k^{eij}\mathbf{A}_k(\underline{\xi}_k^{ei})^T + \mathbf{C}_w^x\right) \ ,$$

which also can be regarded as a bank of independent Kalman prediction steps. Hence, the *predicted density* $\widetilde{f}^p(\cdot)$ results in a Gaussian mixture continuous both in the linear subspace $\underline{x}_k$ and nonlinear subspace $\underline{\eta}_k$,

$$\widetilde{f}^p(\underline{x}_{k+1}, \underline{\eta}_{k+1}) = \sum_{i=1}^{M_D} \sum_{j=1}^{M_G^i} \alpha_k^i \beta_k^{ij} \mathcal{N}\left(\underline{\eta}_{k+1} - \underline{\xi}_{k+1}^{pi}, \mathbf{C}_w^\eta\right) \mathcal{N}\left(\underline{x}_{k+1} - \underline{\mu}_{k+1}^{pij}, \mathbf{C}_{k+1}^{pij}\right) \ . \tag{3.11}$$

The means $\underline{\mu}_{k+1}^{pij}$ and covariance matrices $\mathbf{C}_{k+1}^{pij}$ in the linear subspace are calculated by applying the standard Kalman prediction step. The means $\underline{\xi}_{k+1}^{pi}$ in the nonlinear subspace are derived by simply repositioning the density slices according to the nonlinear system equation (3.1). Thus, the parameters of the predicted density (3.11) are given as follows:

$$\begin{aligned}
\text{Mean vectors} \qquad & \underline{\mu}_{k+1}^{pij} := \mathbf{A}_k(\underline{\xi}_k^{ei})\underline{\mu}_k^{eij} + \mathbf{B}_k(\underline{\xi}_k^{ei})\hat{\underline{u}}_k \\
\text{Covariance matrices} \qquad & \mathbf{C}_{k+1}^{pij} := \mathbf{A}_k(\underline{\xi}_k^{ei})\mathbf{C}_k^{eij}\mathbf{A}_k(\underline{\xi}_k^{ei})^T + \mathbf{C}_w^x \\
\text{Positions of density slices} \qquad & \underline{\xi}_{k+1}^{pi} := \underline{a}_k(\underline{\xi}_k^{ei})
\end{aligned}$$

Here, it is worthwhile mentioning that although $\underline{\xi}_k^{pi}$ represents the individual position of the sliced Gaussian mixture density $f^e(\cdot)$, the $\underline{\xi}_{k+1}^{pi}$ denotes the means of the resulting Gaussian mixture density in nonlinear subspace. The transition of the density slices to a Gaussian mixture density continuous in all subspaces is shown in Figure 3.2 **(b)**-**(c)**.

3.4.2 Combined Measurement/Prediction Step

The purpose of the measurement step is to incorporate the measurements $\hat{\underline{y}}_k$ obtained from a possibly spatially distributed measurement system $\mathcal{M}$ into the estimation process. By this means, the estimation of the system state vector $\underline{z}_k \sim f^e(\underline{z}_k)$ can be further improved. The estimated density $f^e(\underline{z}_k)$ at time step k can be determined by Bayes' formula

$$f^e(\underline{z}_k) = c \cdot f^L(\hat{\underline{y}}_k | \underline{z}_k) \cdot f^P(\underline{z}_k) \ , \tag{3.12}$$

where the coefficient c is a normalization constant. The density function $f^L(\hat{\underline{y}}_k | \underline{z}_k)$ is the so-called *likelihood function* [8, 109] describing the conditional probability for the occurence of the measurement $\hat{\underline{y}}_k$ under the condition $\underline{z}_k$. The additive noise $\underline{v}_k$ subject to the measurement model (3.3) is assumed to be zero-mean white Gaussian as follows

$$\underline{v}_k \sim f_k^w(\underline{v}_k) := \mathcal{N}\left(\underline{v}_k - \underline{\mu}_k^v, \mathbf{C}_k^v\right) \ , \tag{3.13}$$

where $\underline{\mu}_k^v := 0$ is the mean vector and $\mathbf{C}_k^v$ is the covariance matrix. Assuming the measurement noise $\underline{v}_k$ to be given by (3.13), the likelihood function $f^L(\cdot)$ can be derived according to

$$f^L(\hat{\underline{y}}_k | \underline{z}_k) = \mathcal{N}\left(\hat{\underline{y}}_k - \underline{h}_k(\underline{z}_k), \mathbf{C}_k^v\right) \ ,$$

where $\underline{h}_k(\cdot)$ denotes the general nonlinear measurement model. It is obvious that the structure of the likelihood function $f^L(\cdot)$ depends on the structure of the underlying measurement model. By plugging the general-purpose measurement step (3.12) into the general-purpose prediction step (3.7) the individual steps of the estimation process can be performed in a combined fashion, leading to the so-called *combined measurement and prediction step*. The remainder of the section is devoted to the derivation of an efficient update process for the combined measurement and prediction step in terms of the sliced Gaussian mixture densities (3.4).

Combined SGMF measurement/prediction step In the combined estimation step, first, the measurement step is performed on a sliced Gaussian mixture density, followed by the prediction step as introduced in the previous section. This means, the predicted density at time step $k+1$ can be derived by the substitution of Bayes' formula (3.12) into the Chapman-Kolmogorov equation (3.7). Assuming the prior density at time step k is given as a sliced Gaussian mixture density (3.4), then the predicted density $f^P(\underline{x}_{k+1}, \underline{\eta}_{k+1})$ can be derived as follows

$$f^P(\underline{x}_{k+1}, \underline{\eta}_{k+1}) = \int\limits_{\mathbb{R}^{N_x}} \int\limits_{\mathbb{R}^{N_\eta}} f^T(\underline{x}_{k+1}, \underline{\eta}_{k+1} | \underline{x}_k, \underline{\eta}_k) \underbrace{c\, f^L(\hat{\underline{y}}_k | \underline{x}_k, \underline{\eta}_k)\, f^P(\underline{x}_k, \underline{\eta}_k)}_{=: f^e(\underline{x}_k, \underline{\eta}_k)} \,\mathrm{d}\underline{x}_k \mathrm{d}\underline{\eta}_k \ . \tag{3.14}$$

The estimated density $f^e(\underline{x}_k, \underline{\eta}_k)$ can be obtained from the normalized product of the prior density function $f^P(\cdot)$ and the likelihood function $f^L(\cdot)$ incorporating the measurements $\hat{\underline{y}}_k$. In terms of the sliced Gaussian mixture densities (3.4), the *estimated density* $f^e(\cdot)$ is given as

$$f^e(\underline{x}_k, \underline{\eta}_k) = c\, \mathcal{N}\left(\hat{\underline{y}}_k - \mathbf{H}_k(\underline{\eta}_k)\, \underline{x}_k - \underline{h}_k(\underline{\eta}_k), \mathbf{C}_v\right) \cdot \sum_{i=1}^{M} \alpha_k^i \delta\left(\underline{\eta}_k - \underline{\xi}_k^{pi}\right) \cdot \sum_{j=1}^{N^i} \beta_k^{ij} \mathcal{N}\left(\underline{x}_k - \underline{\mu}_k^{pij}, \mathbf{C}_k^{pij}\right)$$

$$= \sum_{i=1}^{M} \alpha_k^{ij} \delta\left(\underline{\eta}_k - \underline{\xi}_k^{pi}\right) \sum_{j=1}^{N^i} \beta_k^{ij} \gamma_k^{ij} \mathcal{N}\left(\underline{x}_k - \underline{\mu}_k^{eij}, \mathbf{C}_k^{eij}\right) \ . \tag{3.15}$$

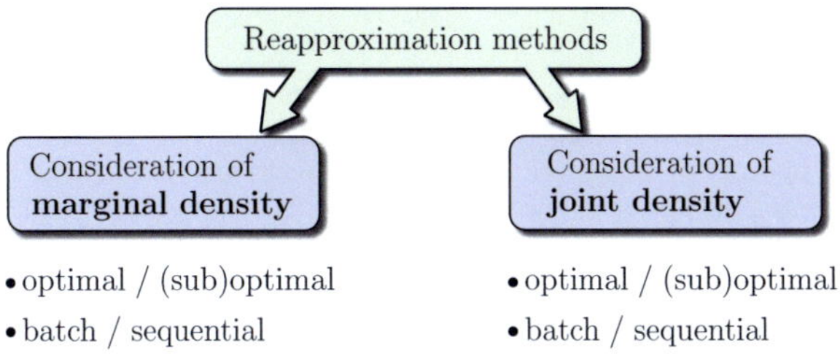

Figure 3.5: Classification of approaches for the approximation of general densities by means of sliced Gaussian mixture densities. During the approximation process the *marginal density* (nonlinear subspace $\underline{\eta}_k$) or the *joint density* (linear subspace $\underline{x}_k$ and nonlinear subspace $\underline{\eta}_k$) can be considered. Furthermore, it can be classified into global *optimal* or *(sub)optimal* approximation, and *batch* or *sequential* approximation.

Thanks to the special structure of the assumed measurement model (3.3) and by representing the prior density $f^p(\cdot)$ as sliced Gaussian mixture densities (3.4), the likelihood function needs to be evaluated only at the positions $\underline{\xi}_k^{pi}$ of the individual density slices. The weights γ_k^{ij}, the mean vectors $\underline{\mu}_k^{eij}$, and the covariance matrices $\mathbf{C}_k^{eij}$ in the estimated density (3.15) can be derived by actually performing the multiplication of the two Gaussian densities and exploiting the sifting properties of the Dirac mixture (as shown in the previous section). This eventually results in the following equations for the density paramters:

$$
\text{Weight of the slices} \qquad \gamma_k^{ij} = \mathcal{N}\left(\underline{\ddot{y}}_k - \underline{h}_k\left(\xi_k^{pi}\right) - \mathbf{H}_k\left(\underline{\xi}_k^{pl}\right)\underline{\mu}_k^{pij}, \mathbf{H}_k\left(\underline{\xi}_k^{pl}\right)\mathbf{C}_k^{plj}\mathbf{H}_k\left(\underline{\xi}_k^{pi}\right)^T + \mathbf{C}_v\right)
$$

$$
\text{Mean vectors} \qquad \underline{\mu}_k^{eij} = \underline{\mu}_k^{pij} + \mathbf{K}_k\left(\underline{\hat{y}}_k - \underline{h}_k\left(\xi_k^{pi}\right) - \mathbf{H}_k\left(\underline{\xi}_k^{pi}\right)\underline{\mu}_k^{pij}\right)
$$

$$
\text{Covariance matrices} \qquad \mathbf{C}_k^{eij} = \mathbf{C}_k^{pij} - \mathbf{K}_k\mathbf{H}_k\left(\underline{\xi}_k^{pi}\right)\mathbf{C}_k^{pij}
$$

$$
\text{Kalman gains} \qquad \mathbf{K}_k = \mathbf{C}_k^{pij}\mathbf{H}_k\left(\underline{\xi}_k^{pi}\right)^T\left(\mathbf{C}_v + \mathbf{H}_k\left(\underline{\xi}_k^{pi}\right)\mathbf{C}_k^{pij}\mathbf{H}_k\left(\underline{\xi}_k^{pi}\right)^T\right)^{-1}
$$

It is worth mentioning that the positions of the density slices $\underline{\xi}_k^{pi}$ are not affected by the measurement step. Rather the mean, the covariance matrices, and the weights of the individual components of the Gaussian mixture are simply updated according to the measurements. In order to perform the combined measurement and prediction step, the estimated density (3.15) has to be substituted into (3.14). Applying the prediction step results in a Gaussian mixture continuous in the linear $\underline{x}_k$ and the nonlinear subspace $\underline{\eta}_k$,

$$
\widetilde{f}^p(\underline{x}_{k+1}, \underline{\eta}_{k+1}) = \sum_{i=1}^{M}\sum_{j=1}^{N^i} \alpha_k^i \beta_k^{ij} \gamma_k^{ij} \mathcal{N}\left(\underline{\eta}_{k+1} - \underline{\xi}_{k+1}^{pi}, \mathbf{C}_w^n\right)\mathcal{N}\left(\underline{x}_{k+1} - \underline{\mu}_{k+1}^{pij}, \mathbf{C}_{k+1}^{pij}\right) \ . \tag{3.16}
$$

The mean $\underline{\mu}_{k+1}^{pij}$ and the covariance matrices $\mathbf{C}_{k+1}^{pij}$ of the predicted density (3.16) for the time step $k+1$ are calculated by applying the equations for the efficient prediction step as introduced in the previous section.

3.5 Reapproximation Step

In the previous section, the efficient estimation update of the sliced Gaussian mixture density (3.4) was introduced, which results in a Gaussian mixture that is continuous in all subspaces. This means, in order to bound the complexity and derive a recursive estimation process, the densities (3.16) and (3.11) after the processing need to be reapproximated by a sliced Gaussian mixture density. The novelty of the methods introduced in this section is the systematic and deterministic (nonrandom) approach for the derivation of the density slice locations based on minimizing a certain distance measure. This results in locations of the density slices with the most support for the approximation of the underlying true density function, and thus less parameters are necessary for a sufficiently accurate result.

The approximation is performed in **three stages**: (1) the approximation of the marginal density in nonlinear subspace by a Dirac mixture density, (2) the extension of the result to sliced Gaussian mixtures over the complete state space, and (3) the reduction of Gaussian mixture components in order to bound the complexity.

1) Approximation of nonlinear subspace   There are several approaches for the approximation of the resulting density function. One possible approach is to derive the location of the slices by only considering the *marginal density* $\widetilde{f}^p(\underline{\eta}_k)$ in the nonlinear subspace [172]. The other more sophisticated possibility is to consider the *joint density* $\widetilde{f}^p(\underline{x}_k, \underline{\eta}_k)$ (linear and nonlinear subspace) using all information available after the processing step in order to derive possibly better locations for the slices. Besides the classification concerning the considered space (marginal subspace or joint space) for the approximation, the approaches can be classified into: batch approximation or sequential approximation. The *batch approximation* [125, 126, 127] is a solution procedure for arbitrary true density functions on the basis of homotopy continuation (progressive Bayes). This procedure results in an optimal solution. The *sequential approximation* [59, 83, 84] is based on inserting one component of the Dirac mixture density at a time. In addition, a classification into *optimal* and *(sub)optimal* approaches is possible. In Figure 3.5 the classification of prospective approaches for the approximation of arbitrary density functions by means of the sliced Gaussian mixture densities is depicted.

Selection of distance measure   For the systematic and deterministic derivation of the density slice locations, the selection of appropriate distance measure plays an essential role. Due to the fact that the sliced Gaussian mixture densities contain discrete functions in the nonlinear subspace, the definition of distance measures in the density space is not appropriate. Basically, the density function used for the approximation is zero at most locations (i.e., nonzero values only at the density slices itself), and thus a comparison and the evaluation of a distance measure in density space at such points does not make much sense. One way to overcome this problem is to choose a distance measure defined in the distribution space, such as the Cramer-von Mises distance. For the one-dimensional case this distance measure is defined as follows

$$D^n = \frac{1}{2} \int_{\mathbb{R}} \left(\widetilde{F}(\eta_k) - F(\eta_k) \right)^2 \, \mathrm{d}\eta_k \;, \tag{3.17}$$

where $\widetilde{F}(\cdot)$ denotes the distribution function to be approximated. Due to the fact that the distance measure (3.17) is not symmetric in the multi-dimensional case, this measure converges to a certain value only when the considered distribution functions are exactly equal. Thus, the derivation of more sophisticated distance measures is necessary in such cases, which is out of the scope of this thesis. A more detailed description can be found in [58, 69].

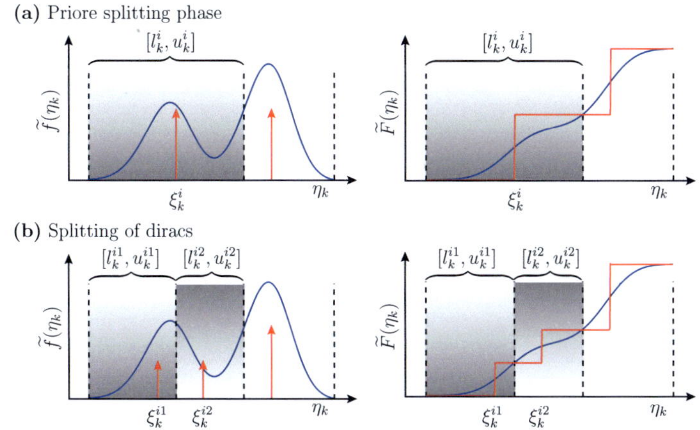

Figure 3.6: Visualization of the approximation process by considering the nonlinear subspace η_k, and thus the determination of the position of the density slices. **(a)** Visualization of Dirac component at assumed position ξ_k^i. **(b)** The Dirac component at location ξ_k^i is replaced by two Dirac components at positions ξ_k^{i1} and ξ_k^{i2}.

Example 3.2: Sequential derivation of slice locations for one-dimensional case

This example is devoted to the brief description of a variation of the sequential greedy algorithm proposed in [59] for deriving the location of the density slices. The description of the method is restricted to the one-dimensional case, however, can be extended to several dimensions. It is assumed that the true density to be approximated is given as a Gaussian mixture density

$$\widetilde{f}(x_k, \eta_k) = \sum_{j=1}^{M_G} \widetilde{\alpha}_k^j \, \mathcal{N}\left(x_k - \widetilde{\mu}_k^j, \widetilde{C}_k^{lj}\right) \mathcal{N}\left(\eta_k - \widetilde{\xi}_k^j, \widetilde{C}_k^{nj}\right) \;,$$

with weighting factors $\widetilde{\alpha}_k^j$, means $\widetilde{\mu}_k^j$ and $\widetilde{\zeta}_k^j$, and covariances $\widetilde{C}_k^{lj}$ and $\widetilde{C}_k^{nj}$. Here, it is important to note that the individual components of the Gaussian densities, each represented as a product of two Gaussians, consist of mutually independent linear and nonlinear parts.

In the sequential algorithm proposed in [59], every density slice corresponds to an interval $[l_k^i, u_k^i]$ in the nonlinear subspace of the state space. Thus, the individual slices approximate the true marginal density $\widetilde{f}(\eta_k)$ only in the corresponding interval. This is shown in Figure 3.6 **(a)**. The key idea for the density approximation, and thus the derivation of appropriate locations for the density slices, is based on splitting the intervals characterized by respective density slices. In the first step, the specific interval for inserting new density slices (or Dirac components) is determined, based on the maximum deviation between the distributions of the true prior and the approximating density function. Here, the distance measure (3.17) is chosen, whereas in the multi-dimensional case respective other measures are necessary, such as the one proposed in [58, 69, 83, 84]. Then, the interval with the highest deviation is chosen for the following splitting phase. This interval corresponds to the region where the approximation deviates most from the true density. The density slice with the position ξ_k^i, weight α_k^i and interval $[l_k^i, u_k]$ is replaced by two respective slices. The new positions ξ_k^{i1} and ξ_k^{i2} are selected to split the probability mass of the true density over the intervals into halves. The derivation of new locations for the density slices is depicted in Figure 3.6 **(b)**. By increasing the number of density slices, the approximation converges towards the true distribution. ∎

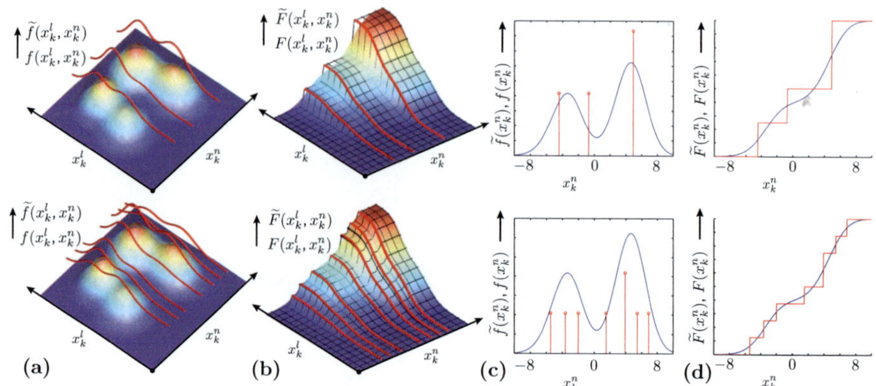

Figure 3.7: Approximation of a Gaussian mixture density $\widetilde{f}(x_k, \eta_k)$ with 4 components for a different number of density slices $M = 3$ and $M = 7$. **(a)–(b)** True joint density $\widetilde{f}(x_k, \eta_k)$ and joint distribution $\widetilde{F}(x_k, \eta_k)$ to be approximated (*surface*) and their respective approximation $f(x_k, \eta_k)$ and $F(x_k, \eta_k)$ (*red lines*). **(c)–(d)** True marginal density $\widetilde{f}(\eta_k)$ and true marginal distribution $\widetilde{F}(\eta_k$ to be approximated (*blue line*), and their respective approximations $f(\eta_k)$ and $F(\eta_k)$ (*red line*).

2) Extension to complete state space   In the previous example, it was described how the locations of the individual density slices are derived based on the minimization of a certain distance measure. After the derivation of the locations, this information needs to be extended to a sliced Gaussian mixture representation over the entire state space, i.e., in the linear and nonlinear subspace. This can be achieved by the evaluation of the Gaussian mixture $\widetilde{f}(x_k, \eta_k)$ at every density slice determined by the aforementioned algorithm, leading to a Gaussian mixture density in the linear subspace

$$f(x_k|\xi_k^i) = \sum_{j=1}^{M_G} \underbrace{c \cdot \widetilde{\alpha}_k^j \mathcal{N}\left(\xi_k^i - \widetilde{\xi}_k^j, \widetilde{C}_k^j\right)}_{=:\beta_k^{ij}} \cdot \mathcal{N}\left(x_k - \widetilde{\mu}_k^j, \widetilde{C}_k^j\right) \tag{3.18}$$

for every density slice $i = 1 \ldots M_D$ with a number of M_G^i individual components. The total number of Gaussian components is denoted as $M_G := \sum_i M_G^i$. The corresponding parameters for the Gaussian components are assigned as follows:

$$\beta_k^{ij} = \frac{\widetilde{\alpha}_k^j \mathcal{N}\left(\xi_k^i - \widetilde{\xi}_k^j, \widetilde{C}_k^j\right)}{\sum_{j=1}^{L} \beta_k^{ij}} \ , \qquad \mu_k^{ij} = \widetilde{\mu}_k^j \ , \qquad \text{and} \qquad C_k^{ij} = \widetilde{C}_k^j \ .$$

For bounding the complexity, the number of components of the resulting Gaussian mixture density (3.18) needs to be reduced by component reduction algorithms, such as the methods presented in [65, 99, 121, 122].

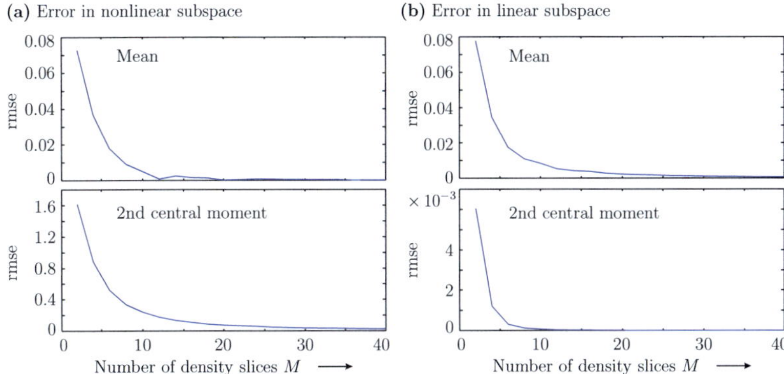

Figure 3.8: Root mean square error (rmse) of mean and 2nd central moment of the approximation with sliced Gaussian mixture. The approximation error is shown in **(a)** nonlinear subspace and **(b)** linear subspace for a growing number of density slices.

Example 3.3: Reapproximation of Gaussian mixture with 4 components

In this example, a Gaussian mixture with 4 components is approximated by a sliced Gaussian mixture. The mean values of the state vector $\underline{z}_k = [x_k,\, \eta_k]^T$ of the individual components are given by

$$\hat{\underline{z}}_k^{(1)} = \begin{bmatrix} 5 \\ -3 \end{bmatrix}, \quad \hat{\underline{z}}_k^{(2)} = \begin{bmatrix} 0 \\ -4 \end{bmatrix}, \quad \hat{\underline{z}}_k^{(3)} = \begin{bmatrix} 5 \\ 4 \end{bmatrix}, \quad \hat{\underline{z}}_k^{(4)} = \begin{bmatrix} -1 \\ 5 \end{bmatrix},$$

the covariance matrices are assumed to be as follows

$$\mathbf{C}_k^{(1)} = \begin{bmatrix} 2 & 0 \\ 0 & 3 \end{bmatrix}, \quad \mathbf{C}_k^{(2)} = \begin{bmatrix} 4 & 0 \\ 0 & 4 \end{bmatrix}, \quad \mathbf{C}_k^{(3)} = \begin{bmatrix} 3 & 0 \\ 0 & 4 \end{bmatrix}, \quad \mathbf{C}_k^{(4)} = \begin{bmatrix} 5 & 0 \\ 0 & 3 \end{bmatrix},$$

and the weights are assumed to be equal to 0.25. The approximation of the Gaussian mixture density for different numbers of density slices is visualized in Figure 3.7. The upper and lower parts show the approximation with $M = 3$ and $M = 5$ slices, respectively. The relative errors of the mean and 2nd central moment of the linear and nonlinear subspace are computed for a growing number of density slices (2–40 components). The root mean square errors (rmse) are displayed in Figure 3.8 **(a)–(b)**. It can be clearly seen, that the relative errors of the systematic reapproximation decrease quite fast in magnitudes in both subspaces. In addition, the relative error of the 2nd central moment in the linear subspace is close to zero. This is due to the exploitation of Gaussian mixture densities with its excellent approximation properties in the linear subspace. ∎

3) Gaussian Mixture Reduction For multiple processing steps in the *Sliced Gaussian Mixture Filter*, the number of overall Gaussian components increases. Let N_k the number of Gaussian mixture components in the time step k and M the number of Dirac impulses (slices), then $N_k = M \cdot N_{k-1} = M^{k-1} \cdot N$. In order to limit the exponentially increasing number of components, a component reduction is required. In general, the component reduction can take place before or after the density approximation. With a reduction before the density approximation, a tradeoff between accuracy and execution time can be made. Component reduction after the density approximation limits the maximum number of Gaussian components and thus, prevents exponential growth in computation time. Different approximation algorithms with a wide range of complexity and approximation quality exist, e.g., [65, 122, 150].

(a) Brute force integration **(b)** MPF (1000 particles) **(c)** SGMF (20 particles)

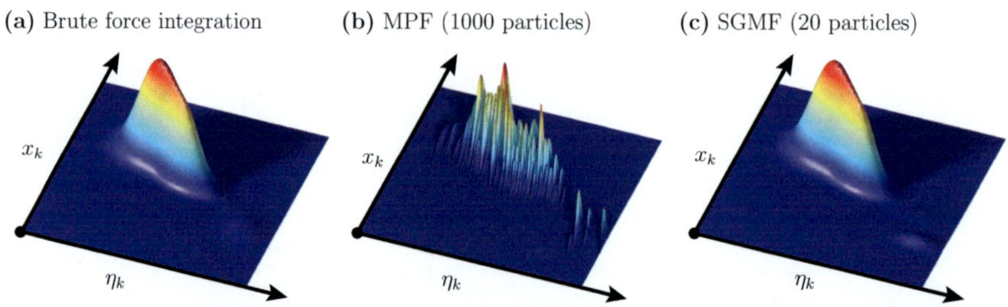

Figure 3.9: Visualization of joint densities for the system description in Example 3.4 after combined filter and prediction step at time step $k = 2$. **(a)** brute force numeric integration, **(b)** marginalized particle filter (1000 particles), and **(c)** sliced Gaussian mixture filter (20 slices).

3.6 Simulation Results

In this section, the performance of the *Sliced Gaussian Mixture Filter* is demonstrated by means of simulation results for the folowing nonlinear dynamic system.

Example 3.4: Nonlinear system with linear substructure
In this example, we consider a nonlinear two-dimensional system with a linear substructure that can be exploited during the estimation process. The system equation is given by

$$\boldsymbol{x}_{k+1} = \underbrace{(0.7 - 0.2\,\boldsymbol{\eta}_k)}_{\mathbf{A}_k^i}\boldsymbol{x}_k + \underbrace{(0.3 + 0.2\,\boldsymbol{\eta})}_{\mathbf{B}_k^i}\hat{u}_k + \boldsymbol{w}_k^x \;, \qquad \boldsymbol{\eta}_{k+1} = \boldsymbol{\eta}_k + \boldsymbol{w}_k^\eta \;,$$

where $\boldsymbol{w}_k^x$ and $\boldsymbol{w}_k^\eta$ are zero mean additive Gaussian noise with variances of $C_w^x = 1$ and $C_w^\eta = 0.5$, respectively. The system input $\hat{u}_k$ is assumed to be $\hat{u}_k = -5\sin(0.2\,k)$. The measurement equation is given by a polynomial of degree 5

$$\hat{y}_k = \underbrace{\boldsymbol{\eta}_k}_{\mathbf{H}_k^i}\boldsymbol{x}_k - 0.32\,(\boldsymbol{\eta}_k)^5 - 1.6\,(\boldsymbol{\eta}_k)^4 - 5.6\,(\boldsymbol{\eta}_k)^2 - 16\,\boldsymbol{\eta}_k - 9.12 + v_k \;,$$

where v_k denotes the measurement noise with a variance of $C_v = 20$. The system was simulated for 20 consecutive time steps and 50 independent Monte-Carlo simulation runs. ∎

The density function after the combined filter and prediction step is calculated by brute force numeric integration for having a ground truth for comparison purposes; see Figure 3.9. In Figure 3.9 **(b)**, the simulation result of the marginalized particle filter with 1000 particles is shown as a histogram of particles in the nonlinear subspace. The corresponding Gaussian components are added up in the linear subspace. Due to the randomly chosen position of the particles, the marginalized particle filter produces a joint density deviating from the true density. The resulting joint density after combined filter and prediction step for the Sliced Gaussian Mixture Filter using 20 slices is depicted in Figure 3.9 **(c)**. It can be seen that the density derived by the Sliced Gaussian Mixture Filter hardly deviates from the brute force solution and appears smoother compared to the density from the marginalized particle filter.

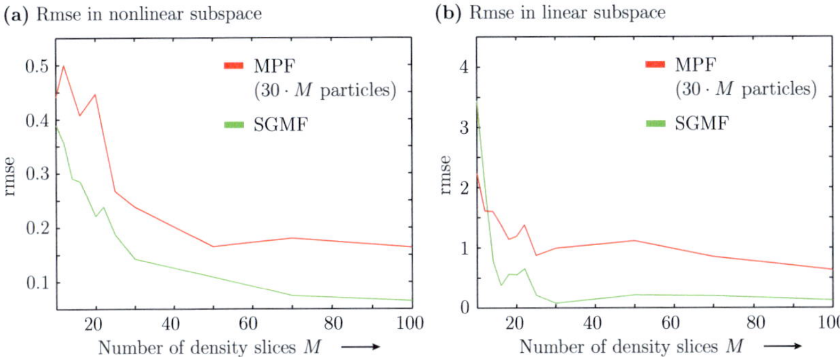

Figure 3.10: Visualization of simulation results of Example 3.4. It is depicted the root mean square of relative errors of mean in nonlinear and linear subspace. Comparison of the Sliced Gaussian Mixture Filter (green) and the marginalized particle filter (red) with 30 times more particles than slices.

The root mean square of the relative error of the mean is shown in Figure 3.10 of nonlinear and linear subspace. The Sliced Gaussian Mixture Filter (SGMF) is compared with the marginalized particle filter (MPF) with 30 times more particles than slices. During the simulation a maximum number of 10 Gaussian components per slice was allowed, whereas 2.37 components were utilized on average. It is obvious that the deviation decreases with growing number of slices. The plateau at the right-hand side of the graph arises from discretization errors in the calculation of the true density function. It can be stated that the SGMF significantly outperforms the MPF in this simulation study. Compared to the SGMF with $M = 30$ slices, the MPF needs far more particles $M \approx 1500$, in order to reach the same error of the mean value. In addition, especially in the linear subspace, the SGMF performs substantially better than the MPF; this is mainly due to the exploitation of Gaussian mixture densities with its good approximation properties in linear subspace. Thanks to the low number of slices compared to the higher number of particles, the Sliced Gaussian Mixture Filter requires less memory storage.

3.7 Summary and Discussion

This chapter was devoted to the exploitation of linear substructures in certain dynamic systems in order to derive a more efficient estimation process. The proposed estimator is based on a novel density representation — *sliced Gaussian mixture density* — consisting of a Gaussian mixture density in the linear subspace and a Dirac mixture density in the nonlinear subspace. The systematic approximation approach reduces a distance measure between the true density and an approximation given as a sliced Gaussian mixture density. It is emphasized that although a particular model structure (3.1) and (3.3) was chosen for the sake of simplicity, the principles of the *S*liced *G*aussian *M*ixture *F*ilter (SGMF) can be applied to more general conditionally linear models. For example, it was assumed that the random variables in linear subspace are uncorrelated to random variables in nonlinear subspace. The extension to the correlated case would be especially interesting for tracking applications, and can be achieved in a straightforward fashion.

There are three key features significantly improving the performance compared to other state-of-the-art estimator: (a) the usage of a special kind of density representation allowing the *systematic decomposition* of the estimation problem, (b) a *systematic (nonrandom) approximation* technique that is (close to) optimal in terms of a certain distance measure, and (c) consideration of *all density slices* enforcing a kind of interaction between the slices in an almost natural way. The improved performance was demonstrated by means of simulated case studies based on a model structure similar to the one for the simultaneous state and parameter estimation of spatially distributed systems, introduced in Chapter 4. This means, the SGMF lays the foundation for deriving an efficient process for the parameter identification of space-time continuous physical systems.

In this thesis, the technique for approximating arbitrary density function using sliced Gaussian mixture densities considered only the marginal density function (i.e., nonlinear subspace). Prospective extension of the proposed novel estimator would be the consideration of the entire joint density (i.e., both in linear and nonlinear subspace). By this means, the accuracy of the approximation could be further improved and less density slices would be necessary to obtain a precise density representation. For additionaly reducing the number of density slices, it is possible to consider both the system equation (transition density) and measurement equation (likelihood) for the determination of optimal position of the slices.

Simultaneous State and Parameter Estimation of Space-Time Continuous Systems

In this chapter, the methodology for the efficient *simultaneous state and parameter estimation* of space-time continuous physical systems is introduced. A common way for the parameter estimation is to augment the system state that characterizes the current state with all the parameters that characterize the dynamic behavior of the system. In most cases, the augmentation results in a *nonlinear system description*, even the original system model was of a linear type. Due to the fact that the conversion of space-time continuous systems yields a high-dimensional system model in state space form, the parameter identification within a Bayesian framework turns out to be a *high-dimensional/nonlinear* problem. In order to derive an efficient process, special estimators are required, such as the *S*liced *G*aussian *M*ixture *F*ilter introduced in the previous chapter. The contributions of the proposed methodology are demonstrated by means of *common tasks* arising in sensor network applications:

- *S*imultaneous *R*econstruction and *I*dentification (SRI method): This task is responsible for the identification of *process parameters* characterizing the dynamic and distributed behavior of the physical system being observed; see Section 4.3. In general, the goal is the derivation of a strong mathematical model with known structure and parameters that can be exploited for performing additional tasks, i.e., node and source localization.

- *S*imultaneous *R*econstruction and *L*ocalization (SRL method): The novel method for the node localization is based on only locally measuring a space-time continuous physical system, i.e., without using global positioning systems; see Section 4.4. Basically, this is achieved by the rigorous exploitation of a mathematical model of the physical system; possibly derived by aforementioned identification process.

- *S*imultaneous *R*econstruction and *S*ource *L*ocalization (SRSL method): This task deals with the efficient localization of spatially distributed sources and leakages driving the physical system; see Section 4.5. Hence, spatially distributed measurements are exploited for identifying locations, for example, of a pollutant concentration. The clear advantage of the simultaneous approach is that besides the location, the actual (often imprecisely known) space-time continuous state of the physical system is estimated.

The *three tasks* for the efficient observation of space-time continuous systems can be performed seperately or in a combined fashion depending on the actual application scenario; visualized in Figure 4.1. For example, sensor nodes with imprecisely known location simultaneously

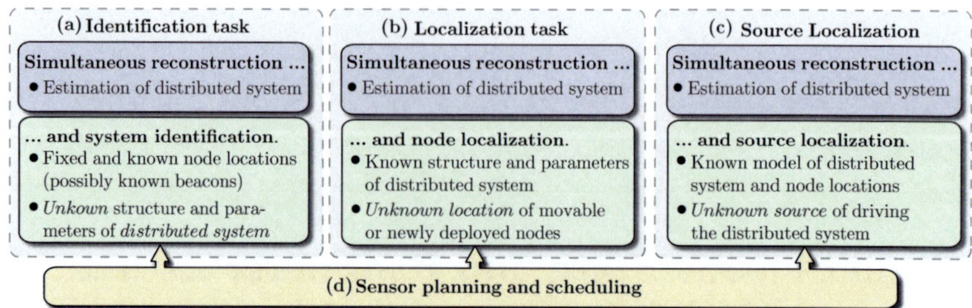

Figure 4.1: Visualization of *three tasks* for the estimation of space-time continuous physical systems. The individual tasks are managed by a planning and scheduling technique. **(a)** The first task consists of the identification of the environment in order to derive a mathematical model of the physical system being monitored (*identification task*). Based on the derived mathematical model **(b)** newly deployed sensor nodes (*node localization task*) and **(c)** sources driving the physical system can be localized (*source localization task*).

identify process parameters of the physical system, perform source and leakage localization (e.g., of a pollutant concentration), and improve their knowledge about their own position based on locally measuring and exchanging information with other nodes. The different tasks are managed by sophisticated planning and scheduling techniques. All the proposed methods on their own provide novel prospects not only for the observation of physical systems but also for sensor network applications in general. Thanks to the *simultaneous approach*, the network is able to estimate the *entire* state of the space-time continuous system, identify *non-measurable* quantities, verify and validate the correctness of the estimation results, and eventually adapt its algorithms and behavior in an autonomous and self-organized fashion.

The methods presented in this chapter were published at [177, 178, 180, 181]. However, explanations for the identification and the novel localization methods are given in a considerably extended way for two-dimensional space-time continuous physical systems, and the performance is demonstrated by respective simulation results.

4.1 State Augmentation of the System Description

It was demonstrated in Chapter 2 that by exploiting *additional background information* about the *physical system* in terms of a mathematical model, more accurate estimates can be derived; especially between the individual nodes. In addition, *non-measurable* quantities can be identified, e.g., additional useful information about the physical system, such as material properties, sources of chemical concentrations or leakages. Moreover, by exploiting mathematical models of the physical system, the individual sensor nodes can be localized by the evaluation of local measurements of the space-time continuous system. This means, one of the most important issues for model-based approaches is the *parameter estimation*, also referred to as *parameter identification* or *inverse problem*. The main goal is the estimation of parameters in the system/measurement model from observed measurements such that the predicted state is close to the observations. The identification of such model parameters becomes even more essential for sensor network applications in harsh and unkown environments, and for unpredictable variations of the space-time continuous system being observed.

Augmented state vector For the simultaneous state and parameter estimation of physical systems, the unknown parameters are treated as additional state variables. By this means, conventional estimation techniques can be used to simultaneously identify parameters, such as parameters in the stochastic partial differential equation (2.1) or node locations, and the state of the space-time continuous system. Hence, an augmented state vector $\underline{z}_k \in \mathbb{R}^{N_z}$ consisting of the system state $\underline{x}_k \in \mathbb{R}^{N_x}$ and the additional unknown parameters $\underline{\eta}_k \in \mathbb{R}^P$ is defined by

$$\underline{z}_k := \left[\underbrace{(\underline{x}_k)^T}_{\text{(Linear) state space}} , \underbrace{\left(\underline{\eta}_k^P\right)^T , \left(\underline{\eta}_k^M\right)^T , \left(\underline{\eta}_k^I\right)^T}_{\text{(Nonlinear) parameter space } \underline{\eta}_k^T} \right]^T \in \mathbb{R}^{N_z} ,$$

where the vector $\underline{\eta}_k^P \in \mathbb{R}^{P_p}$ collects unknown process parameters in the *system model*, such as the diffusion coefficient or the convection field. The random vector $\underline{\eta}_k^M \in \mathbb{R}^{P_m}$ contains unknown parameters in the *measurement model*, such as locations of the individual sensor nodes. The vector $\underline{\eta}_k^I \in \mathbb{R}^{P_i}$ consists of parameters in the *input model*, e.g., locations and intensity of the spatially distributed inputs and leakages.

Augmented system model The augmentation of the state vector $\underline{x}_k$ with the additional parameter vector $\underline{\eta}_k$ being identified leads to an augmented system description. The *augmented lumped-parameter model* of the space-time continuous system can be stated as follows

$$\underbrace{\begin{bmatrix} \underline{x}_{k+1} \\ \underline{\eta}_{k+1}^P \\ \underline{\eta}_{k+1}^M \\ \underline{\eta}_{k+1}^I \end{bmatrix}}_{\underline{z}_{k+1}} = \underbrace{\begin{bmatrix} \mathbf{A}_k(\underline{\eta}_k^P)\,\underline{x}_k + \mathbf{B}_k^u(\underline{\eta}_k^P)\,\hat{\underline{u}}_k(\underline{\eta}_k^I) + \mathbf{B}_k^b(\underline{\eta}_k^P)\,\hat{\underline{b}}_k \\ \underline{a}_k^P(\underline{\eta}_k^P) \\ \underline{a}_k^M(\underline{\eta}_k^M) \\ \underline{a}_k^I(\underline{\eta}_k^I) \end{bmatrix}}_{\underline{a}_k^z(\underline{z}_k,\hat{\underline{u}}_k)} + \underbrace{\begin{bmatrix} \mathbf{B}_k^u(\underline{\eta}_k^P)\,\underline{w}_k^u + \mathbf{B}_k^b(\underline{\eta}_k^P)\,\underline{w}_k^b \\ \underline{w}_k^P \\ \underline{w}_k^M \\ \underline{w}_k^I \end{bmatrix}}_{\underline{w}_k^z} ,$$

$$(4.1)$$

where the matrix $\mathbf{A}_k(\cdot) \in \mathbb{R}^{N_x \times N_x}$ represents the system matrix, $\mathbf{B}_k^u(\cdot) \in \mathbb{R}^{N_x \times N_x}$ is the input matrix, and $\mathbf{B}_k^b(\cdot) \in \mathbb{R}^{N_x \times N_x}$ denotes the boundary matrix. These matrices depend on parameters in the distributed-parameter system (1.2) collected in the *process parameter vector* $\underline{\eta}_k^P$. The *input parameter vector* $\underline{\eta}_k^I$ characterizes the properties of the system input $s(\underline{r}, t)$, e.g., location of spatially distributed sources. The nonlinear functions $\underline{a}_k(\cdot) : \mathbb{R}^P \to \mathbb{R}^P$ describe the dynamic behavior of the parameters to be estimated; see Section 4.4.4. It is important to emphasize that the augmented system model (4.1) contains a high-dimensional linear substructure that can be exploited by the application of a more efficient estimator, as introduced in Chapter 3.

Augmented measurement model The augmentation leads to following *augmented measurement model* characterizing the properties of the spatially distributed measurement system

$$\hat{\underline{y}}_k = \underbrace{\mathbf{H}_k(\underline{\eta}_k^M)\,\underline{x}_k}_{\underline{h}_k(\underline{z}_k)} + \underline{v}_k , \tag{4.2}$$

where $\mathbf{H}_k(\cdot) \in \mathbb{R}^{M \times N_x}$ represents the measurement matrix. This matrix strongly depends on the actual configuration and topology of the measurement system. In particular, the individual node locations $\underline{r}_k^{si} := [r_k^{sx}, r_k^{sy}]^\mathrm{T} \in \mathbb{R}^2$ collected in the *measurement parameter vector* $\underline{\eta}_k^M$ characterizes the measurement matrix $\mathbf{H}_k(\cdot)$, and thus the actual measured values. The structure of the augmented model description (4.1) and (4.2) is shown in Figure 4.2.

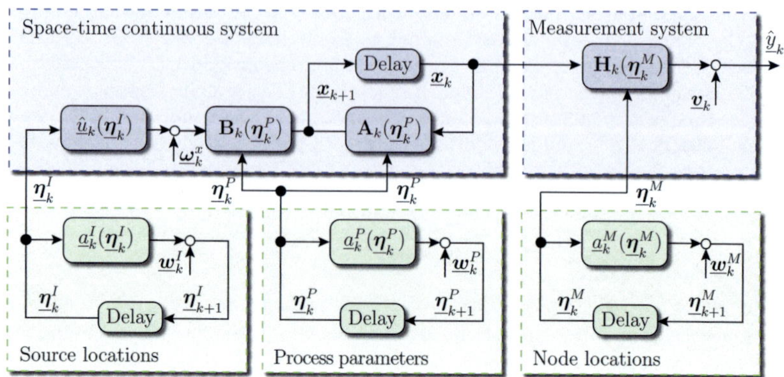

Figure 4.2: Visualization of the augmented system description that contains a high-dimensional linear substructure in terms of the state vector $\underline{x}_k$. The system input $\hat{\underline{u}}_k$ depends on input parameters $\underline{\eta}_k^I$, such as source location or input intensitiy. The process parameter vector $\underline{\eta}_k^P$ affects the system matrix $\mathbf{A}_k$ and the input matrix $\mathbf{B}_k$, and thus the distributed properties and the dynamic behavior. The node locations contained in the parameter vector $\underline{\eta}_k^M$ characterize the measurement matrix $\mathbf{H}_k$.

4.2 Overview and Considered Space-Time Continuous System

This section is devoted to a general overview of the *simultaneous state and parameter estimation process* for observing and identifying *space-time continuous physical systems*. The main goal of the estimation process within a Bayesian framework is to obtain a precise estimate of the augmented state vector $\underline{z}_k \in \mathbb{R}^{N_z}$ in terms of the probability density function $f^e(\underline{z}_k)$. Referring to the augmented system descriptions (4.1) and (4.2), it is obvious that for the parameter estimation, the system and measurement equations are of a *high-dimensional/nonlinear* type. This is mainly due to the *nonlinear relationship* between the state vector $\underline{x}_k \in \mathbb{R}^{N_x}$ with respective parameter vectors $\underline{\eta}_k \in \mathbb{R}^P$; visualized in Figure 4.2.

The linear substructure that is containing in the augmented models (4.1) and (4.2) are exploited by using the SGMF, introduced in Chapter 3. This allows the decomposition of the high-dimensional/nonlinear estimation problem into a linear part (state reconstruction) and a nonlinear part (parameter identification). By this means, an overall more efficient process can be derived for *simultaneously* estimating the state $\underline{x}_k \sim f(\underline{x}_k)$ and the parameter $\underline{\eta}_k \sim f(\underline{\eta}_k)$. The entire process is depicted in Figure 4.3.

Joint densities for the state/parameter estimation Within the proposed SGMF framework, the joint probability density of the state $\underline{x}_k$ and the parameters $\underline{\eta}_k$ are given as a *sliced Gaussian mixture density* according to

$$\underline{z}_k \sim f^p(\underline{x}_k, \underline{\eta}_k) := \sum_{i=1}^{M_D} \sum_{j=1}^{M_G^i} \alpha_k^i \, \beta_k^{ij} \underbrace{\delta\left(\underline{\eta}_k - \underline{\xi}_k^{pi}\right)}_{\text{Parameter subspace}} \underbrace{\mathcal{N}\left(\underline{x}_k - \underline{\mu}_k^{pij}, \mathbf{C}_k^{pij}\right)}_{\text{State subspace}}, \qquad (4.3)$$

where the linear subspace $\mathbb{R}^{N_x}$ is represented by a Gaussian mixture and the nonlinear subspace $\mathbb{R}^P$ by a Dirac mixture density. Thanks to the density representation (4.3) and the special structure of the system (4.1) and (4.2), the state and parameters of space-time continuous systems can be decomposed. The decomposed prediction and measurement step (see Section 3.4)

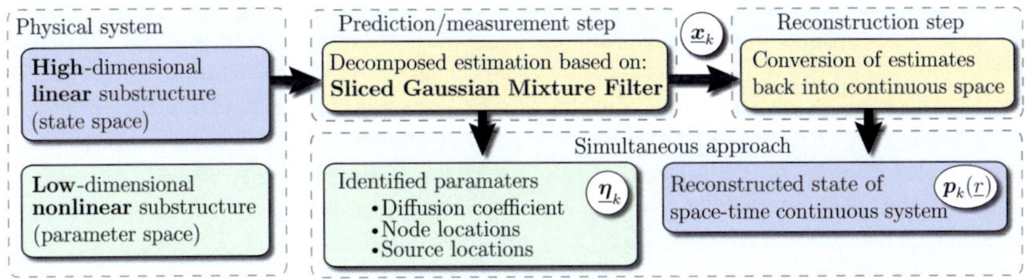

Figure 4.3: General overview of the entire process for the simultaneous state and parameter estimation of space-time continuous physical systems. The high-dimensional linear substructure is exploited by using the Sliced Gaussian Mixture Filter (SGMF) in order to estimate the entire augmented state vector (state/parameter vector) in an efficient and systematic manner. The state vector $\underline{x}_k$ is then used for actually reconstructing the space continuous state $p_k(\underline{r})$ of the physical system. Thanks to the simultaneous approach, additional parameters, such as diffusion coefficient, node locations, and source locations, collected in the parameter vector $\underline{\eta}_k$, are identified.

leads to following *Gaussian mixture density*

$$\underline{z}_{k+1} \sim f^p(\underline{x}_{k+1}, \underline{\eta}_{k+1}) = \sum_{i=1}^{M_D} \sum_{j=1}^{M_G^i} \alpha_k^i \, \beta_k^{ij} \, \gamma_k^{ij} \, \mathcal{N}\left(\underline{\eta}_{k+1} - \underline{\xi}_{k+1}^{pi}, \mathbf{C}_w^{\eta}\right) \mathcal{N}\left(\underline{x}_{k+1} - \underline{\mu}_{k+1}^{pij}, \mathbf{C}_{k+1}^{pij}\right) \,,$$

(4.4)

which consists of continuous densities in all subspaces, i.e., in the linear subspace $\mathbb{R}^{N_x}$ as well as in the nonlinear subspace $\mathbb{R}^P$. For the recursive estimation, this density function needs to be re-approximated by the sliced Gaussian mixture density (4.3); see Section 3.5 for more details.

Marginal density of parameter and space-time continuous state The processing based on decomposing the estimation problem allows the efficient derivation of the joint density $f^p(\underline{x}_k, \underline{\eta}_k)$ representing the augmented state vector $\underline{z}_k := [(\underline{x}_k)^T \, (\underline{\eta}_k)^T]^T$. The parameters $\underline{\eta}_k \sim f^p(\underline{\eta}_k)$ can be identified by simply marginalizing over the state vector $\underline{x}_k$, according to

$$\underline{\eta}_k \sim f^p(\underline{\eta}_k) = \int_{\mathbb{R}^{N_x}} f^p(\underline{x}_k, \underline{\eta}_k) \, \mathrm{d}\underline{x}_k = \sum_{i=1}^{M_D} \alpha_k^i \, \mathcal{N}\left(\underline{\eta}_k - \underline{\xi}_k^{pi}, \mathbf{C}_w^{\eta}\right) \,,$$

which obviously can be performed in a very efficient manner by simply summing over the individual density slices.

For the space-time continuous state $\boldsymbol{p}_k(\underline{r}) \sim f^p(p_k|\underline{r})$, an additional, more involved conversion step into the continuous space is necessary. This step can also be regarded as a so-called *interpolation step* allowing the derivation of an estimate of the distributed state at any desired location $\underline{r} := [x, y] \in \mathbb{R}^2$. Similar to the conversion introduced in Section 2.5.3, the probability density function $f^p(p_k|\underline{r})$ for the system state can be obtained by

$$\boldsymbol{p}_k(\underline{r}) \sim f^p(p_k|\underline{r}) = \int_{\mathbb{R}^{N_x}} \int_{\mathbb{R}^P} f^C(p_k - \underline{\Psi}(\underline{r})^{\mathrm{T}} \underline{x}_k) f^p(\underline{x}_k, \underline{\eta}_k) \mathrm{d}\underline{x}_k \mathrm{d}\underline{\eta}_k \,,$$

(4.5)

where $f^C(\cdot)$ represents the transition density for the conversion process (2.30). Using the expressions (2.33) for the mean and the variance of the Gaussian mixture density resulting from the conversion step, the parameters of the probability density function (4.5) can be efficiently derived in a similar way. Then, an estimate of the physical system in terms of $f^p(p_k|\underline{r})$ can be obtained at any desired spatial coördinate $\underline{r}$ in the area of interest; see Figure 4.3.

Considered space-time continuous physical system As proof of concept, the novel prospects of the proposed methods for the *simultaneous state and parameter identification* of space-time continuous systems are demonstrated and evaluated using the same example scenario. In the following, the process parameters of the underlying physical system are stated:

Example 4.1: Considered physical system for the parameter estimation

Throughout this chapter, the underlying space-time continuous system is represented by the two-dimensional convection-diffusion equation (2.1), introduced in Example 2.1. Unless stated otherwise, the parameters of the physical system are assumed to be as follows

$$\text{Dirichlet/Neumann conditions} \qquad g_D = 20\,^\circ\text{C} \; , \quad g_N = 0\,^\circ\text{C}\,\text{m}^{-1}$$

$$\text{Model parameters of physical system} \qquad \alpha_{\text{true}} = 1.0\,\text{m}^2\,\text{h}^{-1} \; , \quad \gamma_{\text{true}} = 1.0\,\text{m}^3\,^\circ\text{C}\,\text{cal}^{-1}$$

$$\text{Homogeneous convection field} \qquad \underline{v}(\underline{r},t) = \begin{bmatrix} 8 \; , & 8 \end{bmatrix}^{\text{T}}\,\text{m}\,\text{h}^{-1}$$

$$\text{Spatially distributed system input} \qquad \hat{s}(\underline{r},t) = 4 \cdot 10^3 \left(e^{-\frac{(0.5-x)^2}{0.1} - \frac{(0.5-y)^2}{0.0005}} + e^{-\frac{(1.5-x)^2}{0.0005} - \frac{(1.5-y)^2}{0.1}} \right)$$

$$C^s(\underline{r},t) = 0.5\,\text{cal}^2\,\text{m}^{-6}\,\text{h}^{-2}$$

The mathematical model of the physical system is converted into a lumped-parameter system description based on *piecewise linear* shape functions, i.e., using the finite-element method. The parameters of the spatial decomposition and the temporal discretization are given by $N_x = 225$, $N_{el} = 384$ (spatial decomposition) and $\Delta t = 0.001\,\text{h}$ (temporal discretization). Similar to the conversion of the stochastic partial differential equation (2.1), the corresponding noise term of the system input $s(\underline{r},t)$ represented by the mutually independent spatially distributed variance $C^s(\underline{r},t)$ needs to be converted. In the homogeneous case (as considered in this work), this conversion can be specifically achieved as described in Chapter 2. Here, the covariance matrix of the boundary condition noise is assumed to be $\widetilde{\mathbf{C}}^b(t_k) = 0.05 \cdot \mathbf{I}_{N_x}\,\text{cal}^2\,\text{m}^{-6}\,\text{h}^{-2}$ and the covariance matrix of the spatially distributed measurement system is given by $\mathbf{C}^v_k = 0.5 \cdot \mathbf{I}_{N_y}\,\text{K}^2$. ∎

4.3 Application 1: Identification of Process Parameters

The model-based *state reconstruction* of space-time continuous physical systems by means of a sensor network is based on a mathematical model that describes the dynamic behavior and distributed properties. Assuming an appropriate and sufficiently accurate model description, the physical system is uniquely characterized by so-called *process parameters* and *boundary conditions*, and thus can be reconstructed by means of the methods proposed in Chapter 2. However, in practical implementations the process parameters, such as diffusion coefficient, might not be known in advance and usually need to be identified. It was clearly shown in Section 2.6.2 that deviating process parameters result in a degradation of the reconstruction accuracy. This makes the *process parameter identification* one of the most important issues concerning the model-based observation of space-time continuous physical systems. For sensor network applications, the parameter identification becomes even more essential due to the harsh environment, and unpredictable variations of the physical system being monitored. It is important to emphasize that inherently existing uncertainties not only in the measurements but also in the assumed model structure need to be considered in a systematic way during the identification process.

The main goal of the *identification stage* is to use measurements in order to estimate imprecisely known or completely unknown process parameters $\underline{\eta}^P_k \sim f(\underline{\eta}^P_k)$ in the system model (1.2). This process yields parameter estimates such that the estimated state $\underline{p}_k(\underline{r}) \sim f(p_k|\underline{r})$ sufficiently accurate explains the observations obtained by the sensor network [138]. The space-time discrete samples measured by the individual sensor nodes are incorporated into the mathematical model in order to improve its accuracy in terms of estimated process parameters [118, 119]. Here, the identification of parameters characterizing the dynamic and distributed properties is called *S*imultaneous *R*econstruction and *I*dentification method (SRI method), see Figure 4.1 **(a)**.

Density parameters for *SRI method* The augmentation of the state $\underline{x}_k$ with the purpose of identifying unknown process parameters $\underline{\eta}_k^P$ leads to a nonlinear system description that in general requires the employment of *nonlinear Bayesian estimators*. However, in this research work, the high-dimensional linear substructure containing in the nonlinear probabilistic system model (4.1) is systematically exploited by the SGMF; see Section 4.2 for a more detailed description. In the case of precisely known parameters $\underline{\eta}_k^M$ in the measurement model (i.e, precisely known location $\underline{r}_k^S$ of the sensor nodes), the density parameters of the predicted density function (3.11) are given as follows

- The parameters of the resulting predicted density $f^p(\underline{x}_{k+1}, \underline{\eta}_{k+1}^P)$ for the *prediction step* are given as follows

$$\text{Mean vectors} \qquad \underline{\mu}_{k+1}^{pij} = \mathbf{A}_k\left(\underline{\xi}_k^i\right)\underline{\mu}_k^{eij} + \mathbf{B}_k^u\left(\underline{\xi}_k^i\right)\hat{\underline{u}}_k + \mathbf{B}_k^b\,\hat{\underline{b}}_k$$

$$\text{Covariance matrices} \qquad \mathbf{C}_{k+1}^{pij} = \mathbf{A}_k\left(\underline{\xi}_k^i\right)\mathbf{C}_k^{eij}\mathbf{A}_k\left(\underline{\xi}_k^i\right)^T + \mathbf{B}_k^u\left(\underline{\xi}_k^i\right)\mathbf{C}_k^u\mathbf{B}_k^u\left(\underline{\xi}_k^i\right)^T$$

$$\text{Positions of density slices} \qquad \underline{\xi}_{k+1}^i = \underline{a}_k^P\left(\underline{\xi}_k^i\right)$$

- For the *combined measurement/prediction step*, the parameters of the estimated probability density function $f^e(\underline{x}_k, \underline{\eta}_k^P)$ can be derived by

$$\text{Weights of the slice} \qquad \gamma_k^{ij} = \mathcal{N}\left(\hat{\underline{y}}_k - \mathbf{H}_k\underline{\mu}_k^{pij}, \mathbf{H}_k\mathbf{C}_k^{pij}\mathbf{H}_k^T + \mathbf{C}_k^v\right)$$

$$\text{Mean vectors} \qquad \underline{\mu}_k^{eij} = \underline{\mu}_k^{pij} + \mathbf{K}_k\left(\hat{\underline{y}}_k - \mathbf{H}_k\underline{\mu}_k^{pij}\right)$$

$$\text{Covariance matrices} \qquad \mathbf{C}_k^{eij} = \mathbf{C}_k^{pij} - \mathbf{K}_k\mathbf{H}_k\mathbf{C}_k^{pij}$$

$$\text{Kalman gains} \qquad \mathbf{K}_k = \mathbf{C}_k^{pij}\mathbf{H}_k^T\left(\mathbf{C}_k^v + \mathbf{H}_k\mathbf{C}_k^{pij}\mathbf{H}_k^T\right)^{-1}$$

Example 4.2: Identification of diffusion coefficient

In the following study, the performance of the method for identifying process parameters $\underline{\eta}_k^P$ based on the SGMF is demonstrated. The underlying physical system is assumed to be modelled by the convection-diffusion equation (2.1) with nominal parameters stated in Example 4.1. For visualization purposes, the numeric solution of the considered partial differential equation is shown in Figure 4.4 for the deterministic case. As an example of a *process parameter* $\underline{\eta}_k^P$ being identified, in this simulated case study the *diffusion coefficient* α_{true} is chosen, the true parameter is $\alpha_{true} = 1.0\,\mathrm{m^2\,h^{-1}}$. The main goal here is to identify the diffusion coefficient α_k and simultaneously reconstruct the initially unknown state $p(\underline{r}, t)$. In this particular case, the system matrix $\mathbf{A}_k(\cdot)$ and the input matrix $\mathbf{B}_k^u(\cdot)$, which generally depend on process parameters $\underline{\eta}_k^P$, can be derived as follows

$$\mathbf{A}_k\left(\underline{\xi}_k^i\right) = \mathbf{I} - \mathbf{M}_G^{-1}(\mathbf{N}_G + \xi_k^i\,\mathbf{D}_G)\Delta t \qquad , \qquad \mathbf{B}_k^u\left(\underline{\xi}_k^i\right) = \gamma\,\Delta t\,\mathbf{I}\ .$$

The convection field, and thus the convection matrix $\mathbf{N}_G$ is assumed to be known; see (2.19) and (2.20) in Section 2.3.5 for a more detailed description on deriving the aforementioned matrices. ∎

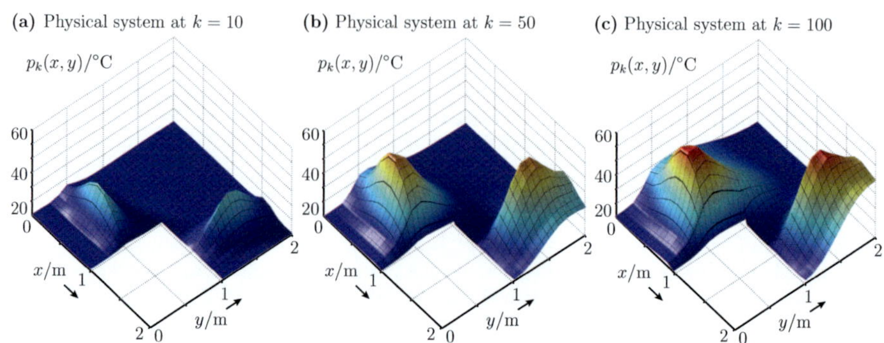

(a) Physical system at $k = 10$ **(b)** Physical system at $k = 50$ **(c)** Physical system at $k = 100$

Figure 4.4: Visualization of the considered physical system for the identification of the process parameter α. The parameters and assumptions of the simulated case study are stated in Example 4.2. Depicted is the numeric solution (deterministic case) at time step **(a)** $k = 10$, **(b)** $k = 50$, and **(c)** $k = 100$.

Reconstruction with deviating diffusion coefficient   In the case of precisely known process parameters characterizing the underlying space-time continuous system (2.1), the framework introduced in Chapter 2 could be applied for the reconstruction of the space-time continuous system state $p(\cdot)$. It was already demonstrated in Section 2.6.2 that the proposed model-based approach requires a rather precise description about the physical system being observed. If any assumption about the structure or about the process parameters is violated, the performance of the estimation result can quickly degrade leading to poor reconstruction results. However, in many cases, the real physical system deviates from the nominal model; this is especially the case for sensor networks deployed in harsh and unknown environments.

Before the proposed simultaneous approach for the identification of process parameters $\underline{\eta}_k^P$ is demonstrated, the degradation in the case of ignoring deviating parameters is shown in terms of Example 4.2. For that reason, the state reconstruction is performed assuming a nominal parameter set according to $\alpha_{\mathrm{model}} \in \{0.1, 0.2, \ldots, 2.0\} \; \mathrm{m^2\,h^{-1}}$. For each assumed nominal diffusion coefficient α_{model} in the model (2.1), totally $M_{\mathrm{MC}} = 200$ independent simulation runs have been performed, resulting in 200 true realizations $\widetilde{\underline{x}}_k^i$ of the physical system. The root mean square error e_k^x (rmse) and the error variance C_x^{rmse} of the estimated state vector $\underline{x}_k$ are approximated by calculating the average according to (2.34). The mean $\hat{e}_k^x$ of the state vector rmse based on deviating nominal diffusion coefficients α_{model} is depicted in Figure 4.5. It can be easily seen that the more the assumed diffusion coefficient α_{model} deviates from the true parameter, the more the performance of the reconstruction result degrades. In addition, the accuracy of the reconstructed space-time continuous system (2.1) seems to be more sensitive to coefficients α_{model} that are assumed being too low rather than ceofficients that are too high.

Simultaneous approach (SRI method)   In the following, the performance of the SGMF-based parameter identification applied to space-time continuous physical systems (2.1) is demonstrated. In particular, the accuracy of the identified process parameter $\underline{\eta}_k^P$ needs to be investigated in comparison to another nonlinear estimation method; the marginalized particle filter (MPF). In Figure 4.6 **(a)** an example simulation run for the estimation of the parameter $\eta_k^P = \alpha_k$ derived by the SGMF (20 slices) and the MPF (40 particles) is visualized. It is obvious that after a certain transition time the SGMF offers a nearly exact parameter estimation, while the

(a) Mean of state vector rmse   **(b)** Sectional drawing with error variances

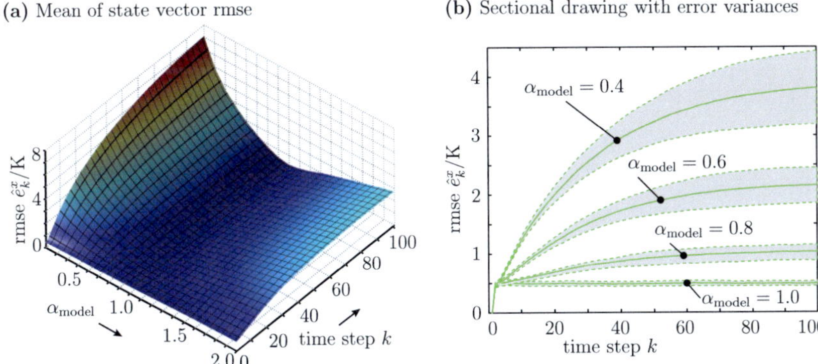

Figure 4.5: Root mean square error e_k^x (rmse) for the reconstruction based on incorrect nominal diffusion coefficient over $M_{\text{MC}} = 200$ independent simulation runs. The true diffusion coefficient is assumed to be $\alpha_{\text{true}} = 1.0\,\text{m}^2\,\text{h}^{-1}$. **(a)** Mean $\hat{e}_k^x$ of the state vector rmse for different nominal diffusion coefficients α_{model}. It is obvious that with the deviation of the parameter the performance quickly degrades. **(b)** Mean $\hat{e}_k^x$ and standard deviation $\sqrt{C_x^{\text{rmse}}}$ of state vector rmse for different nominal parameters $\alpha_{\text{model}} \in \{0.4, 0.6, 0.8, 1.0\}\,\text{m}^2\,\text{h}^{-1}$.

MPF slightly jitters. In addition, although less parameters are required, the SGMF converges faster to the true parameter than an identification process based on MPF.

The mean $\hat{e}_k^\alpha$ and variance C_α^{rmse} of the root mean square error e_k^α (rmse) of the diffusion coefficient α, and the error averaged over time is approximated by calculating according to

$$
\hat{e}_k^\alpha = \frac{1}{N_{\text{MC}}} \sum_{i=1}^{N_{\text{MC}}} |\alpha_{\text{true}} - \hat{\alpha}_k^{ei}| \; , \quad
C_\alpha^{\text{rmse}} = \frac{1}{N_{\text{MC}} - 1} \sum_{i=1}^{N_{\text{MC}}} (e_k^{\alpha i} - \hat{e}_k^{\alpha i})^2 \; , \quad
e_{\text{T}}^{\alpha i} = \frac{1}{N_t} \sum_{k=1}^{N_t} |\alpha_{\text{true}} - \hat{\alpha}_k^{ei}| \; ,
$$

$$(4.6)$$

where $\hat{\alpha}_k^{ei}$ is the mean of the estimated diffusion coefficient for the i-th simulation run. The mean and standard deviation of the rmse e_k^α of the diffusion coefficient considering all 50 performed simulation runs is depicted in Figure 4.6 **(b)**. The error $e_{\text{T}}^{\alpha i}$ of all 50 runs is visualized in Figure 4.6 **(c)**. From these results it can be clearly seen that the SGMF-based identification in most cases outperforms the MPF. This is basically due to the systematic (non-random) positioning of the density slices in the case of SGMF, while the slices for the MPF are placed randomly; see Chapter 3. In Figure 4.6 **(d)**, the error (i.e., error mean $\hat{e}_k^x$ and variance C_x^{rmse}) between a reconstruction process based on incorrect parameters and the proposed simultaneous approach is compared. The significantly improved performance clearly justifies the systematic consideration of uncertainties in parameters during the reconstruction as proposed in this work.

4.4 Application 2: Node Localization based on Local Observations

The sensor data derived from the individual nodes in most applications has only limited utility without precise information about their locations. The knowledge about the locations of the individual nodes of the spatially distributed measurement system is particularly important for the accurate reconstruction of space-time continuous systems. This was already demonstrated in the simulated case study in Section 2.6.3. Manually measuring the location of every individual node in the entire sensor network becomes infeasible, especially when the number of sensor

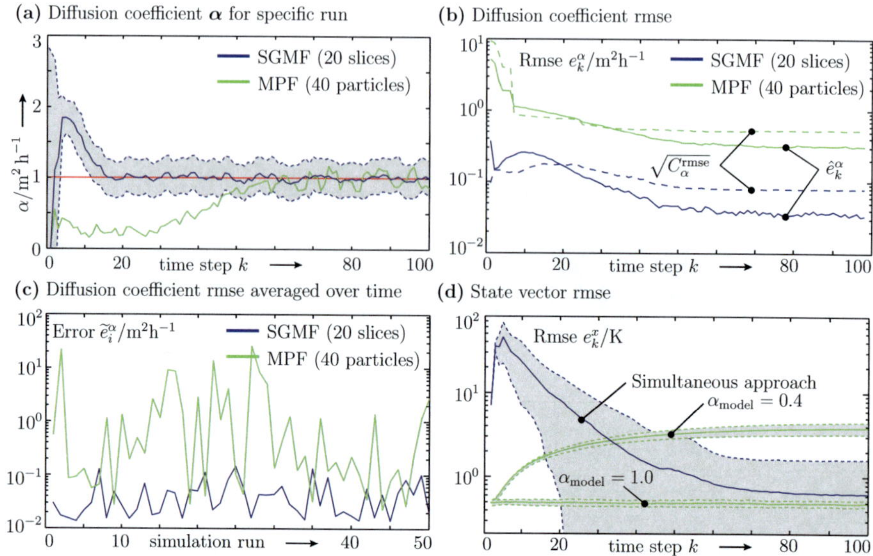

Figure 4.6: Comparison of the Sliced Gaussian Mixture Filter (SGMF) using 20 slices and the marginalized particle filter (MPF) using 40 particles for the identification of the true diffusion coefficient $\alpha_{\mathrm{true}} = 1.0\mathrm{m}^2\,\mathrm{h}^{-1}$. (a) Mean/variance of the diffusion coefficient α for a specific run. (b) Mean and standard deviation of the root mean square error e_k^α (rmse) of diffusion coefficient considering all performed simulation runs. (c) Diffusion coefficient rmse $e_k^{i\alpha}$ averaged over time for all runs. (d) Mean $\hat{e}_k^x$ and standard deviation $\sqrt{(C_x^{\mathrm{rmse}})}$ of state vector rmse; compared is the reconstruction based on deviating parameters and the proposed simultaneous approach.

nodes is large, the nodes are inaccessible or in the case of mobile sensor deployments. Hence, the aforementioned issues make the localization problem one of the most important tasks to be considered in the area of sensor networks. In this section, a novel approach for localizing nodes in a sensor network is proposed — the so-called **S**imultaneous **R**econstruction and **L**ocalization method (*SRL method*); see Figure 4.1 **(b)**. The novelty is the localization based only on local observations of a space-time continuous physical system while rigorously exploiting background knowledge about the dynamic and the distributed behavior.

In general, the main goal of a localization and positioning system is to provide an estimate about the location of the individual nodes in the sensor network in the area of interest. There are several ways to classify the huge diversity of localization methods. In this thesis, these methods are classified into *active* localization methods and *passive* localization methods:

- **Active localization methods:** Active localization methods obtain an estimate of the sensor node location based on signals that are artificially stimulated and measured by the network itself or by a global positioning system; see Figure 4.7. The stimuli usually used in such scenarios consist of artificially generated acoustic events or radio signals. It is obvious that the active localization is performed in fairly controlled and well accessible environments. As it stands, these circumstances incur significant installation and maintenance costs. A comprehensive survey on active localization methods can be found in [62].

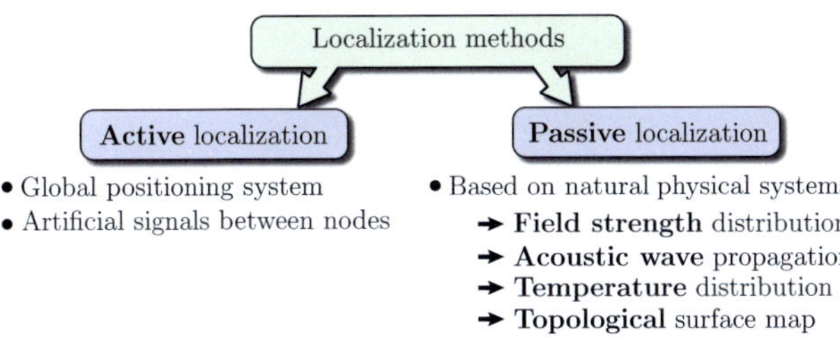

Figure 4.7: Classification of localization methods: **(a)** Active localization, such as methods based on artificial signals between nodes and global positioning systems, and **(b)** passive localization, such as methods based on locally measuring a naturally existing space-time continuous physical system (considered in this thesis).

- **Passive localization methods:** In the case of passive localization methods, which on the contrary occur in a non-controlled and a possibly inaccessible environment, the stimuli necessary for the localization process occur naturally. In Figure 4.7 prospective examples of natural physical systems that can be used as stimuli for localization purposes are stated. The clear advantage of using passive methods for the localization is that they do not need additional infrastructure. This certainly keeps the installation and maintenance costs at a very low level. In addition, these methods become particularly important for applications where global positioning systems are simply not available. This is for example the case for sensor networks that monitor the snow cover [61], for applications in deep sea, for indoor localization [115, 137, 147], or in the case of robotic-based localization [88].

There are various techniques and methods that can be considered for localization systems using different kind of infrastructures in different scenarios. In general, for the estimation of a space-time continuous physical system, the existing infrastructure could consist of a number of sensor nodes both with *known locations* and with *unknown or uncertain locations*. For the minimization of the installation and maintenance costs, it is beneficial to develop a method that requires no additional hardware such as a global positioning system or other heavy infrastructure. Moreover, there are various application scenarios without possible access to a global positioning system, such as the indoor localization of mobile phones [146, 147] or sensor networks deployed deep inside the snowpack for predicting snow avalanche risks (see Section 1.1).

4.4.1 Key Idea of the Proposed Passive Localization Method

In this research work, a novel *passive localization process* is developed that does not require global positioning systems or the localization based on landmarks. The key contribution of the proposed localization approach is the rigorous exploitation of a *strong mathematical model* of the physical system in terms of stochastic partial differential equations (1.2). By this means, individual nodes would be able to localize themselves in a non-controlled environment using only local observations of a space-time continuous physical system. The use of such a model for node localizations was proposed in [61]; however, there was no consideration of uncertainties naturally occuring in the measurements and in the used mathematical models. The *simultaneous approach* based on the SGMF that is proposed in this thesis allows the systematic consideration of uncertainties. This approach is called *simultaneous reconstruction and localization method* (SRL method); see Figure 4.1 **(b)**.

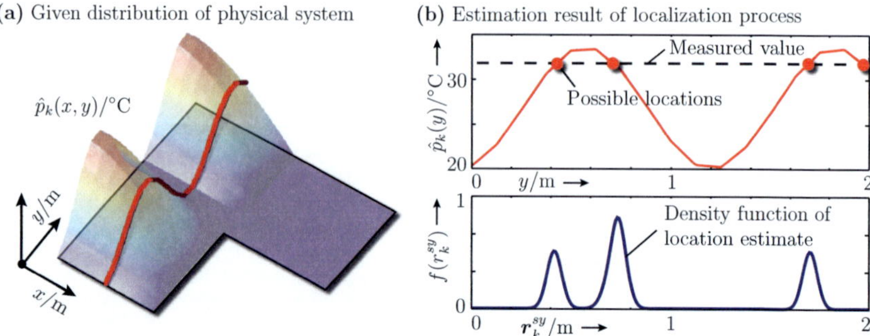

Figure 4.8: Visualization of the key idea of the **SRL method**, which is based on locally measuring a space-time continuous physical system. **(a)** Space continuous mean $\hat{p}_k(x, y)$ of a physical system that is characterized by a strong mathematical model describing the dynamic and distributed behavior. **(b)** Sectional drawing of the system at a specific location in x-direction. Depicted are the possible locations (deterministic case) and the respective density function $f(r_k^{sy})$ (stochastic case) based on a specific measured value of the physical system.

In addition, for the state reconstruction of space-time continuous systems, the precise knowledge about the node locations is essential for obtaining precise estimation results. However, by using any kind of positioning system, uncertainties in the location estimate inherently remain. In order to obtain *consistent* and in particular *accurate reconstruction results*, these uncertainties in the node location need to be systematically considered during the reconstruction process. The SGMF-based simultaneous reconstruction and localization approach, not only allows (a) the *localization of sensor nodes*, but also (b) the systematic consideration of uncertainties in the node locations during the *state reconstruction process*; as proposed in Chapter 2.

The key idea of the proposed localization approach is depicted in Figure 4.8. Roughly speaking, for localizing individual sensor nodes, the space-time continuous representation of the physical system is exploited in an *inverse manner*. This means, locally measured physical quantities are used to obtain possible locations where the measured values could have been generated. In the considered stochastic approach an expression for the location $\underline{r}_k^{si} := [r_k^{sx}, r_k^{sy}] \in \mathbb{R}^2$ of the i-th sensor node being identified is obtained in terms of density functions. Hence, collecting the node locations in the parameter vector $\underline{\eta}_k^M \in \mathbb{R}^{2 \cdot M}$ according to (2.24), the probability density function $f^e(\underline{\eta}_k^M)$ needs to be derived. It is shown that the localization problem can be formulated as a *simultaneous state and parameter estimation* problem: with the finite-dimensional state vector $\underline{x}_k$ representing the space-time continuous physical system and with the individual node locations $\underline{r}_k^{si}$ contained in the parameter vector $\underline{\eta}_k^M$. By this means, the sensor nodes are localized and the state of the physical system is reconstructed in a simultaneous fashion. The improved knowledge about the observed physical system can be exploited for other nodes to localize themselves using only local observations.

4.4.2 Identification/Calibration Stage

The first stage is the *identification/calibration stage*, which is responsible for building a sufficiently accurate probabilistic model of the considered space-time continuous system and its environment. This can be regarded as a system identification and training phase; see Figure 4.1 **(a)**. For the derivation of a sophisticated model (structure and parameters) describing the underlying physical system exploited for the localization, a series of calibration measurements is required. This can be performed by using a certain number of nodes sensing the space-time continuous system at known locations. In this work, these nodes are assumed to be responsible only for identifying the underlying physical system, however, not necessarily for the actual localization process. At each sensor node with the precisely known position $\underline{r}_k^{\mathrm{BS}i} := [r_k^{bx}, r_k^{by}]^{\mathrm{T}} \in \mathbb{R}^2$, a realization of the physical system is locally measured. The positions of the sensor nodes are collected in the *known location vector* $\underline{r}_k^{\mathrm{BS}} \in \mathbb{R}^{2 \cdot M_{\mathrm{BS}}}$ as follows

$$\underline{r}_k^{\mathrm{BS}} := \left[(\underline{r}_k^{\mathrm{BS}1})^{\mathrm{T}} \ , \ (\underline{r}_k^{\mathrm{BS}2})^{\mathrm{T}} \ , \ \ldots \ , \ (\underline{r}_k^{M_{\mathrm{BS}}})^{\mathrm{T}} \right]^{\mathrm{T}} \in \mathbb{R}^{2 \times M_{\mathrm{BS}}} \ ,$$

where M_{BS} denotes the total number of sensor nodes with known location considered for the identification/calibration stage.

For physical systems that are distributed over a wide area, gathering the measurements for the identification stage can become tedious. However, the automation of this process can be achieved using mobile devices (with accurate navigation system) moving in the area of interest in an autonomous and self-organized manner. Such a system, for example, was proposed in [120], where mobile robots autonomously collect information about the signal strength distribution that can be used for indoor localization purposes [115, 117].

The identification stage strongly differs in the way it actually makes use of the measurements obtained. In general, the localization based on *static/distributed* as well as *dynamic/distributed* physical systems would be of interest. Depending on the type of the physical system, the description being obtained during the identification stage is different. For static systems a model only in terms of a probability density function is required, whereas for dynamic systems additional parameters describing the dynamic behavior need to be identified.

Static physical systems   In the case of localizing the individual sensor nodes based on a *static physical system*, the identification stage consists only of finding an appropriate model description in terms of the conditional density function $\boldsymbol{p}(\underline{r}) \sim f^e(p|\underline{r})$. This description characterizes the *spatial distribution* of the considered physical quantity and its underlying uncertainty in the area of interest. In this sense, for each position $\underline{r} \in \mathbb{R}^2$ a probability density function $f^e(\cdot)$ about the spatially distributed system $\mathcal{P}$ is obtained. In Figure 4.9, a descriptive example of such model is depicted that can be used for the localization in the one-dimensional case. There are several ways for the actual derivation of the model describing the spatial distribution of the physical quantity. For example, this can be achieved by *data-driven approaches* [47], which use the calibration measurements to directly estimate the underlying probability density function $f^e(p|\underline{r})$ of the static/distributed physical system. Another way is to use *probabilistic learning techniques*, such as the **S**imultaneous **P**robabilistic **L**ocalization and **L**earning method (*SPLL method*) proposed in [110] that additioinaly allows the simultaneous localization during the identification and calibration stage.

Dynamic physical systems   For *dynamic physical systems*, it is not sufficient to derive a description only about the current spatial distribution of the physical quantity, rather additional parameters characterizing the dynamic behavior are necessary. The main advantage of exploiting dynamic systems for the localization is that additional information about the dynamic allows excluding specific values of the otherwise possibly ambiguous location estimates. However, this advantage is opposed by the more sophisticated and costly identification/calibration stage that usually must be accomplished before or simultaneous to the actual localization stage. This means, the identification of the parameters of the model description (1.2) for the underlying physical system is required. This can be achieved by the *SRI approach* proposed in Section 4.3.

4.4.3 Localization Stage

Then, during the *localization stage*, the previously created and identified model is exploited to estimate the location of individual sensor nodes by local measurements of the physical system. This stage can be seen as the application stage performing the actual localization task based on locally measuring the physical system. It is important to emphasize that after a prior identification of the model structure, in general, it is possible to perform the identification of model parameters, the state reconstruction, and the localization of sensor nodes in a *simultaneous fashion*. The separation of the identification/localization stage is made here only for clearly and independently stating the individual basic ingredients of the SRL method.

In the localization stage, the individual sensor nodes with unknown or imprecisely known location $\underline{r}_k^{si} \in \mathbb{R}^2$ are locally measuring the underlying space-time continuous system, e.g., temperature distribution or signal strength distribution. The locations of the M sensor nodes being identified are collected in the location parameter vector $\underline{\eta}_k^M \in \mathbb{R}^{2 \cdot M}$ according to (2.24). Based on the measurements and on the model description generated in the preceding identification/calibration stage, the location of these sensor nodes are estimated in terms of the density function $f^e(\underline{\eta}_k^M)$. Hence, the main goal of the *SRL method* is to estimate the augmented state vector $\underline{z}_k := \left[(\underline{x}_k)^T \quad (\underline{\eta}_k^M)^T \right]^T$ including the state of the physical system and the node locations.

In the special case of the *pure* localization method, i.e., precisely known process parameters $\underline{\eta}_k^P$ and input model parameters $\underline{\eta}_k^I$, the complexity of the augmented probabilistic *system description* (4.1) can be reduced leading to a *high-dimensional linear* system model. The only nonlinear structure here is possibly contained in the function $\underline{a}_k^M(\cdot)$ describing the dynamic properties of the individual sensor nodes. On the contrary, the augmented *measurement model* (4.2) turns out to be a *nonlinear relationship*, mainly due to the multiplication of the node locations $\underline{\eta}_k^M$ to be identified with the finite-dimensional state vector $\underline{x}_k \in \mathbb{R}^{N_x}$. The structure of the measurement matrix $\mathbf{H}(\cdot)$ and especially the dependency on the individual node locations $\underline{r}_k^{si}$ collected in the parameter vector $\underline{\eta}_k^M$ is illustrated in Example 2.3.

Density parameters for *SRL method* In the estimation process, the high-dimensional linear substructure contained in the nonlinear generative measurement model (4.2) is systematically exploited by the Sliced Gaussian Mixture Filter (SGMF); see Section 4.2 for a more detailed description. In the case of a known strong mathematical description of the underlying physical system (i.e., known model parameters $\underline{\eta}_k^P$ and input parameters $\underline{\eta}_k^I$), then the density parameters of the predicted density function (3.11) are given as follows:

- For the *prediction step* the parameters of the resulting predicted density $f^p(\underline{x}_{k+1}, \underline{\eta}_{k+1}^M)$ can be derived by

$$\begin{aligned}
\text{Mean vectors} \qquad & \underline{\mu}_{k+1}^{pij} = \mathbf{A}_k \underline{\mu}_k^{eij} + \mathbf{B}_k^u \underline{\hat{u}}_k + \mathbf{B}_k^b \underline{\hat{b}}_k \\
\text{Covariance matrices} \qquad & \mathbf{C}_{k+1}^{pij} = \mathbf{A}_k \mathbf{C}_k^{eij} \mathbf{A}_k^T + \mathbf{B}_k^u \mathbf{C}_k^{uij} \mathbf{B}_k^{uT} + \mathbf{B}_k^b \mathbf{C}_k^{bij} \mathbf{B}_k^{bT} \\
\text{Positions of density slices} \qquad & \underline{\xi}_{k+1}^i = \underline{a}_k^M \left(\underline{\xi}_k^i \right)
\end{aligned}$$

- In the case of available measurements $\underline{\hat{y}}_k$ the parameters of estimated density $f^e(\underline{x}_k, \underline{\eta}_k^M)$ in terms of the *combined measurement step* are given by

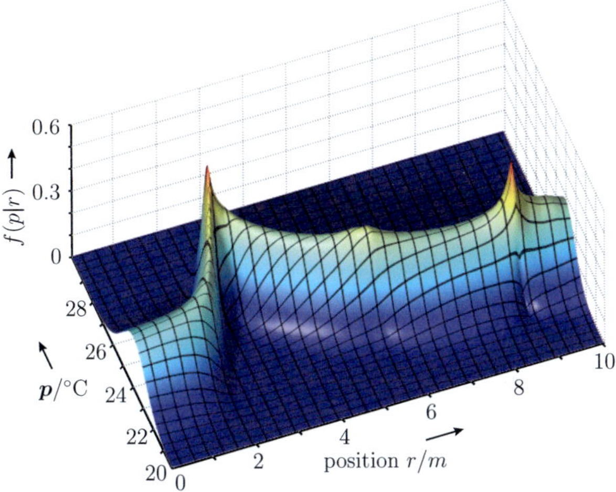

Figure 4.9: Visualization of a model that can be used for the *SRL method* based on *static physical systems*. The model is given in terms of a conditional density function $f(p|\underline{r})$ over the position $\underline{r}$ and the space-time continuous state $p(\cdot)$; here depicted for the one-dimensional case for simplicity purposes only.

Weights of the slices	$\gamma_k^{ij} = \mathcal{N}\left(\underline{\hat{y}}_k - \mathbf{H}_k\left(\underline{\xi}_k^i\right)\underline{\mu}_k^{pij}, \mathbf{H}_k\left(\underline{\xi}_k^i\right)\mathbf{C}_k^{pij}\mathbf{H}_k\left(\underline{\xi}_k^i\right)^T + \mathbf{C}_k^v\right)$
Mean vectors	$\underline{\mu}_k^{eij} = \underline{\mu}_k^{pij} + \mathbf{K}_k\left(\underline{\hat{y}}_k - \mathbf{H}_k\left(\underline{\xi}_k^i\right)\underline{\mu}_k^{pij}\right)$
Covariance matrices	$\mathbf{C}_k^{eij} = \mathbf{C}_k^{pij} - \mathbf{K}_k\mathbf{H}_k\left(\underline{\xi}_k^i\right)\mathbf{C}_k^{pij}$
Kalman gains	$\mathbf{K}_k = \mathbf{C}_k^{pij}\mathbf{H}_k\left(\underline{\xi}_k^i\right)^T\left(\mathbf{C}_k^v + \mathbf{H}_k\left(\underline{\xi}_k^i\right)\mathbf{C}_k^{pij}\mathbf{H}_k\left(\underline{\xi}_k^i\right)^T\right)^{-1}$

4.4.4 Tracking of Movable Sensor Nodes

This section is devoted to some remarks on extending the proposed *SRL method* to the tracking of movable sensor nodes; so-called sensor-actuator nodes. In general, such networks of sensor-actuator nodes can be used for the intelligent exploration of space-time continuous systems where the individual nodes autonomously move in the area of interest. By cruising in the entire area in an intelligent manner, the movable sensor-actuator nodes gather specific information (in terms of state/parameter vectors) about the physical system being observed. The goal for example could consist of optimizing a certain object function, such as minimizing the variance field (state estimation) or maximizing the information gain (parameter identification). In [63] a control algorithm is proposed for a swarm of robots with the purpose to minimize the variance of a specific information field. However, the implemented mathematical model describing the grow of the uncertainty does not consider physical background knowledge. Thus, it does not sufficiently take the dynamic/distributed behavior of the space-time continuous system into account. The performance of such exploration systems could be significantly improved by employing the systematic approach proposed in this thesis in order to obtain a precise and a physically correct estimation of the underlying random field.

Motion models For aforementioned application scenarios the accurate localization and especially the tracking of the movable sensor-actuator nodes plays an important role. In general, any tracking algorithm makes specific assumptions about the motion behavior of the object to be tracked. By this means, additional background knowledge is exploited to obtain an improved location estimate, i.e., some restrictions on the new position estimate are imposed. Depending on the actual application, there are various mathematical models of motion behaviors. A comprehensive survey on different *kinematic motion models* with emphasizing applications to human motion tracking can be found in [149]. Employing *dynamic motion models* can improve the accuracy of the tracking algorithm in many cases.

Assuming a holonomic motion behavior, i.e., independent motion in all directions, then the *dynamics* of the entire sensor-actuator network consisting of M individual nodes can be described by following motion model,

$$
\begin{bmatrix} \boldsymbol{\eta}_{k+1}^{M} \\ \dot{\boldsymbol{\eta}}_{k+1}^{M} \end{bmatrix} = \underbrace{\begin{bmatrix} \mathbf{I} & \Delta t \cdot \mathbf{I} \\ \mathbf{0} & \left(1 - \frac{\Delta t f}{m}\right) \cdot \mathbf{I} \end{bmatrix} \begin{bmatrix} \boldsymbol{\eta}_{k}^{M} \\ \dot{\boldsymbol{\eta}}_{k}^{M} \end{bmatrix}}_{a_k(\boldsymbol{\eta}_{k+1}^{M}, \dot{\boldsymbol{\eta}}_{k+1}^{M})} + \begin{bmatrix} \mathbf{0} \\ \frac{\Delta t}{m} \end{bmatrix} \left(\hat{\boldsymbol{u}}_{k}^{M} + \boldsymbol{w}_{k}^{M}\right) , \tag{4.7}
$$

where m denotes the mass of the individual sensor-actuator nodes, Δt represents the temporal discretization constant and f is the so-called viscous-friction coefficient. The state of this model consists of the *node location vector* $\boldsymbol{\eta}_{k}^{M} \in \mathbb{R}^{2 \cdot M}$ and the *velocity vector* $\dot{\boldsymbol{\eta}}_{k}^{M} \in \mathbb{R}^{2 \cdot M}$ and is driven by the input vector $\hat{\boldsymbol{u}}_{k} \in \mathbb{R}^{2 \cdot M}$. The employment of the model (4.7) into the augmented system model (4.1) for tracking movable sensor-actuator nodes is conceptually straightforward.

4.4.5 Simulation Results

In this section, the performance of the *SRL method* that is based on locally measuring a space-time continuous physical system is descriptively demonstrated by *two simulated case studies;* based on (a) *static/distributed* and (b) *dynamic/distributed* physical systems. As proof of concept, the spatially distributed measurement system is assumed to consist of *one single sensor node* to be localized. This can be regarded as a worst case scenario meaning the localization is performed only based on the physical system without using additional information from other nodes or a global positioning system. Here, it is noted that in the case of available additional information that are possibly obtained from other localization techniques then these information can be used to further improve the location estimate. Also, the extension to localize more than one sensor node at once is straightforward.

Example 4.3: Localization exploiting models of static/distributed physical systems

In this example, the space-time continuous system that is exploited for the localization of one single sensor node is assumed to be *static*, i.e., *time-invariant*. In practical implementations, the model description in terms of the space-time continuous state $p(x, y) \in \mathbb{R}^2$ could be obtained using the methods proposed in [47, 110]. Here, the mean and variance is given as

$$\text{Mean physical system} \qquad \hat{p}(x, y)/\,^\circ\text{C} = \begin{cases} 20 - 20 \sin\left(1.5x - 1.5\right)\left(\sin(5y + 5) + 1\right) & x < 1 \\ 20 & x \geq 1 \end{cases}$$

$$\text{Variance physical system} \qquad C(x, y) = 100\,\text{K}^2 ,$$

(a) Static space-time continuous system   **(b)** Density of location estimate

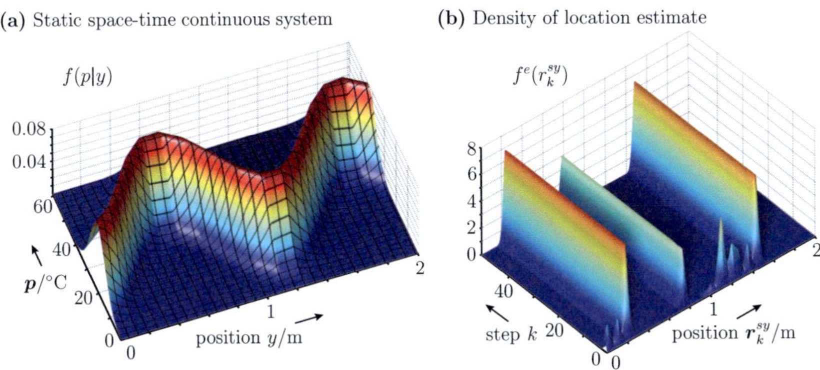

Figure 4.10: Simulation results for the localization of one single sensor node at r_k^{sy} based on locally measuring a *static physical system*. **(a)** Visualization of the physical model description in terms of the conditional density function $f(p|y)$. **(b)** Resulting probability density function $f^e(r_k^{sy})$ for the estimated node location.

where the space-time continuous mean $\hat{p}(\cdot)$ is visualized in Figure 4.8. A sectional drawing of the density function $f^e(p|y)$ along the y-direction exploited for the localization is depicted in Figure 4.10 **(a)**. The distributed measurement system to be localized consists of one single node with following *true node location* $r_{\text{true}}^M := [0.4\,\text{m},\ 0.8\,\text{m}]^{\text{T}}$ and sensor variance $C_k^v = 0.1\,\text{K}^2$ of the local measurement. The goal in this case study is to localize the sensor node in the y-direction using the *SRL approach* proposed in this chapter. The resulting high-dimensional nonlinear estimation problem is performed by means of the Sliced Gaussian Mixture Filter (SGMF) with a total number of $M_D = 40$ density slices. The localization results are shown in Figure 4.10 **(b)**. It can be clearly seen that all three possible locations are represented in terms of the probability density function $f^e(r_k^{sy})$. More important, it does not lead to a degeneration of particular locations, which automatically would result in unjustifiable improvements of the estimated location or even worse to a tracking of completely wrong locations. ■

Example 4.4: Localization exploiting models of dynamic/distributed physical systems

This example is devoted to a demonstration of the *SRL method* exploiting *dynamic*/distributed physical systems; in particular systems governed by the convection-diffusion equation (2.1). The goal here is to localize the sensor node with initially unknown location (true node location is $r_{\text{true}}^{sy} = 0.8\,\text{m}$) using local measurements of the space-time continuous physical system. The model parameters of the physical system that are exploited for the localization are given in Example 4.1 and the initial conditions are stated in Example 4.3. The boundary conditions, the assumed convection field, and the spatially distributed inputs are depicted in Figure 2.4. For visualization purposes, the spatial distribution of the physical system and its development over time is shown in Figure 4.11. It is assumed that the measurement system to be localized consists only of one single sensor node locally measuring the space-time continuous physical system. Furthermore, the sensor node has only very uncertain knowledge about the initial spatially distributed state of the physical system; see Figure 4.13 **(f)**. The simulation results are discussed in the following. ■

Reconstruction based on incorrect locations   As it was already demonstrated in Section 2.6.2, the reconstruction process of space-time continuous physical systems requires rather

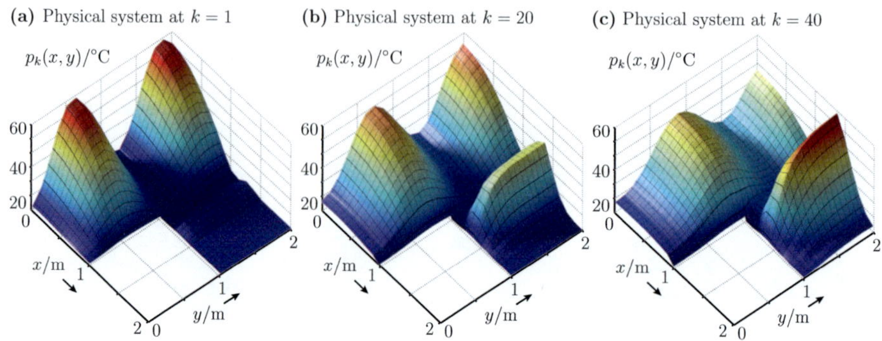

Figure 4.11: Simulated case study for the localization based on dynamic physical systems. Numeric solution of the space-time continuous system (deterministic case) at time step **(a)** $k = 10$, **(b)** $k = 20$, and **(c)** $k = 40$.

precise models, both of the physical system and the measurement system itself. If any assumption about the model parameters (or model structure) is violated, the performance of the reconstruction can quickly degrade. However, in many cases, the locations of sensor nodes (in particular randomly deployed or movable nodes) contain some uncertainties or even could be *completely unknown*. The degradation leading to poor performance is illustrated in the following. For that reason, the reconstruction of the distributed system is performed on the basis of a Kalman filter with nominal parameters for the sensor location r^{sy}_{model}, according to

$$r^{sy}_{\mathrm{model}} \in \{0.1\,,\, 0.2\,,\, \ldots\,,\, 1.9\}\ \mathrm{m}\ .$$

For each assumed node location, a total number of $M_{\mathrm{MC}} = 200$ independent simulation runs have been performed, resulting in 200 true realizations $\widetilde{\underline{x}}^i_k$ of the physical system. The root mean square error e^x_k (rmse) and the error variance C^{rmse}_x are approximated by calculating the average according to (2.34). The mean and standard deviation of rmse e^x_k of the estimated state vector $\underline{x}_k$ based on deviating node locations is shown in Figure 4.12. It can be easily seen that the more the assumed node location r^{sy}_{model} deviates from the true location r^{sy}_{true}, the more the performance of the reconstruction result degrades. In addition, obviously the actual spatial distribution of the physical system influences the resulting errors for deviating node locations. Roughly speaking, when the temporal process at the deviated node location is similar to the process at the true location, then obviously a smaller reconstruction error is caused. This degradation clearly justifies the systematic consideration of location uncertainties during the reconstruction process; as demonstrated in the remainder of this section.

Simultaneous approach (SRL method)   The aforementioned approaches (i.e., SGMF and MPF) for the passive node localization are compared based on 50 independent simulation runs. In particular, the accuracy of the estimated location $r^{sy}_k \sim f(r^{sy}_k)$ is investigated. The estimation of the unknown location r^{sy}_k is depicted in Figure 4.13 **(a)** for one specific simulation run. It can be clearly seen that after a certain transition time the SRL method based on the SGMF (with 40 slices) offers a nearly exact location estimate. The complete density function $f^e(r^{sy}_k)$ for the estimated location evolving over time is depicted in Figure 4.13 **(d)** for a specific run. The ambigious distribution of the physical system being observed results in a multimodal density function for the estimated location r^{sy}_k. This undoubtedly explains the higher uncertainty at the beginning of the simulation. However, by exploiting more and more measurements and

(a) Mean of state vector rmse   (b) Sectional drawing with error variances

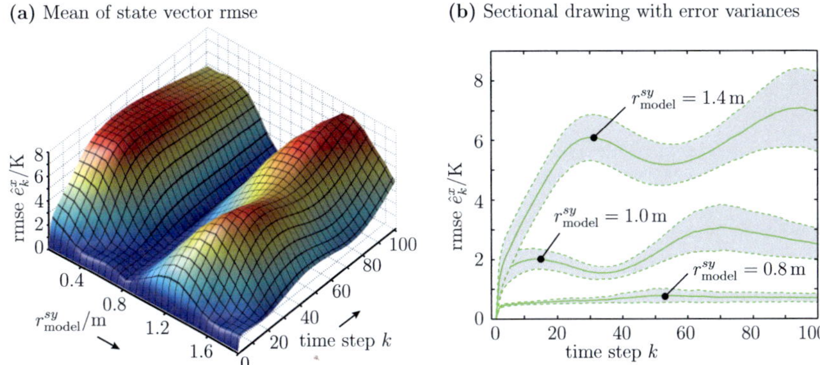

Figure 4.12: Root mean square error e_k^x (rmse) for the reconstruction based on incorrect nominal node location over $M_{\mathrm{MC}} = 200$ independent simulation runs. The true node location is assumed to be $r_{\mathrm{true}}^{sy} = 0.8\,\mathrm{m}$. **(a)** Mean $\hat{e}_k^x$ of the state vector rmse for different assumed node locations. It is obvious that with the deviation of the location the performance quickly degrades. **(b)** Mean $\hat{e}_k^x$ and standard deviation $\sqrt{C_x^{\mathrm{rmse}}}$ of state vector rmse for different incorrect node locations $r_{\mathrm{model}}^{sy} \in \{0.8, 1.0, 1.4\}$ m.

information about the dynamic system, the estimate of the location changes from a multimodal to a unimodal function. Thus, the estimate becomes more accurate; see Figure 4.13 **(a)**.

The mean $\hat{e}_k^{r^{sy}}$ and variance $C_{r^{sy}}^{\mathrm{rmse}}$ of the root mean square error $e_k^{r^{sy}}$ (rmse) of the node location r_k^{sy} can be calculated similar to (4.6). The error averaged over time is calculated according to

$$e_{\mathrm{T}}^{r^{sy}} = \frac{1}{N_{\mathrm{t}} - 50} \sum_{k=50}^{N_{\mathrm{t}}} |r_{\mathrm{true}}^{sy} - \hat{r}_k^{esy}| \,,$$

where $\hat{r}_k^{esy}$ is the mean of the estimated location for the i-th simulation run. The mean and standard deviation of the rmse $e_k^{r^{sy}}$ of node location considering all 50 performed simulation runs is visualized in Figure 4.13 **(b)**. The error $e_{\mathrm{T}}^{r^{sy}}$ of the location estimate after a certain transition time (i.e., $k > 50$) of all 50 simulation runs are depicted in Figure 4.13 **(c)**. From these two figures, it can be clearly seen that the SGMF-based localization (40 slices) in most cases results in a more accurate location estimate than in the case of using MPF (200 particles), although a lower number of density slices are used. This higher accuraciy is basically due to the systematic approach for finding optimal placements of the density slices in the case of SGMF, while the slices for the MPF are placed randomly. It is well-known that this randomness results in a degeneration and impoverishment of certain particles. Even more severe, due to the multimodal density function for the location estimate at the beginning of the simulation (see Figure 4.13 **(e)**), this fact causes the degeneration of entire modes. To visualize this, the mean from the MPF-based localization is shown in Figure 4.13 **(a)** for different simulation runs; two results show where the estimate get stuck in wrong modes. It is obvious that in certain cases the MPF sticks to the wrong location due to the degeneration of specific modes.

In Figure 4.13 **(d)**, the error (i.e., error mean $\hat{e}_k^x$ and variance C_x^{rmse}) between a reconstruction process based on incorrect node locations and the proposed simultaneous approach is compared. The improved accuracy clearly justifies the systematic consideration of uncertainties in the node location during the state reconstruction. Thanks to the *simultaneous property* of the SRL method, not only can the sensor node be accurately localized, but also the estimate of the space-time continuous physical system can be further improved. The improvement of the reconstruction result is obvious by comparing the two plots in Figure 4.13 (**f**). It is important to emphasize that the physical system can be reconstructed at the actual measurement point as well as at non-measurement points. The improved knowledge in the entire area of interest can be exploited by other sensor nodes to localize themselves.

In this thesis, the localization was restricted to one single sensor node locally measuring the space-time continuous system. However, the method can be extended to more sensor nodes with both uncertain location and precisely known location in a straightforward fashion. In addition, it is believed that using more than one sensor node, the performance of the localization and reconstruction process can be significantly improved since more information about the physical system is available, and thus can be exploited for more accurate estimation results. The already precisely localized sensor nodes, e.g., sensor beacons or base stations, can be used to reconstruct the physical system and by this means support the localization of individual sensor nodes deployed between the beacons.

4.5 Application 3: Source and Leakage Localization

In many application scenarios the task consists of localizing a certain source of a space-time continuous physical system. For example, the detection of disposal sites on the ocean floor [67], the localization of landmines using chemical sensors [68], the detection of leakages in storage facilities for radioactive waste [3], or biochemical concentrations [108, 155]. In such scenarios, sensor networks with their spatially distributed sensing properties offer novel prospects for accurately localizing sources and leakages.

In order to derive accurate localization results, usually, physical background knowledge in terms of mathematical models needs to be exploited. Hence, in this research work, a method for source and leakage localization is proposed that is based on combining the state reconstruction (Chapter 2) resulting in physically correct estimation results of the physical system and the efficient non-linear estimator SGMF (Chapter 3). This means, the goal is the reconstruction of the space-time continuous system state $\boldsymbol{p}(\boldsymbol{r}, t) \sim f(p|\underline{r}, t)$ as well as the space-time continuous input $\boldsymbol{s}(\boldsymbol{r}, t) \sim f(s|\underline{r}, t)$ in a simultaneous fashion. This can also be considered as the *model-based reconstruction of spatially distributed system inputs*. Here, the identification of parameters characterizing the dynamic and distributed properties of sources/leakages is called *S*imultaneous *R*econstruction and *S*ource *L*ocalization method (SRSL method)

Density parameters for SRSL method Similar to previous cases, the augmentation of the high-dimensional state vector $\underline{x}_k$ with the purpose of identifying input parameters $\underline{\eta}_k^I$ leads to a nonlinear system description. The high-dimensional linear substructure contained in the resulting augmented system model is systematically exploited by the SGMF, introduced in Section 4.2. The parameters of the predicted density function (3.11) are given as follows

- For the *prediction step* the parameters of the resulting predicted density $f^p(\underline{x}_{k+1}, \underline{\eta}_{k+1}^I)$ can be derived by

$$
\begin{aligned}
\text{Mean vectors} \quad & \underline{\mu}_{k+1}^{pij} = \mathbf{A}_k \underline{\mu}_k^{eij} + \mathbf{B}_k^u \, \hat{\underline{u}}_k\left(\underline{\xi}_k^i\right) + \mathbf{B}_k^b \hat{\underline{b}}_k \\
\text{Covariance matrices} \quad & \mathbf{C}_{k+1}^{pij} = \mathbf{A}_k \mathbf{C}_k^{eij} \mathbf{A}_k^{\,T} + \mathbf{B}_k^u \mathbf{C}_k^{uij} \mathbf{B}_k^{u\,T} + \mathbf{B}_k^b \mathbf{C}_k^{bij} \mathbf{B}_k^{b\,T} \\
\text{Positions of density slices} \quad & \underline{\xi}_{k+1}^i = \underline{a}_k^I\left(\underline{\xi}_k^i\right)
\end{aligned}
$$

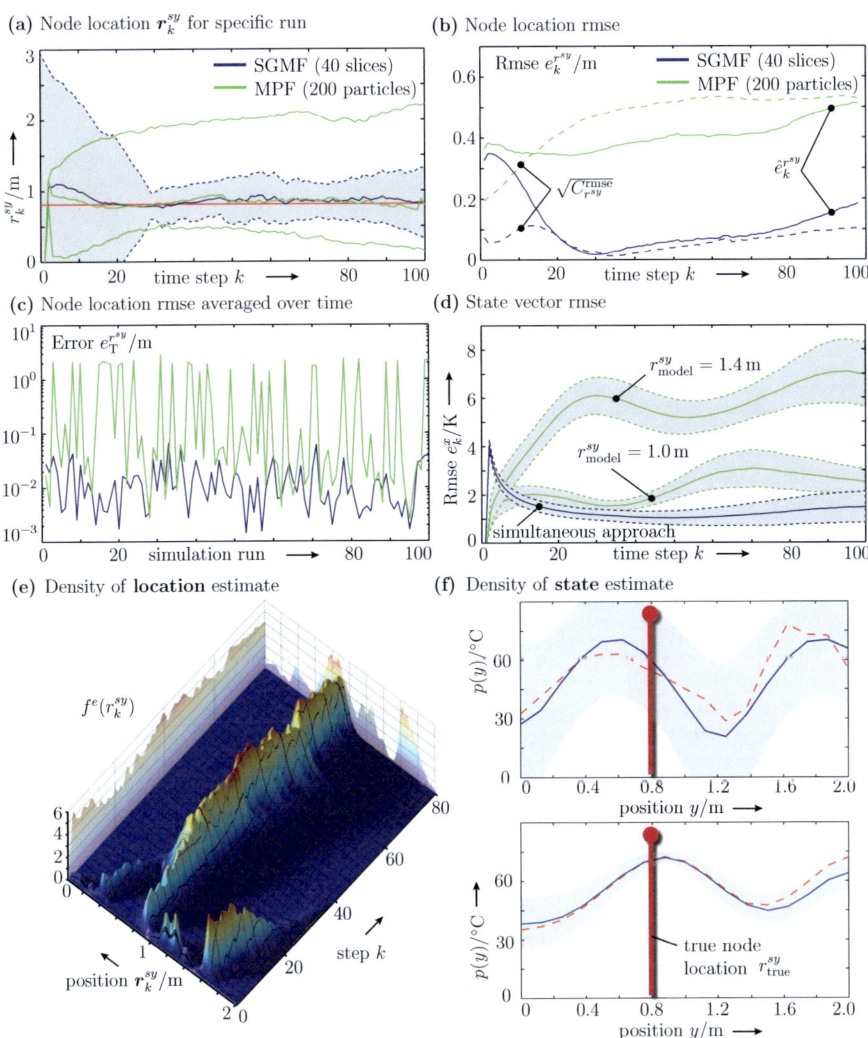

Figure 4.13: Comparison of the Sliced Gaussian Mixture Filter (SGMF) using 40 slices and the marginalized particle filter (MPF) using 200 particles for the localization of one single sensor node; true location $r_{\text{true}}^{sy} = 0.8\,$m. **(a)** Mean/variance of node location $\boldsymbol{r}_k^{sy}$ for a specific simulation run. **(b)** Mean and standard deviation of the root mean square error $e_k^{r^{sy}}$ (rmse) of node location considering all performed simulation runs. **(c)** Location rmse e_{T}^{sy} averaged over time for all runs. **(d)** Mean $\hat{e}_k^x$ and standard deviation $\sqrt{C_x^{\text{rmse}}}$ of state vector rmse; compared is the reconstruction based on deviating node locations and the proposed simultaneous approach. **(e)** Resulting density function $f^e(r_k^{sy})$ for estimated node location $\boldsymbol{r}_k^{sy}$ over time for specific simulation run. **(f)** Realization of the distributed physical system (red dotted) and its estimated mean (blue). The confidence interval of the estimated physical system (gray shaded area) can be significantly improved thanks to the *simultaneous* approach.

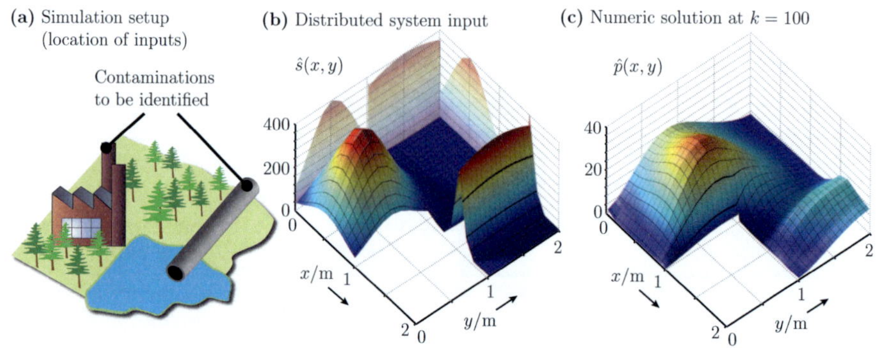

(a) Simulation setup (location of inputs)

Contaminations to be identified

(b) Distributed system input

$\hat{s}(x,y)$

(c) Numeric solution at $k = 100$

$\hat{p}(x,y)$

Figure 4.14: Visualization of the simulation results for the identification of local system inputs. **(a)** Simulation setup with location of contaminations to be identified. **(b)** True assumed distributed system input $\hat{s}(x,y)$. **(c)** Stationary solution ($k = 300$) of the space-time continuous physical system in the deterministic case.

Example 4.5: Localization of spatially distributed input

In the following simulated case study, the performance of the proposed method for localizing spatially distributed sources is demonstrated. The underlying space-time continuous system is assumed to be modelled by the convection-diffusion equation (2.1) with nominal parameters stated in Example 4.1. The space-time continuous input $s_{\text{true}}(x,y)$ being estimated is assumed to be given by

$$s_{\text{true}}(x,y) = 4 \cdot 10^2 \left(\exp\left\{ -\frac{(q^{1y} - x)^2}{0.2} - \frac{(q^{1y} - y)^2}{0.2} \right\} + \exp\left\{ -\frac{(q^{2x} - x)^2}{0.01} - \frac{(q^{2y} - y)^2}{2} \right\} \right) \tag{4.8}$$

where the center of the two sources are $q^{1x} = q^{1y} = 0.5\,\text{m}$ and $q^{2x} = q^{2y} = 1.5\,\text{m}$. The system input $s_{\text{true}}(x,y)$ is visualized in Figure 4.14 **(a)**-**(b)**. The boundary conditions and the assumed convection field are shown in Figure 2.4. The space-time continuous state $p(\underline{r},t)$ resulting from the assumed input is depicted in Figure 4.14 **(c)** for the deterministic case for visualization purposes only. The spatially distributed measurement system consists of different number of nodes randomly deployed in the domain of interest, according to

$$S \in \{10, 20, \ldots, 100\} \ .$$

The main goal here is to reconstruct the *entire* space-time continuous input $s(\underline{r},t)$ and simultaneously reconstruct the initially unknown state $p(\underline{r},t)$. In terms of the simultaneous state and parameter estimation framework (see Section 4.1), there are generally two different approaches, (a) the direct identification of the input vector $\underline{u}_k$ (results shown in Figure 4.15), and (b) the identification of input model parameters $\underline{\eta}_k^I$ characterizing the input vector (results shown in Figure 4.16). This is explained and demonstrated in more detail in the remainder of this section. ∎

Direct identification The first approach for the model-based source localization is the estimation of the state vector $\underline{x}_k \in \mathbb{R}^{N_x}$ augmented with their *corresponding direct input vector* $\underline{u}_k \in \mathbb{R}^{N_x}$. This means, the system input necessary for the system model (4.1) is directly parameterized according to $\underline{u}_k(\underline{\eta}_k^I) = \underline{\eta}_k^I$. It is important to emphasize that in this case the

(a) Mean of estimated input map   **(b)** Rmse for input and state estimate (vs. node number)

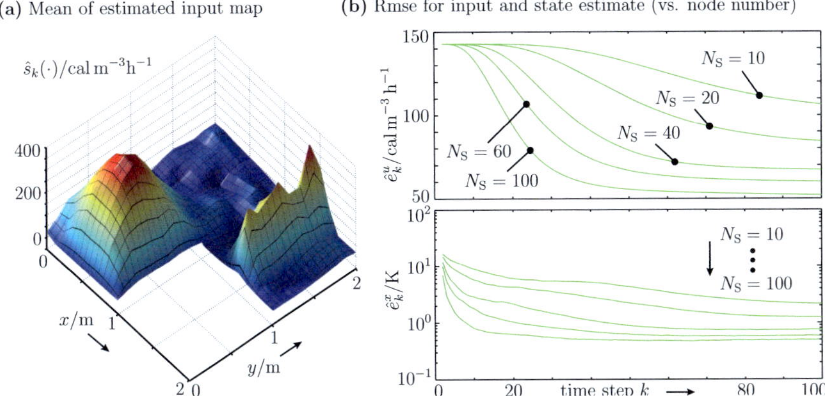

Figure 4.15: Simulation results for the ***direct identification approach*** in order to reconstruct the entire spatially distributed system input. **(a)** Resulting mean of input $\hat{s}(x, y)$ using $N_\mathrm{S} = 100$ randomly deployed sensor nodes. **(b)** Mean of the root mean square error (rmse) e_k^u and e_k^x of the space-time discrete input vector $\underline{u}_k$ and state vector $\underline{x}_k$, respectively. The results are shown for different number of sensor nodes $N_\mathrm{S} \in \{10, 20, 40, 60, 100\}$. Obviously, a high number of nodes is necessary to obtain a sufficiently accurate estimate.

augmented system model (4.1) remains a *linear description* with following structure

$$\begin{bmatrix} \underline{x}_{k+1} \\ \underline{\eta}_{k+1}^I \end{bmatrix} = \begin{bmatrix} \mathbf{A}_k & \mathbf{B}_k^u \\ \mathbf{0} & \mathbf{I} \end{bmatrix} \cdot \begin{bmatrix} \underline{x}_k \\ \underline{\eta}_k^I \end{bmatrix} + \begin{bmatrix} \mathbf{B}_k^b \, (\hat{\underline{b}}_k + \underline{w}_k) \\ \underline{w}_k^I \end{bmatrix} \; ;$$

however, obviously the dimension is double the original problem. Hence, the linear Kalman filter [132] can be used for estimating the augmented system state $\underline{z}_k := [(\underline{x}_k)^\mathrm{T}, (\underline{\eta}_k^I)^\mathrm{T}]^\mathrm{T}$, which contains the state vector and its corresponding input vector; see (2.28) and (2.29).

The reconstructed system input $s(x, y)$ that is obtained after the conversion of the estimated input vector $\underline{\eta}_k^I = \underline{u}_k$ into the continuous space (similar to (2.30)) is visualized in Figure 4.15 **(a)**. The root mean square error (rmse) both of the space-time discrete state vector $\underline{x}_k$ and the space-time discrete input vector $\underline{u}_k$ can be obtained as stated in (2.34). The results are shown in Figure 4.15 **(b)**. From these figures, it is obvious that a high number of sensor nodes is required in order to obtain a sufficiently accurate estimate of the system input $s(\cdot)$. Moreover, using a lower number of nodes causes a low convergence rate.

Identification of the input model   The direct identification of the input vector $\underline{u}_k$ results in a low convergence rate and still requires a high number of sensor nodes. This is mainly caused by the fact that the correlation between the individual components of the space-time discrete input vector is too weak, and thus local measurements have only locally restricted influence on the estimation results. The convergence rate and the accuracy can be significantly improved by making specific assumptions about the space-time continuous input $s(x, y)$ being reconstructed, i.e., imposing some restrictions. This can be achieved by exploiting additional physical background knowledge in terms of a *input model.* This means, the space-time continuous system input $s(\underline{\eta}_k^I, x, y)$ does depend on model descriptions, and thus does depend on the so-called *input parameter vector* $\underline{\eta}_k^I$. This vector includes parameters such as intensity or location of the individual sources or leakages. In this case, the resulting augmented system model (4.1) turns out to be *nonlinear* due to the nonlinear relationship between the system state $\underline{x}_k$ and the parameter being identified. In a similar way to the SRI-method and the SRL-method, the linear substructure is exploited using the SGMF; see Chapter 3.

The mathematical model of the space-time discrete input vector $\underline{u}_k$ that is parameterized by the vector $\underline{\eta}_k^I$ being estimated can be obtained by a spatial decomposition of the space-time continuous input $s(\underline{\eta}_k^I, x, y)$; see Section 2.3.3. This results in a system input according to

$$\underline{u}_k\left(\underline{\eta}_k^I\right) = \Delta t\, \mathbf{M}_G^{-1}\, \underline{\widetilde{s}}\left(\underline{\eta}_k^I, t\right) \ ,$$

where $\underline{\widetilde{s}}(\cdot)$ denotes the system input being integrated over the used shape functions; see (2.10). This parameterization of the system input $\underline{u}_k(\underline{\eta}_k^I)$ can be used for the *simultaneous reconstructuction* of the state and the *localization* of spatially distributed sources and leakages.

Depending on the actual application, there are various mathematical models that can be used for describing the dynamic and distributed properties of the system input. For example, for modelling point-wise sources Dirac functions could be used and in the case of spatially distributed sources continuous functions are required, such as exponential functions. Moreover, the spatially distributed source can be assumed to be *stationary* or *time-variant*. In the time-variant case, the dynamic behavior of the source location needs to be sufficiently described by a dynamic motion model; similar to (4.7).

Here, we assume to have given a *stationary spatially distributed source* that can be described according to (4.8) with imprecisely known location $\eta_k^I := q^{1y}$ in the y-direction. The main goal is to localize the spatially distributed source in the y-direction and simultaneously reconstruct the distributed physical system. In Figure 4.16 **(a)**, an example simulation run for the estimation of the source location derived by the SGMF (using 40 slices) is visualized. It can be clearly seen that after a certain transition time the SGMF-based source localization method offers a nearly exact estimation result. The estimation error e_T^q of the source location q^{1y} averaged over the simulation time is visualized in Figure 4.16 **(b)** for all 30 runs. The mean of the root mean square error (rmse) both of the space-time discrete state vector $\underline{x}_k$ and input vector $\underline{u}_k$ derived according to (2.34) are depicted in Figure 4.16 **(c)-(d)**. Compared to directly identifying the input vector $\underline{u}_k$, the identification based on an appropriate input model results in an higher convergence rate and in lower reconstruction errors. This is the case for both the *state reconstruction and the input reconstruction*. From these results, it is obvious that exploiting additional background knowledge about the general behavior of the source and using the SGMF-based identification approach significantly improves the state and input reconstruction.

In this simulated case study, the reconstruction of the space-time continuous system input $s(\cdot)$ was restricted to a mathematical description that is parameterized by one single parameter; here, the location in the y-direction. The extension to more parameters is conceptually straight-forward. Then, spatially distributed sources described by arbitrary functions with an arbitrary number of input model parameters can be reconstructed. Even the extension to multi-source localization is possible with the proposed methods for the *system conversion* and the efficient state/parameter estimation based on the Sliced Gaussian Mixture Filter (SGMF).

4.6 Summary and Discussion

In this chapter, the methodology for the *simultaneous state and parameter estimation* of space-time continuous physical systems was introduced. Basically, the finite-dimensional system

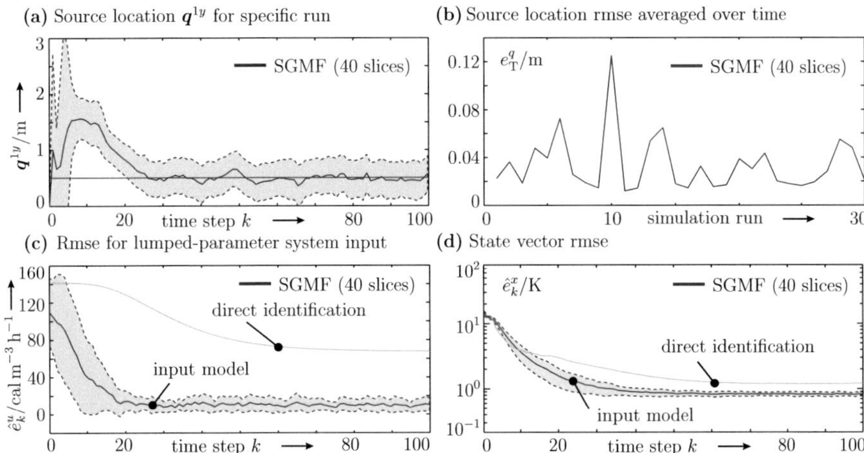

Figure 4.16: Simulation results for the **_identification of the input model_** using $N_\mathrm{S} = 40$ randomly deployed sensor nodes. **(a)** Mean/variance of the estimated source location q^{1y} for a specific simulation run. The assumed true location is assumed to be given as $q^{1y}_\mathrm{true} = 0.5\,\mathrm{m}$. **(b)** Source location rmse e^{y1}_T averaged over time for all runs. **(c)** Mean and standard deviation of the root mean square error e^u_k (rmse) of the resulting space-time discrete input vector $\underline{u}_k$, and **(d)** rmse of the estimated state vector $\underline{x}_k$.

state vector is augmented with the parameters that characterize the dynamic behavior and distributed properties both of the physical system and the measurement system. Due to the fact that the spatial decomposition and temporal discretization of space-time continuous physical systems results in a high-dimensional model, the augmentation leads to a _high-dimensional and nonlinear_ model. Based on the proposed novel estimator — _**S**liced **G**aussian **M**ixture **F**ilter_ — the linear substructure contained in the finite-dimensional model is exploited. By this means an overall more efficient parameter estimation process is obtained. The novel prospects were demonstrated in an exemplary fashion by applying the proposed methodology to the most common tasks in sensor network applications: **(a)** the identification of process parameters, **(b)** the localization of sensor nodes by locally measuring a space-time continuous physical system, and **(c)** the localization of sources and leakages. In particular, the passive localization approach — _**S**imultaneous **R**econstruction and **L**ocalization (SRL method)_ — is not restricted to sensor network applications but also offers new possibilities for indoor localization techniques. In such application scenarios, usually, the objects being localized are not able to access a global positioning system. For example, cell phones can be localized based on locally measuring the signal strength distribution transmitted by specific base stations.

CHAPTER 5

Decentralized State Reconstruction of Space-Time Continuous Systems

This chapter addresses the problem of the decentralized estimation of space-time continuous systems. The centralized approach for the state reconstruction (as introduced in Chapter 2) is not scalable for large sensor networks or physical systems that are characterized by a large state vector. All information has to be transmitted to a powerful central processing node, and thus requires an extensive amount of communication bandwidth and processing power. Hence, in order to obtain an efficient estimation process, *decentralized processing* of the information *locally* on each sensor nodes is preferred. The main challenge is that the decentralized approach leads to stochastic dependencies between the individual estimates that may either be too expensive to maintain or are simply not available for several reasons. Unfortunately, these dependencies in terms of *joint probability density function* are required for fusing local estimates. As a consequence, the density that describes the joint statistics of all estimates in the network needs to be reconstructed or an appropriate so-called bounding density needs to be derived. In this chapter, methods are introduced that allow the *decentralized estimation* of space-time continuous systems while systematically considering the imprecisely known dependencies.

In the case of *Gaussian probability density functions*, stochastic dependencies can be uniquely described by the *classical correlation coefficient*. For decentralized estimation, this correlation coefficient between the considered estimates is often assumed to be completely unknown, although prior knowledge in terms of constraints may be available. The constraints can be classified into three types: (a) *completely unknown* correlation, (b) *symmetric* correlation constraints, and (c) *asymmetric* correlation constraints. Using just the natural bound of the coefficient leads to quite conservative and usually not sufficient results. The novel estimator — *Covariance Bounds Filter (CBF)* — that is introduced in this chapter allows the systematic consideration of such prior knowledge about the correlation constraints and leads to correct and consistent estimation results. This estimator is based on a *systematic separation* of the covariance matrix to be bounded into two components. The *first component* consists of a matrix with completely unknown cross-correlations, meaning the unknown coefficients may vary in the entire natural bound. The *second component* consists of matrices that need to be derived on the basis of the given correlation constraints.

Based on the Covariance Bounds Filter, a novel framework for the *decentralized state reconstruction* of space-time continuous physical systems is proposed. The decentralized approach consists of **three stages** shown in Figure 5.1 and briefly described in the following:

1. *Conversion* of the mathematical model of the physical system being reconstructed from a space-time continuous form into a discrete system in state-space form (see Section 2.3).

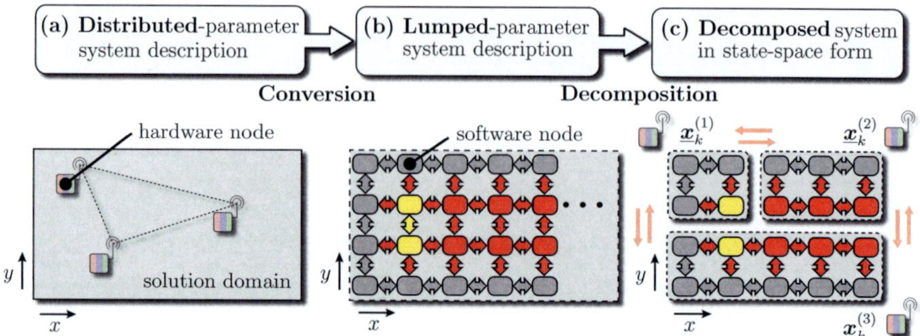

Figure 5.1: Visualization of the *three stages* toward a fully decentralized state reconstruction of *space-time continuous systems*: **(a)**⇒**(b)** Conversion of the mathematical model into a space-time discrete system in state-space form, **(b)**⇒**(c)** decomposition of the system model into subsystems, and decomposition of the probability density function for the decentralized estimation.

2. *Decomposition* of the space-time discrete system model into appropriate subsystems in order to allocate the system description to the spatially distributed sensor nodes.

3. *Decomposition* of the underlying probability density function and employment of an appropriate decentralized estimator, such as the Covariance Bounds Filter.

The methods for the decentralized reconstruction of space-time continuous systems were published at [169, 173]. However, explanations are stated in a considerably extended way and further simulation results clarify the properties of the proposed methods.

5.1   Related Work

Centralized reconstruction of space-time continuous systems   In the case of a *centralized reconstruction approach*, as introduced in Chapter 2, the nodes locally collect measurements and propagate the corresponding information through the network to a central processing node. At the central node, the information obtained from all sensor nodes are fused at once; see Figure 5.10 **(a)**. In this case, the physical system can be reconstructed by applying a standard estimator[1] to the entire global state vector and storing the associated correlations between the individual sensor nodes. However, this approach for the reconstruction requires a powerful central processing node, and an extensive amount of communication bandwidth. For practical applications, a decentralized approach for the reconstruction is more efficient, which implies that the individual substate vectors are maniuplated separately at each reconstruction step.

Decentralized reconstruction approaches   For the *decentralized reconstruction* of space-time continuous physical systems, the individual sensor nodes solely rely on their local measurements. Hence, the reconstruction process occurs locally on the sensor nodes without a central processing node. There are *two types of sources of unknown correlations* in sensor network applications. The *first* type is inherent to the system and caused by partially stochastic dependent noise sources for different sensor nodes. In other words, there are usually additional external disturbances affecting more than one sensor. Even for ideal sensor properties, this already would lead

---

1   It is refered to Section 2.5 and Section 3.4 for the *linear* and *nonlinear case*, respectively.

to a partially stochastic correlation between the measured states. The decentralized estimation process itself causes a *second* source of imprecisely known correlation. The physical quantity is measured and processed only locally. Then, the individual sensor nodes exchange their local estimates in order to improve their estimate. In this case, the estimation results become automatically stochastically correlated after the first fusion of individual estimates. Applying the Kalman filter for decentralized problems while ignoring the existing dependencies between the individual states leads to overoptimistic, even wrong estimation results. The imprecisely known correlations need to be systematically considered during the reconstruction in order to get correct and consistent estimation results.

Decentralized Kalman filtering One possibility would be based on a *fully-connected topology*, where every node transmits local information to *all* other nodes in the network and a centralized reconstruction is performed on each node [102]. In such cases, the communication and computational load is high and compared to the centralized approach no significant reduction is achieved. For that reason, in most cases, it is more beneficial when individual sensor nodes exploit only local estimates and estimates of their corresponding *adjacent neighbors* without storing any information about the correlations, as visualized in Figure 5.10 **(b)**.

Channel Filter The *channel filter* [141] exploits the fact that the mutual information between any nodes can be uniquely calculated in the case of a *tree-connected topology*. Only in such cases does a single path exist between any pair of sensor nodes in the network. Based on this, the information that is common between *all the nodes* is maintained, and thus can be removed in the processing of the estimates. However, there are several limitations with this approach. The channel filter cannot be applied to arbitrary connection topology, e.g., network topology containing cycles. This is the main justification for the following robust estimators that can be applied to *any network topology*. In addition, for non-Gaussian densities there exists no closed form solution, and thus computational expensive numerical methods are required [105, 106].

Covariance Intersection and its generalization The main challenge for a *fully decentralized reconstruction* (in terms of a Bayesian approach) is that due to the process itself, imprecisely known correlations between the states are caused, i.e., their joint statistics are simply not available. In that case, classical filtering techniques like the Kalman filter conveniently assume uncorrelated joint densities leading automatically to unjustified improvements of estimation results. For coping with this problem, estimators based on *Covariance Intersection* [29, 32, 30, 73, 140] were derived. The key idea of this estimator that is robust against imprecisely known correlations is certainly not new; it was already published in a more general context of robust estimation of uncertain dynamic systems [130]. The objective is to derive a *consistent estimate*[1] when the respective random variables are linearly combined. The fusion result depends on a parameter that has to be optimized in order to derive a tight bound. Typically, the objective function for this optimization is chosen to be the determinant or trace of the resulting covariance matrix. A closed form solution exists for the trace as the objective function [103]. This estimator has found wide applications in localization and navigation [7, 13, 153] and in particular in simultaneous localization and mapping applications [26, 75, 140]. The equivalence to the log-linear combination of two Gaussian density functions, and thus its relationship to the Chernoff information is shown in [66]. Given this relationship and using exponential mixture densities, a generalization to any probability density functions may be possible [71, 70]. However, the only justification of the generalization on the basis of the Chernoff information to arbitrary density functions would be the observations stated in [66].

---

1 The term *consistent estimate* here means an upper bound in the positive definite sense.

Covariance Bounds Filter (CBF)   More general set-based approaches for robust estimation can be systematically derived based on so-called *Covariance Bounds* [54, 55, 53]. It is noted that the proof of consistent estimation results of all the aforementioned Covariance Intersection algorithms is restricted to the measurement step, i.e., fusion of random variables. Whereas the method based on Covariance Bounds allow to cope with unknown correlations, both for the *measurement step* and the *prediction step*, as well as allow the consideration of *uncertainties in the model*. In addition, the systematic approach allows to find bounding densities even with constrained correlations, as introduced within this research work (see Section 5.4). The applicability to simultaneous localization and mapping, and a demonstration of its improved performance compared to the Covariance Intersection is demonstrated in [57].

Distributed optimization problem   Besides aforementioned Bayesian estimation approaches, there are other methods tackling the problem of the decentralized estimation of space-time continuous systems. In [17, 113], the problem of decentralized parameter identification is stated as a distributed optimization problem minimizing a certain cost function of interest. Although these algorithms are distributed, they do not provide a recursive characteristic, and thus require an extensive amount of data. The algorithm introduced in [96] is both decentralized and recursive. However, it addresses only the estimation of stationary physical systems.

5.2   Conversion and Decomposition of the System Description

Conversion of space-time continuous system   The estimation of space-time continuous systems based on a mathematical model in distributed-parameter form is quite complex. Hence, in order to cope with this problem, the system model needs to be converted from the distributed-parameter form into a lumped-parameter form; see Section 2.3. It was shown that based on these methods, the solution domain Ω can be spatially decomposed resulting in a *global state vector* $\underline{x}_k$ that characterizes the state of the physical system. The individual entries $\underline{x}_k^i$ can be regarded as so-called *software nodes*, since they are only necessary for describing the system in a finite-dimensional state space. Here, it is noted that for any numerical method for solving partial differential equations (see Section 2.3), the resulting state vector $\underline{x}_k$ can always be rearranged and separated so that the state at a certain node i can be derived by considering their respective adjacent nodes only. This means, the propagation of *local* estimates over space and time can be conveniently described by a lattice structure as shown in Figure 5.2 **(b)**.

Throughout this chapter, the following system is considered in order to show the key idea and novelties of the proposed decentralized estimation process for spatially distributed systems.

Example 5.1: Considered space-time continuous physical system
In general, the methods introduced in this chapter can be applied to convection-diffusion equations (2.1) and to general linear partial differential equations (1.2). For simplicity reasons, we restrict our attention to the following one-dimensional diffusion equation,

$$\mathbb{L}(\boldsymbol{p}(r,t)) = \frac{\partial \boldsymbol{p}(r,t)}{\partial t} - \alpha(r,t)\frac{\partial^2 \boldsymbol{p}(r,t)}{\partial r^2} - \boldsymbol{s}(r,t) = 0 \; , \tag{5.1}$$

where the diffusion coefficient $\alpha(r,t)$ could be both time and space varying; compare (2.1). The simplest method for the system conversion is the finite-difference method. In order to solve the partial differential equation (5.1), the derivatives are approximated according to

$$\frac{\partial \boldsymbol{p}(r,t)}{\partial t} \approx \frac{\boldsymbol{p}_{k+1}^i - \boldsymbol{p}_k^i}{\Delta t} \; , \qquad \frac{\partial^2 \boldsymbol{p}(r,t)}{\partial r^2} \approx \frac{\boldsymbol{p}_k^{i+1} - 2\boldsymbol{p}_k^i + \boldsymbol{p}_k^{i-1}}{\Delta h^2} \; , \tag{5.2}$$

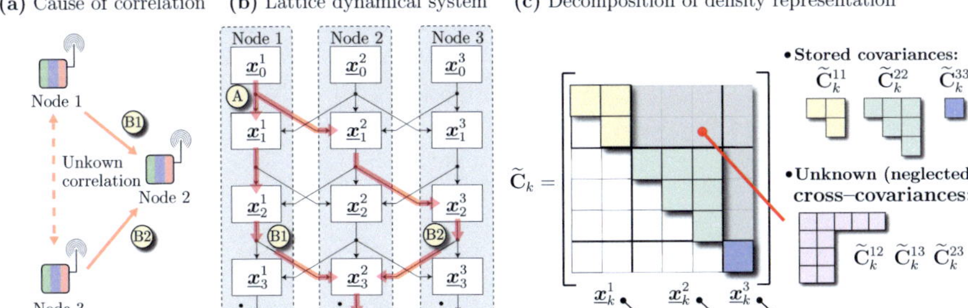

Figure 5.2: **(a)** Each sensor locally collects measurements and propagates *local estimates* to adjacent nodes. In a *fully decentralized* propagation through the network, the correlations between the individual estimates are not stored. **(b)** Lattice dynamical system for visualizing the decentralized reconstruction process and for describing the cause of unknown correlations, e.g., information from Node 1 at point **A** is counted twice at **B1** and **B2**. **(c)** *Decomposition* of the *probability density function*. The covariance matrix $\widetilde{\mathbf{C}}_k$ is decomposed in the same way as the system decomposition, where covariances $\widetilde{C}_k^{ii}$ are stored and the cross-covariances $\widetilde{C}_k^{ij}$ with $i \neq j$ are neglected.

where Δt is the sampling time and Δh the spatial sampling period. The superscript i and the subscript k in p_k^i denote the value of the physical system at discretization node i and at time step k. The diffusion coefficient is assumed to be space-time variant, and the individual coefficients α_k^i at locations i are collected in the vector $\underline{\alpha}_k = \left[\alpha_k^1, \ldots, \alpha_k^{N_x}\right]^{\mathrm{T}}$. Then, the conversion results in the following system matrix $\mathbf{A}_k \in \mathbb{R}^{N_x \times N_x}$

$$\mathbf{A}_k = \frac{\Delta t}{\Delta h^2} \begin{bmatrix} -2\alpha_k^1 & 1 & 0 & \cdots & & 0 \\ 1 & -2\alpha_k^2 & 1 & \cdots & & 0 \\ \vdots & \ddots & \ddots & \ddots & & \vdots \\ 0 & \cdots & 1 & -2\alpha_k^{N_x-1} & 1 \\ 0 & \cdots & & 0 & 1 & -2\alpha_k^{N_x} \end{bmatrix} + \mathbf{I} , \tag{5.3}$$

where $\mathbf{I} \in \mathbb{R}^{N_x \times N_x}$ represents the identity matrix. The state of the physical system is characterized by the *global state vector* $\underline{x}_k = \left[p_k^1, \ldots, p_k^{N_x}\right]^{\mathrm{T}}$. For the conversion of the entire space-time continuous system, the input function $s(r, t)$ needs to be discretized in the same way as the system state. This leads to the input vector $\underline{u}_k = \left[s_k^1, \ldots, s_k^{N_x}\right]^{\mathrm{T}}$. The input matrix $\mathbf{B}_k$ that relates the system input $\underline{u}_k$ to the corresponding state vector $\underline{x}_k$ is given by a diagonal matrix with the sampling time Δt as diagonal entries, according to $\mathbf{B}_k = \mathrm{diag}\left\{\Delta t, \ldots, \Delta t\right\}$. ∎

Decomposition of resulting space-time discrete system (linear case) For physical systems that are spatially distributed over a large area, the dimension of the *global state vector* $\underline{x}_k$ may become very large. In the case of a *centralized estimation approach*, the entire state vector needs to be communicated and processed at once, and thus yields high communication costs and high computational load. As a first step toward a *decentralized estimation* approach, a *decomposition* of the space-time discrete system into appropriate *subsystems* is of major significance. Basically, the *software nodes* that are obtained from the conversion process are allocated to respective *hardware nodes* (depending on their location), i.e., the system description is mapped to the sensor network. For the system decomposition, the *global state vector* $\underline{x}_k$ is decomposed

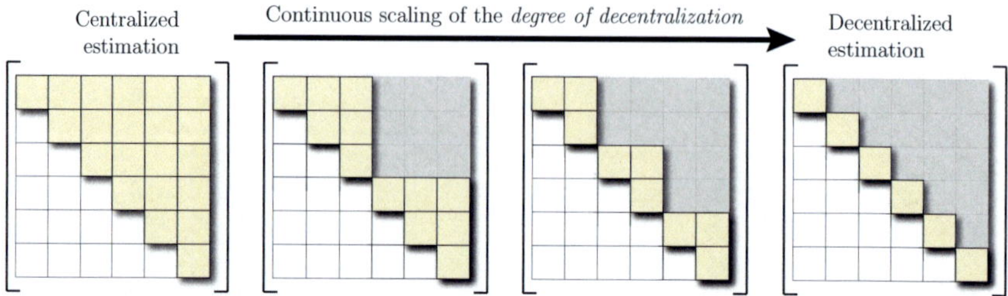

Figure 5.3: The decomposition of the system model and the underlying probability density function allows the continuous scaling between the *centralized approach* and the *decentralized approach*. By this means, additional knowledge about the correlation structure within the network can be exploited. The structure of the decomposed covariance matrix $\tilde{\mathbf{C}}_k$ strongly depends on the actual application.

into appropriate *substate vectors* $\underline{x}_k^i$, according to

$$\underline{x}_k = \left[\left(\underline{x}_k^1\right)^{\mathrm{T}}, \ldots, \left(\underline{x}_k^i\right)^{\mathrm{T}}, \ldots, \left(\underline{x}_k^{N_C}\right)^{\mathrm{T}} \right]^{\mathrm{T}} ,$$

where the individual substate vectors $\underline{x}_k^i$ may be allocated to appropriate hardware nodes. The variable N_C denotes the number of substate vectors. The decomposition of the state vector and the allocation to sensor nodes is depicted in Figure 5.1 **(c)**.

Based on the decomposition of the state vector, the mathematical system model needs to be decomposed into appropriate *subsystems*. In the case of *linear system/measurement models* (i.e., reconstruction of linear partial differential equations) the i-th substate vector $\underline{x}_k^i$ and the i-th measurement vector $\hat{\underline{y}}_k^i$ are stated as follows,

$$\underline{x}_{k+1}^i = \sum_{j=1}^{N_C} \mathbf{A}_k^{ij}\, \underline{x}_k^j + \sum_{j=1}^{N_C} \mathbf{B}_k^{ij} \left(\hat{\underline{u}}_k^j + \underline{w}_k^j\right) , \qquad \hat{\underline{y}}_k^i = \sum_{j=1}^{N_C} \mathbf{H}_k^{ij}\, \underline{x}_k^j + \underline{v}_k^i , \tag{5.4}$$

where $\mathbf{A}_k^{ij}$, $\mathbf{B}_k^{ij}$ and $\mathbf{H}_k^{ij}$ are the respective submatrices of the global matrices $\mathbf{A}_k$, $\mathbf{B}_k$ and $\mathbf{H}_k$. It is important to emphasize that generally, the decomposition of the space-time discrete system model into the decomposed system model (5.4) is achieved in an exact fashion, i.e., no approximation is required. However, for certain applications it might be more beneficial to ignore negligible subsystems in (5.4), for instance when certain submatrices $\mathbf{A}_k^{ij}$ are (close to) zero. This certainly could lead to a more efficient estimation process. The decomposition of *nonlinear system models*[1] is conceptually straightforward.

In the *deterministic case*, i.e., the uncertainties in the models and in the measurements are not considered, the decomposed system description (5.4) can be directly used for reconstructing the space-time continuous system in a decentralized fashion. Hence, the propagation of the system state can be exactly derived. In the *stochastic case*, an additional decomposition of the *underlying probability density function* is necessary in order to arrive at a fully decentralized approach. This decomposition is explained in the following section.

---

[1] This would be required for the parameter identification of space-time continuous systems in a decentralized fashion.

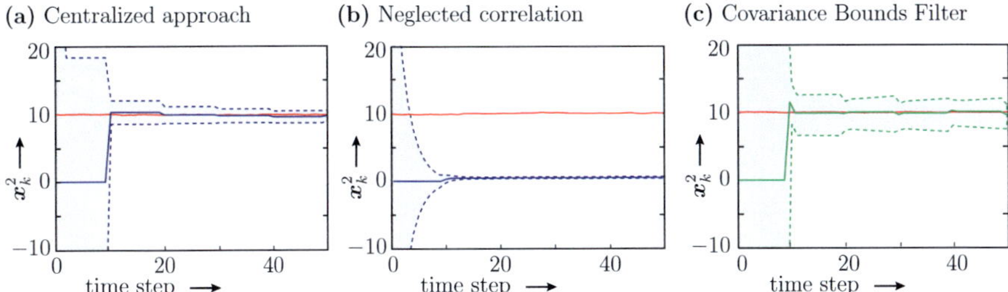

Figure 5.4: Visualization of the effect of neglecting unknown correlations during the propagation of information through the network: **(a)** centralized Kalman filter, **(b)** decentralized Kalman filter with neglecting correlations, and **(c)** Covariance Bounds Filter (CBF).

5.3 Decomposition of Probability Density Functions

This section is devoted to the systematic decomposition of probability density functions. In order to derive a fully decentralized estimation process, the density function has to be decomposed in such a way that it matches the decomposed system equations (5.4). In the *centralized approach*, all information about the space-time continuous system and the measurements has to be collected and processed at a central processing node. In the case of a *decentralized estimation*, the individual substate vectors $\underline{x}_k^i$ are manipulated separately at each processing step, instead of the entire global vector at once. By this means, it is possible to perform the state estimation process locally on each hardware node. Moreover, only local estimates need to be communicated between adjacent nodes, which dramatically reduces communication load. Before the decentralized state reconstruction is derived, the underlying probability density function is required to be decomposed. This is described in more detail in the remainder of this section, both for the (a) Gaussian and (b) non-Gaussian case.

(a) Gaussian density case For a fully decentralized reconstruction of space-time continuous physical systems, it is beneficial not to store the occurring correlations between the individual estimates. In the case of Gaussian probability density functions, the cross-covariances $\widetilde{\mathbf{C}}_k^{ij}$ between the substate vectors $\underline{x}_k^i$ and $\underline{x}_k^j$ with $i \neq j$ are not stored within the sensor network. Hence, their covariance matrix is characterized by

$$\widetilde{\mathbf{C}}_k = \mathrm{Cov}\left\{\underline{x}_k^i, \underline{x}_k^j\right\} = \begin{cases} \widetilde{\mathbf{C}}_k^{ij} & \text{for } i = j \\ \text{unknown} & \text{for } i \neq j \end{cases}. \tag{5.5}$$

This certainly reduces the computational burden, memory resources, and communication activities between the individual nodes to a minimum. The structure of the covariance matrix $\widetilde{\mathbf{C}}_k$ of the entire network is depicted in Figure 5.2 **(c)**.

It is noted that the entire covariance matrix $\widetilde{\mathbf{C}}_k$ is usually decomposed so that prior information about the correlation is sufficiently considered, i.e., collected in the submatrices $\widetilde{\mathbf{C}}_k^{ij}$. This means, the decomposition of the system into subsystems and the underlying probability density function allows a continuous scaling between the *centralized approach* and the *decentralized approach*. The structure of the covariance matrix for different *degrees of decentralization* that has to be chosen depending on the application is shown in Figure 5.3.

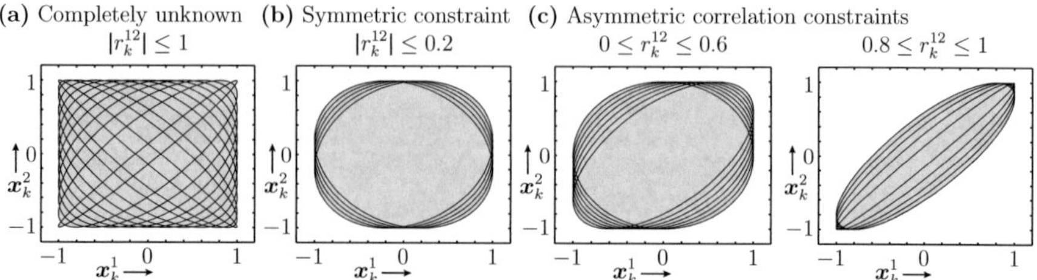

(a) Completely unknown $|r_k^{12}| \leq 1$ **(b)** Symmetric constraint $|r_k^{12}| \leq 0.2$ **(c)** Asymmetric correlation constraints $0 \leq r_k^{12} \leq 0.6$ $0.8 \leq r_k^{12} \leq 1$

Figure 5.5: Union of the ellipses corresponding to the joint covariances of two scalar random variables x_k^1 and x_k^2 with imprecisely known correlation. **(a)** Completely unknown correlation, **(b)** Symmetric correlation constraints, and **(c)** asymmetric constraints for correlation coefficient r.

Example 5.2: Comparison of different reconstruction approaches

The following example is considered to visualize the effect of neglecting unknown correlations during the decentralized reconstruction of a space-time continuous system. The system description (5.1) is converted into state-space form consisting of only *three nodes* for illustration purposes. The boundary conditions are assumed to be $g_N = 0$ at both ends. Applying the finite differences (5.2) and considering the boundary conditions leads to a system matrix $\mathbf{A}_k$ with a structure that is similar to (5.3). The initial state vector is assumed to be $\hat{\underline{x}}_k = [0, 0, 0]^{\mathrm{T}}$ and the true state to be $\widetilde{\underline{x}}_k = [10, 10, 10]^{\mathrm{T}}$. The estimated state vector $\underline{x}_k^e$ can be propagated through the system equation to the next time step by means of the Kalman prediction step,

$$\hat{\underline{x}}_{k+1} = \mathbf{A}_k \hat{\underline{x}}_k^e \, , \qquad \mathbf{C}_{k+1}^p = \mathbf{A}_k \mathbf{C}_k^e \mathbf{A}_k^{\mathrm{T}} \, , \qquad \text{with} \qquad \mathbf{A}_k = \frac{\Delta t}{\Delta h^2} \begin{bmatrix} -2\alpha_k^1 & 2 & 0 \\ 1 & -2\alpha_k^2 & 1 \\ 0 & 2 & -2\alpha_k^3 \end{bmatrix}$$

where $\hat{\underline{x}}_{k+1}^p$ and $\mathbf{C}_{k+1}^p$ denote the predicted mean and covariance matrix, respectively. Furthermore, it is assumed that at time steps $k \in \{10, 20, 30, 40, 50\}$ a Kalman filter step is performed.

The simulation results are shown in Figure 5.4. In the case of *centralized estimation*, the entire covariance matrix $\mathbf{C}_k^e$ is stored and considered in the reconstruction process. Hence, the resulting estimates can be regarded as a reference solution; shown in Figure 5.4 **(a)**. In the *decentralized approach*, the cross-covariances $\mathbf{C}_k^{ij}$ with $i \neq j$ are not stored, and thus cannot be considered in the prediction step. Simply assuming the individual states $\underline{x}_k^i$ to be uncorrelated leads to over-optimistic results, as shown in Figure 5.4 **(b)**. It is obvious that due to the *unjustified improvement* of the variances, the filter step at $k = 10$ has almost no influence. In comparison, robust estimators based on covariance bounds (introduced in Section 5.4) *systematically* consider the unknown correlations, and thus provide a consistent and conservative result, see Figure 5.4 **(c)**. ∎

(b) Non-Gaussian density case In the case of non-Gaussian density functions, the joint densities $f^e(\underline{x}_k^i, \underline{x}_k^j)$ are not stored in the network, instead only the marginal densities $f^e(\underline{x}_k^i)$ are stored on the individual sensor nodes. However, for the processing of the individual estimates, the joint statistics is required to be known. Hence, the reconstruction of the joint density and the derivation of so-called bounding densities are necessary. In Chapter 6, the reconstruction of possible joint densities $f^e(\underline{x}_k^i, \underline{x}_k^j)$ based on given marginal densities $f^e(\underline{x}_k^i)$ is introduced. These so-called *parameterized joint densities* lay the foundation for a decentralized estimation process for non-Gaussian density functions.

5.4 The Covariance Bounds Filter (CBF)

In this section, the mathematical constructs for deriving consistent filters that are able to cope with imprecisely known correlations are derived. In many research works dealing with decentralized estimation, it is usually assumed that the correlations between the considered random vectors are unconstrained and completely unknown, i.e., the maximum absolute correlation coefficient is less than or equal to one (i.e., $r \in [-1, 1]$) [53, 75]. Using just the natural bound of the correlation coefficient would lead to quite conservative and usually not sufficient estimation results. For many real world scenarios, additional knowledge about the correlation coefficient can be exploited to find tighter bounds [55]. In general, it is possible to distinguish three types of uncertain correlations with increasing complexity:

1. *Completely unknown correlation:* Here, no additional knowledge is available, and thus the correlation coefficient can be constrained only by the natural bound $r_k^{12} \in [-1, 1]$. The following condition is obtained

$$\mathbf{C}_k^{12} \left(\mathbf{C}_k^{11}\right)^{-1} \mathbf{C}_k^{21} \leq \mathbf{C}_k^{22} \; . \tag{5.6}$$

All the off-diagonal matrices $\mathbf{C}_k^{12}$ that satisfy this relation are valid in the case of completely unknown correlation. The union of all valid joint covariance matrices is aligned with the coördinate axes and leads to a hyper-square, as it can be seen in Figure 5.5 **(a)**.

2. *Symmetric correlation constraints:* In many cases, the correlation coefficient can be constrained by a symmetric bound $|r_k^{12}| \leq r_{max}^{12} \leq 1$. For a given maximum correlation level r_{max}^{12} between two random vectors, valid cross covariance matrices are given by

$$\mathbf{C}_k^{12} \left(\mathbf{C}_k^{11}\right)^{-1} \mathbf{C}_k^{21} \leq r_{\max}^{12} \mathbf{C}_k^{22} \; . \tag{5.7}$$

The union of all valid joint covariances that satisfy the relation (5.7) is axes-aligned; visualized in Figure 5.5 **(b)** for the scalar case.

3. *Asymmetric correlation constraints:* In the most general case, the correlation coefficient is constrained according to $-1 \leq r_{min}^{12} \leq r_k^{12} \leq r_{max}^{12} \leq 1$. The asymmetric case is more difficult to cope with since the resulting set corresponding to all valid joint covariances is not axis aligned anymore; see Figure 5.5 **(c)** for the scalar case.

5.4.1 Completely Unknown Correlation

Before the most general case of correlation constraints is considered, the covariance bounds for completely unknown correlations are discussed. Here, we assume to have given N_C *random vectors* with expected values and individual covariances

$$\mathrm{E}\left\{\underline{x}_k^i\right\} = \hat{\underline{x}}_k^i \; , \qquad \mathrm{Cov}\left\{\underline{x}_k^i\right\} = \widetilde{\mathbf{C}}_k^{ii} \; ,$$

where the estimates $\underline{x}_k^i$ are correlated with *completely unknown correlations*. For the reconstruction of space-time continuous systems, the individual state vectors $\underline{x}_k^i$ contain the *local estimates* of the physical system being reconstructed, e.g., local temperature or humidity values. The main goal is to find a set of bounding covariance matrices $\mathbf{C}_k^{\mathrm{B}}$ so that

$$\mathbf{C}_k^{\mathrm{B}} \geq \widetilde{\mathbf{C}}_k \; ,$$

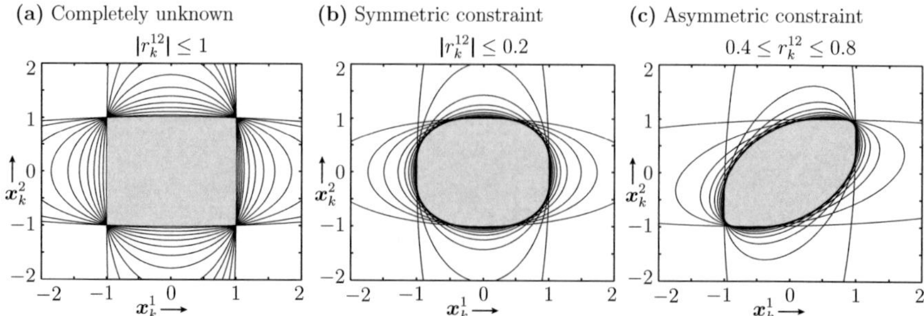

Figure 5.6: Visualization of covariance bounds for different correlation constraints, (a) completely unknown correlation, (b) symmetrically constrained correlation, and (c) asymmetrically constrained correlation.

for all valid joint covariances $\widetilde{\mathbf{C}}_k$. Similar to the proof stated in [55, 130], it can be shown that given a positive definite symmetric matrix $\widetilde{\mathbf{C}}_k$ with completely unknown correlations (5.5), a "larger" matrix, the so-called *covariance bound* can be parameterized by

$$\mathbf{C}_k^{\mathrm{B}}(\underline{\kappa}_k) = \mathrm{diag}\left\{ \frac{1}{\kappa_k^1}\widetilde{\mathbf{C}}_k^{11} , \ \ldots \ , \ \frac{1}{\kappa_k^{N_C}}\widetilde{\mathbf{C}}_k^{N_C N_C} \right\} , \qquad \text{with } 0 < \kappa_k^i < 1 , \quad \sum_{i=1}^{N_C} \kappa_k^i = 1 . \quad (5.8)$$

The individual parameters κ_k^i are collected in the vector $\underline{\kappa}_k$. Similar parameterizations of the bounds can be found in the case of constrained correlations, i.e., *symmetric constraints* or *asymmetric constraints*; see Section 5.4.2.

Example 5.3: Two random variables

In this example, the covariance bounds (5.8) are visualized for the special case of two random variables. The covariances are assumed to be given as $\widetilde{C}_k^{11} = \widetilde{C}_k^{22} = 1$. The set of all valid covariance matrices $\widetilde{\mathbf{C}}_k$ are parameterized by $r_k^{12} \in [-1, 1]$, and their corresponding covariance bounds $\mathbf{C}_k^{\mathrm{B}}$ are parameterized by $\kappa_k \in (0, 1)$ as follows

$$\widetilde{\mathbf{C}}_k = \begin{bmatrix} \widetilde{C}_k^{11} & r_k^{12}\sqrt{\widetilde{C}_k^{11}\widetilde{C}_k^{22}} \\ r_k^{12}\sqrt{\widetilde{C}_k^{11}\widetilde{C}_k^{22}} & \widetilde{C}_k^{22} \end{bmatrix} , \qquad \mathbf{C}_k^{\mathrm{B}}(\kappa_k) = \begin{bmatrix} \frac{1}{\kappa_k}\widetilde{C}_k^{11} & 0 \\ 0 & \frac{1}{1-\kappa_k}\widetilde{C}_k^{22} \end{bmatrix} .$$

The ellipses of valid covariance matrices are depicted for some r_k^{12} in Figure 5.5 **(a)**. The covariance matrix $\mathbf{C}_k^{\mathrm{B}}$ that bounds the union of all valid matrices can be derived using (5.8) with $\kappa_k^1 := \kappa_k$ and $\kappa_k^2 := 1 - \kappa_k$. Ellipsoids of the covariance bounds are visualized for some κ_k in Figure 5.6 **(a)**. ■

5.4.2   Arbitrary Correlation Constraints

This section is devoted to the generalization of the covariance bounds to the case of N_C *random vectors* with unknown but *arbitrarily constrained correlation*. The covariance bounds for symmetric correlation constraints is introduced in [55]; however, the proposed method is restricted to only *two random vectors*. The method proposed in this research work allows the derivation of covariance bounds for N_C *random vectors* with *arbitrary correlation constraints*.

The key idea is a systematic *separation* of the covariance matrix $\widetilde{\mathbf{C}}_k$ to be bounded into *two components*. The *first component* consists of a matrix with completely unknown cross-correlations, which means the unknown coefficients vary in the entire natural bound, i.e., $r_k^{ij} \in [-1, 1]$. The *second component* consists of matrices that are derived on the basis of the individual covariance matrices and the given cross-correlation constraints of the matrix being bounded. To be more specific, the matrix $\widetilde{\mathbf{C}}_k$ can be represented as follows

$$\widetilde{\mathbf{C}}_k = \mathbf{U}_k + \sum_{i=1}^{N_K} \mathbf{K}_k^i \, , \tag{5.9}$$

where $\mathbf{U}_k$ denotes the matrix with completely unknown cross-correlation and $\mathbf{K}_k^i$ are matrices that need to be derived depending on the given correlation constraints, i.e., symmetric or asymmetric constraints.

Based on the aforementioned separation principle, the covariance bounds can be obtained by employing the parameterization introduced in the pevious section. This means, the matrix $\mathbf{U}_k$ is bounded by $\mathbf{C}_k^{\mathrm{B}}$ according to (5.8). This leads to following general structure of the *covariance bounds for arbitrarily constrained correlations*

$$\mathbf{E}_k^{\mathrm{B}}(\underline{\kappa}_k) = \mathbf{C}_k^{\mathrm{B}}(\underline{\kappa}_k) + \sum_{i=1}^{N_K} \mathbf{K}_k^i \, , \qquad \text{with} \qquad \mathbf{C}_k^{\mathrm{B}} \geq \mathbf{U}_k \, .$$

Here, it is important to note that the individual matrices $\mathbf{K}_k^i$ do not necessarily need to represent covariance matrices, and thus are not required to be positive definite. However, the sum of the matrices $\mathbf{K}_k^i$ need to be positive definite in order to ensure that $\mathbf{E}_k^{\mathrm{B}}$ is "larger" than $\widetilde{\mathbf{C}}_k$.

Covariance bounds for symmetrically constrained correlation In this section, the covariance bounds $\mathbf{E}_k^{\mathrm{B}}$ are derived that bound a covariance matrix $\widetilde{\mathbf{C}}_k$ with correlations that are *symmetrically constrained*. As introduced in the previous section, this can be achieved by finding a proper representation of the matrices $\mathbf{U}_k$ and $\mathbf{S}_k := \mathbf{K}_k^1$ parameterized by given values of the constraints. The following parameterization is proposed

$$\mathbf{U}_k^{ij} = \begin{cases} \beta_k^i \, \widetilde{\mathbf{C}}_k^{ij} & \text{for } i = j \\ \widetilde{\mathbf{C}}_k^{ij} & \text{for } i \neq j \end{cases} , \qquad \mathbf{S}_k^{ij} = \begin{cases} (1 - \beta_k^i) \, \widetilde{\mathbf{C}}_k^{ij} & \text{for } i = j \\ 0 & \text{for } i \neq j \end{cases} , \tag{5.10}$$

where the parameters β_k^i need to be derived in the interval $\beta_k^i \in [0, 1]$ depending on the correlation constraints. This parameter can be regarded as a coefficient scaling between the entries in the unknown covariance matrix $\mathbf{U}_k$ and in the matrix $\mathbf{S}_k$. Roughly speaking, the parameters β_k^i are responsible for transfering the knowledge about the correlation constraints into the known matrix $\mathbf{S}_k$, so that the correlations in the matrix $\mathbf{U}_k$ can be assumed to be *completely unknown*, i.e., vary in the entire interval $r \in [-1, 1]$.

In the following, it is shown how the individual parameters β_k^i has to be chosen depending on given values of the correlation constraints. For keeping the notation simple only two entries of the matrix $\widetilde{\mathbf{C}}_k$ to be bounded are considered. With respect to the proposed matrix separation (5.9) and its actual parameterization (5.10), the matrix $\widetilde{\mathbf{C}}_k$ can be separated according to

$$\begin{aligned}
\begin{bmatrix} \widetilde{\mathbf{C}}_k^{ii} & \widetilde{\mathbf{C}}_k^{ij} \\ \widetilde{\mathbf{C}}_k^{ji} & \widetilde{\mathbf{C}}_k^{jj} \end{bmatrix} &= \begin{bmatrix} \mathbf{U}_k^{ii} & \mathbf{U}_k^{ij} \\ \mathbf{U}_k^{ji} & \mathbf{U}_k^{jj} \end{bmatrix} + \begin{bmatrix} \mathbf{S}_k^{ii} & \mathbf{S}_k^{ij} \\ \mathbf{S}_k^{ji} & \mathbf{S}_k^{jj} \end{bmatrix} \\
&= \begin{bmatrix} \beta_k^i \, \widetilde{\mathbf{C}}_k^{ii} & \mathbf{U}_k^{ij} \\ \mathbf{U}_k^{ji} & \beta_k^j \, \widetilde{\mathbf{C}}_k^{jj} \end{bmatrix} + \begin{bmatrix} (1 - \beta_k^i) \, \widetilde{\mathbf{C}}_k^{ii} & \mathbf{0} \\ \mathbf{0} & (1 - \beta_k^j) \, \widetilde{\mathbf{C}}_k^{jj} \end{bmatrix} \, .
\end{aligned} \tag{5.11}$$

The aim is to derive the coefficients β_k^i in such way that the correlation in the matrix $\mathbf{U}_k$ is completely unknown, in other words the information about the constraints is moved into the matrix $\mathbf{S}_k$. This means, valid cross covariance matrices in $\mathbf{U}_k$ are characterized by

$$\mathbf{U}_k^{ij} \left(\mathbf{U}_k^{ii}\right)^{-1} \mathbf{U}_k^{ji} \leq \mathbf{U}_k^{jj} \, ,$$

which means that the correlation are completely unknown. Using the parameterization proposed in (5.10) in terms of the parameter β_k^i eventually yields

$$\widetilde{\mathbf{C}}_k^{ij} \left(\widetilde{\mathbf{C}}_k^{ii}\right)^{-1} \widetilde{\mathbf{C}}_k^{ji} \leq \beta_k^i \beta_k^j \widetilde{\mathbf{C}}_k^{jj} \, , \qquad \text{with} \qquad \left(r_{max}^{ij}\right)^2 = \beta_k^i \beta_k^j \, , \tag{5.12}$$

where r_{max}^{ij} is the given maximum correlation level between the individual random vectors, as defined in (5.7). Hence, the parameters β_k^i need to be chosen so that (5.12) holds. In order to derive sufficient β_k^i that depend on the given maximum correlation level r_{max}^{ij}, the nonlinear system of equations needs to be solved. This is demonstrated by following two examples.

Example 5.4: Two random variables (symmetric constraints)

In this example, the proposed parameterization of the covariance bounds is applied to the case of two random vectors $\underline{x}_k^1 \in \mathbb{R}^{N_x^1}$ and $\underline{x}_k^2 \in \mathbb{R}^{N_x^1}$. Their joint density is characterized by the covariance matrix $\widetilde{\mathbf{C}}_k$ with a given maximum correlation level $r_{\max}^{12}$. By assuming $\beta_k^1 = \beta_k^2 = \beta_k$ and using the system of equations (5.12), the parameter for the matrix separation (5.11) results in $\beta_k = r_{\max}^{12}$. By using (5.8) the covariance bounds $\mathbf{E}_k^B$ can be derived as follows

$$\mathbf{E}_k^B = \begin{bmatrix} \frac{\kappa_k^1 - r_{\max}^{12}\kappa_k^1 + r_{\max}^{12}}{\kappa_k^1} \widetilde{\mathbf{C}}_k^{11} & \mathbf{0} \\ \mathbf{0} & \frac{\kappa_k^2 - r_{\max}^{12}\kappa_k^2 + r_{\max}^{12}}{\kappa_k^2} \widetilde{\mathbf{C}}_k^{22} \end{bmatrix} \, , \qquad \text{with} \qquad \kappa_k^1 + \kappa_k^2 = 1 \, ,$$

where the parameters of the covariance bounds are defined as $\kappa_k^1 = \kappa_k$ and $\kappa_k^2 = 1 - \kappa_k$. In the following, only the scalar case is shown for simplicity, i.e., covariances are given by $\widetilde{C}_k^{11} = \widetilde{C}_k^{22} = 1$. In Figure 5.5 **(b)**, the set of all valid covariance matrices are visualized for a given symmetrically constrained correlation $|r_k^{12}| \leq 0.2$. The corresponding covariance bounds $\mathbf{E}_k^B$ parameterized by κ_k are shown in Figure 5.6 **(b)**. It is obvious that in this example bounding densities can be derived that include the set of all valid densities (gray-shaded area). ∎

Special case: three random vectors In general, for deriving the parameters β_k^i that characterize the structure of the covariance bounds $\mathbf{E}_k^B$, the system of equations (5.12) needs to be solved. In the following, this is shown for the special case of three random vectors. Assuming the maximum correlation r_{max}^{ij} to be positive, the system of equations can be stated as

$$\underbrace{2 \log r_{max}^{ij}}_{=:\tilde{r}_{max}^{ij}} = \underbrace{\log \beta_k^i}_{=:\tilde{\beta}_k^i} + \underbrace{\log \beta_k^j}_{=:\tilde{\beta}_k^j} \, . \tag{5.13}$$

The individual correlation levels $\tilde{r}_{max}^{ij}$ and the parameters $\tilde{\beta}_k^j$ can be rearranged to respective vectors $\underline{\tilde{r}}_k$ and $\underline{\tilde{\beta}}_k$. By using the matrix $\mathbf{T}$ that contains zeros and ones according to (5.13) leads to following linear equations to be solved

$$\mathbf{T}\underline{\tilde{\beta}}_k = \underline{\tilde{r}}_k \, , \qquad \underline{\tilde{\beta}}_k = \mathbf{T}^{-1} \underline{\tilde{r}}_k \, . \tag{5.14}$$

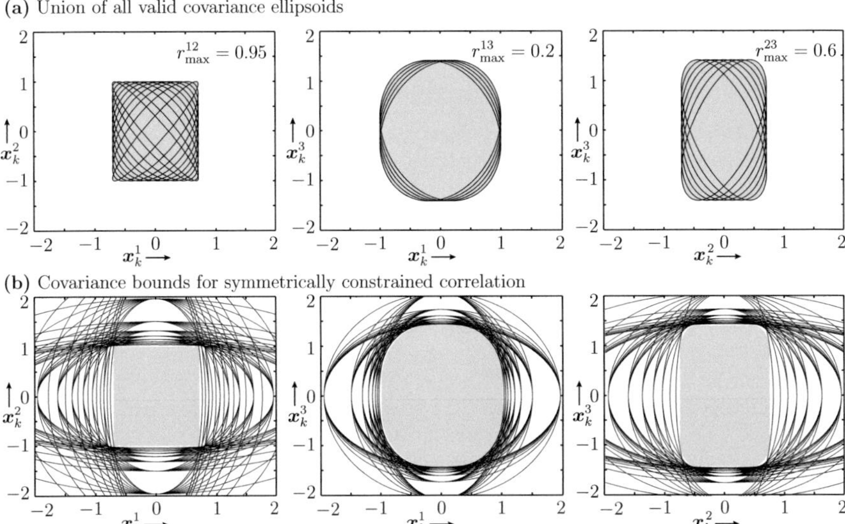

(a) Union of all valid covariance ellipsoids

(b) Covariance bounds for symmetrically constrained correlation

Figure 5.7: Visualization of covariance bounds for the case of three random scalars with symmetrically constrained correlation, i.e., $r_{\max}^{12} = 0.95$, $r^{13} = 0.2$, and $r^{23} = 0.6$. **(a)** Marginal densities of the union of all valid covariance ellipsoids. **(b)** Covariance bounds for symmetrically constrained correlation for various parameters κ_1 and κ_2.

In the case of three random vectors the matrix $\mathbf{T}$ is a square matrix, and thus this equation can be readily solved. This results in the following parameters of the known matrix $\mathbf{K}_k$

$$\beta_k^1 = \frac{r_{\max}^{12} r_{\max}^{13}}{r_{\max}^{23}} \,, \qquad \beta_k^2 = \frac{r_{\max}^{12} r_{\max}^{23}}{r_{\max}^{13}} \,, \qquad \beta_k^3 = \frac{r_{\max}^{13} r_{\max}^{23}}{r_{\max}^{12}} \,. \tag{5.15}$$

It is obvious that there exists only one solution and the result can be easily verified by the general system of equations (5.12) that must hold. The parameters β_k^1, β_k^2, and β_k^3 can be used to derive the separated covariance matrix according to (5.11). Replacing the matrix $\mathbf{U}_k$ with the covariance bounds (5.8) for completely unknown correlations, the covariance bound $\mathbf{E}_k^{\mathrm{B}}$ for symmetrically constrained correlation can be obtained. This result can be extended to N_C random vectors by replacing the inverse matrix $\mathbf{T}^{-1}$ with Moore-Penrose matrix inverse $\mathbf{T}^\dagger$.

Example 5.5: Three random variables (symmetric constraints)

This example is devoted to the visualization of the derived covariance bounds in the case of three random vectors. The parameter for the matrix separation (5.11) can be obtained using (5.15). Similar to Example 5.4, the covariance bounds $\mathbf{E}_k^{\mathrm{B}}$ can be derived by equation (5.8), and yields

$$\mathbf{E}_k^{\mathrm{B}} = \begin{bmatrix} \frac{r_{\max}^{12} r_{\max}^{13} + \kappa_k^1 (r_{\max}^{23} - r_{\max}^{12} r_{\max}^{13})}{r_{\max}^{23} \kappa_k^1} \widetilde{\mathbf{C}}_k^{11} & 0 & 0 \\ 0 & \frac{r_{\max}^{12} r_{\max}^{23} + \kappa_k^2 (r_{\max}^{13} - r_{\max}^{12} r_{\max}^{23})}{r_{\max}^{13} \kappa_k^2} \widetilde{\mathbf{C}}_k^{22} & 0 \\ 0 & 0 & \frac{r_{\max}^{13} r_{\max}^{23} + \kappa_k^3 (r_{\max}^{12} - r_{\max}^{13} r_{\max}^{23})}{r_{\max}^{12} \kappa_k^3} \widetilde{\mathbf{C}}_k^{33} \end{bmatrix} \,,$$

with $0 < \kappa_k^i < 1$ and $\kappa_k^3 := 1 - \kappa_k^1 - \kappa_k^2$. For simplicity reasons only the scalar case is depicted in this example, although the same parameterization can be used in the vector case. The following variances and correlation constraints are used

$$\text{Known variances} \qquad \widetilde{C}_k^{11} = 0.5 \ , \quad \widetilde{C}_k^{22} = 1 \ , \quad \widetilde{C}_k^{33} = 2 \ ,$$

$$\text{Correlation constraints} \qquad r_{\max}^{12} = 0.95 \ , \quad r_{\max}^{13} = 0.2 \ , \quad r_{\max}^{23} = 0.6$$

In Figure 5.7 **(a)**, the set of all valid covariance matrices are visualized for a given symmetrically constrained correlation. The corresponding covariance bounds $\mathbf{E}_k^{\mathrm{B}}$ parameterized by κ_k^1 and κ_k^2 are shown in Figure 5.7 **(b)**. It is obvious that covariance bounds can be derived that include the set of all valid matrices that satisfy the given correlation constraints. ■

Covariance bounds for asymmetrically constrained correlation In this section, the covariance bounds $\mathbf{E}_k^{\mathrm{B}}$ are derived that bound a covariance matrix $\widetilde{\mathbf{C}}_k$ with *asymmetrically constrained* cross-covariances. For simplicity, only the *scalar case* is considered, the vector case is more involved and beyond the scope of this thesis. The constraints discussed so far result in covariance bounds that are axis-aligned. In contrast, in the asymmetric case the set of all possible covariance matrices cannot be regarded as axis-aligned anymore, and thus off-diagonal entries in the covariance bounds are required.

A proper representation can be derived by finding the matrices $\mathbf{U}_k$, $\mathbf{S}_k := \mathbf{K}_k^1$, and $\mathbf{A}_k := \mathbf{K}_k^2$ in a similar way to the symmetric case. The following parameterization is proposed

$$U_k^{ij} = \begin{cases} \beta_k^i \, \widetilde{C}_k^{ij} & \text{for } i = j \\ \widetilde{C}_k^{ij} & \text{for } i \neq j \end{cases} , \quad S_k^{ij} = \begin{cases} (1 - \beta_k^i) \, \widetilde{C}_k^{ij} & \text{for } i = j \\ 0 & \text{for } i \neq j \end{cases} , \quad A_k^{ij} = \begin{cases} 0 & \text{for } i = j \\ A_k^{ij} & \text{for } i \neq j \end{cases} ,$$

$$(5.16)$$

where the parameters β_k^i and the off-diagonal entries A_k^{ij} in the matrix $\mathbf{A}_k$ need to be derived depending on the given constrained correlations. It is obvious that the entries in $\mathbf{A}_k$ can be regarded as coefficients that characterize the alignment arising from the *asymmetric constraints* of the covariance matrix. Once this alignment is found, the parameters β_k^i transfer the knowledge about the *symmetric constrained correlation* into the known matrix $\mathbf{S}_k$. Then the correlations in the matrix $\mathbf{U}_k$ can be assumed to be *completely unknown*, i.e., its coefficient varies in the entire range $r \in [-1, 1]$.

In the following, it is demonstrated how the parameters β_k^i and A_k^{ij} can be derived depending on given values of the correlation constraints. In order to keep the notation simple only two entries of the matrix $\widetilde{\mathbf{C}}_k$ are considered. With respect to the proposed matrix separation (5.9) and its parameterization (5.16), the matrix $\widetilde{\mathbf{C}}_k$ can be separated according to

$$\begin{aligned} \begin{bmatrix} \widetilde{C}_k^{ii} & \widetilde{C}_k^{ij} \\ \widetilde{C}_k^{ji} & \widetilde{C}_k^{jj} \end{bmatrix} &= \begin{bmatrix} U_k^{ii} & U_k^{ij} \\ U_k^{ji} & U_k^{jj} \end{bmatrix} + \begin{bmatrix} S_k^{ii} & 0 \\ 0 & S_k^{jj} \end{bmatrix} + \begin{bmatrix} 0 & A_k^{ij} \\ A_k^{ij} & 0 \end{bmatrix} \\ &= \begin{bmatrix} \beta_k^i \widetilde{C}_k^{ii} & U_k^{ij} \\ U_k^{ji} & \beta_k^j \widetilde{C}_k^{jj} \end{bmatrix} + \begin{bmatrix} (1 - \beta_k^i) \widetilde{C}_k^{ii} & 0 \\ 0 & (1 - \beta_k^j) \widetilde{C}_k^{jj} \end{bmatrix} + \begin{bmatrix} 0 & A_k^{ij} \\ A_k^{ij} & 0 \end{bmatrix} . \end{aligned} \qquad (5.17)$$

The main goal is to derive the coefficients β_k^i and A_k^{ij} in such way that the correlation in the matrix $\mathbf{U}_k$ is completely unknown. Roughly speaking, the information about the asymmetric constraints is transfered into the matrices $\mathbf{S}_k$ and $\mathbf{A}_k$. With respect to the separated matrix

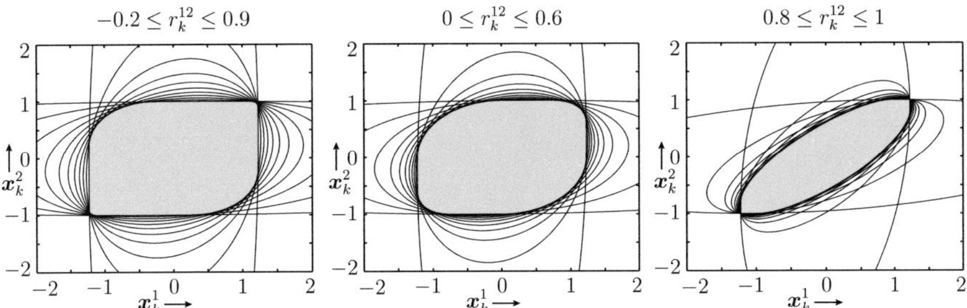

Figure 5.8: Various covariance bounds for the joint covariances of two scalar random variables with imprecisely known correlation. Asymmetric constraints: **(a)** $0.2 \leq r_k^{12} \leq 0.9$, **(b)** $0 \leq r_k^{12} \leq 0.6$, and **(c)** $0.8 \leq r_k^{12} \leq 1$.

equation (5.17) the off-diagonal entries can be stated as follows

$$\underbrace{r_{\max}^{ij}\sqrt{\widetilde{C}_k^{ii}\widetilde{C}_k^{jj}}}_{\widetilde{C}_k^{ij}} = \underbrace{\sqrt{\beta_k^i\beta_k^j}\sqrt{\widetilde{C}_k^{ii}\widetilde{C}_k^{jj}}}_{U_k^{ij}} + A_k^{ij} \ , \qquad r_{\min}^{ij}\sqrt{\widetilde{C}_k^{ii}\widetilde{C}_k^{jj}} = -\sqrt{\beta_k^i\beta_k^j}\sqrt{\widetilde{C}_k^{ii}\widetilde{C}_k^{jj}} + A_k^{ij} \ ,$$

where the imprecisely known correlation coefficient r_k^{ij} in the matrix $\widetilde{\mathbf{C}}_k$ were assumed to be $r_k^{ij} = r_{\max}^{ij}$ and $r_k^{ij} = r_{\min}^{ij}$, respectively. The substraction and addition of these equations results in the following equations for deriving the coefficients β_k^{ij} and A_k^{ij}

$$A_k^{ij} = \underbrace{\frac{r_{\max}^{ij} + r_{\min}^{ij}}{2}}_{=:r_{\mathrm{avrg}}^{ij}}\sqrt{\widetilde{C}_k^{ii}\widetilde{C}_k^{jj}} \ , \qquad \underbrace{\left(\frac{r_{\max}^{ij} - r_{\min}^{ij}}{2}\right)^2}_{=:(r_{\mathrm{d}}^{ij})^2} = \beta_k^i\beta_k^j \ , \tag{5.18}$$

where r_{avrg}^{ij} is the so-called *averaged correlation coefficient* and r_{d}^{ij} denotes the *difference correlation coefficient*. The equations for A_k^{ij} can be readily solved, whereas for the derivation of the parameters β_k^i the nonlinear system of equations needs to be solved. This was introduced for the *symmetric case* in the previous section. The derivation of covariance bounds is demonstrated by the following two examples, (a) two random variables and (b) three random variables.

Example 5.6: Two random variables (asymmetric constraints)

In this example, the proposed parameterization of the covariance bounds is applied to the case of two random variables $x_k^1 \in \mathbb{R}$ and $x_k^2 \in \mathbb{R}$. Their joint density is characterized by the covariance matrix $\widetilde{\mathbf{C}}_k$ with a minimum and maximum correlation coefficient $r_{\min}^{12}$ and $r_{\max}^{12}$, respectively. By using the system of equations (5.18) and by assuming $\beta_k^1 = \beta_k^2 = \beta_k$, the parameter for the matrix separation leads to $\beta_k = r_{\mathrm{d}}^{12}$. Then, the covariance bounds $\mathbf{E}_k^{\mathsf{B}}$ can be derived as follows

$$\mathbf{E}_k^{\mathsf{B}} = \begin{bmatrix} \frac{\kappa_k^1 - r_{\mathrm{d}}^{12}\kappa_k^1 + r_{\mathrm{d}}^{12}}{\kappa_k^1}C_k^{11} & r_{\mathrm{avrg}}^{12}\sqrt{C_k^{11}C_k^{22}} \\ r_{\mathrm{avrg}}^{12}\sqrt{C_k^{11}C_k^{22}} & \frac{\kappa_k^2 - r_{\mathrm{d}}^{12}\kappa_k^2 + r_{\mathrm{d}}^{12}}{\kappa_k^2}C_k^{22} \end{bmatrix} \quad \text{with } r_{\mathrm{avrg}}^{12} = \frac{r_{\max}^{12} + r_{\min}^{12}}{2} \ , \quad r_{\mathrm{d}}^{12} = \frac{r_{\max}^{12} - r_{\min}^{12}}{2} \ ,$$

where the parameters of the covariance bounds are defined as $\kappa_k^1 = \kappa_k$ and $\kappa_k^2 = 1 - \kappa_k$. The covariances are given by $\widetilde{C}_k^{11} = 1.5$ and $\widetilde{C}_k^{22} = 1$. In Figure 5.5 **(c)**, the set of all valid covariance matrices are visualized for different asymmetrically constrained correlation. The covariance bounds $\mathbf{E}_k^{\mathsf{B}}$ parameterized by κ_k are shown in Figure 5.8. ∎

(a) Union of all valid covariance ellipsoids

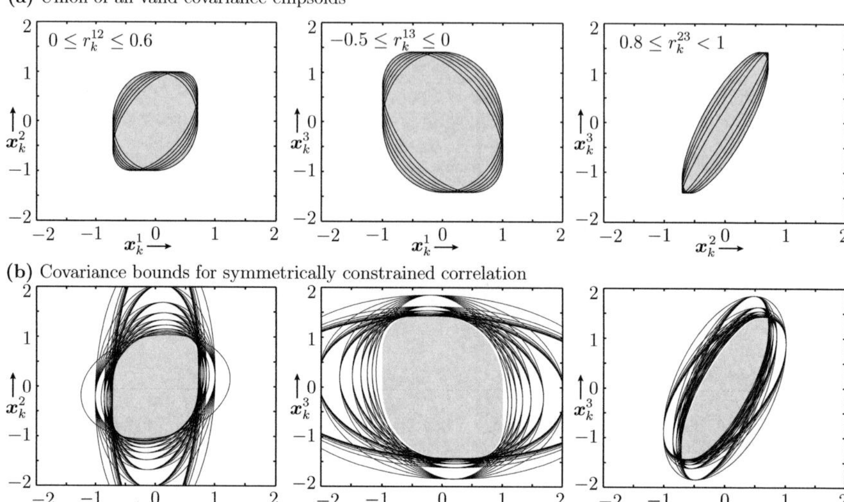

(b) Covariance bounds for symmetrically constrained correlation

Figure 5.9: Visualization of covariance bounds for the case of three random scalars with asymmetrically constrained correlation. **(a)** Marginal densities of the union of all valid covariance ellipsoids. **(b)** Covariance bounds for symmetrically constrained correlation for various parameters κ_1 and κ_2.

Example 5.7: Three random variables (asymmetric constraints)

This example is devoted to the visualization of the derived covariance bounds for the case of three random variables. In the case of three random variables, the equation (5.18) for deriving the coefficients β_k^{ij} can be solved, similar as described in the symmetric case. This results in following parameters of the matrix $\mathbf{S}_k$

$$\beta_k^1 = \frac{r_\mathsf{d}^{12} r_\mathsf{d}^{13}}{r_\mathsf{d}^{23}} \; , \qquad \beta_k^2 = \frac{r_\mathsf{d}^{12} r_\mathsf{d}^{23}}{r_\mathsf{d}^{13}} \; , \qquad \beta_k^3 = \frac{r_\mathsf{d}^{13} r_\mathsf{d}^{23}}{r_\mathsf{d}^{12}} \; . \tag{5.19}$$

These equations can be used to obtain the parameters for the matrix separation (5.16). Similar to Example 5.5 the covariance bounds $\mathbf{E}_k^\mathsf{B}$ can be derived as folows

$$\mathbf{E}_k^\mathsf{B} = \begin{bmatrix} \frac{r_\mathsf{d}^{12} r_\mathsf{d}^{13} + \kappa_k^1 (r_\mathsf{d}^{23} - r_\mathsf{d}^{12} r_\mathsf{d}^{13})}{r_\mathsf{d}^{23} \kappa_k^1} \widetilde{C}_k^{11} & r_\mathrm{avrg}^{12} \sqrt{\widetilde{C}_k^{11} \widetilde{C}_k^{22}} & r_\mathrm{avrg}^{13} \sqrt{\widetilde{C}_k^{11} \widetilde{C}_k^{33}} \\ r_\mathrm{avrg}^{12} \sqrt{\widetilde{C}_k^{11} \widetilde{C}_k^{22}} & \frac{r_\mathsf{d}^{12} r_\mathsf{d}^{23} + \kappa_k^2 (r_\mathsf{d}^{13} - r_\mathsf{d}^{12} r_\mathsf{d}^{23})}{r_\mathsf{d}^{13} \kappa_k^2} \widetilde{C}_k^{22} & r_\mathrm{avrg}^{23} \sqrt{\widetilde{C}_k^{22} \widetilde{C}_k^{33}} \\ r_\mathrm{avrg}^{13} \sqrt{\widetilde{C}_k^{11} \widetilde{C}_k^{33}} & r_\mathrm{avrg}^{23} \sqrt{\widetilde{C}_k^{22} \widetilde{C}_k^{33}} & \frac{r_\mathsf{d}^{13} r_\mathsf{d}^{23} + \kappa_k^3 (r_\mathsf{d}^{12} - r_\mathsf{d}^{13} r_\mathsf{d}^{23})}{r_\mathsf{d}^{12} \kappa_k^3} \widetilde{C}_k^{33} \end{bmatrix} \; ,$$

with $0 < \kappa_k^i < 1$ and $\kappa_k^3 := 1 - \kappa_k^1 - \kappa_k^2$. The averaged correlation r_avrg^{ij} and the difference correlation r_d^{ij} can be obtained by using (5.18). The following variances and correlation constraints are used

$$\text{Known variances} \qquad \widetilde{C}_k^{11} = 0.5 \; , \quad \widetilde{C}_k^{22} = 1 \; , \quad \widetilde{C}_k^{33} = 2 \; ,$$

$$\text{Correlation constraints} \qquad 0 \leq r_k^{12} \leq 0.6 \; , \quad 0.5 \leq r_k^{13} \leq 0 \; , \quad 0.8 \leq r_k^{23} < 1 \; ,$$

In Figure 5.9 **(a)**, the set of all valid covariance matrices are visualized for a given symmetrically constrained correlation. The corresponding covariance bounds $\mathbf{E}_k^\mathsf{B}$ parameterized by κ_k^1 and κ_k^2 are shown in Figure 5.9 **(b)**. ∎

5.5 Process of the Decentralized State Reconstruction

In this section the *Covariance Bounds Filter* (CBF) is employd for the decentralized state reconstruction of space-time continuous phyiscal systems. By this means, an estimation process can be derived that is robust against unknown (or imprecisely known) correlations, and thus yields correct and consistent reconstruction results. The severe effect of simply neglecting unknown cross-correlations and the resulting over-optimistic, even wrong results were shown in Example 5.2. The decentralized reconstruction process on the basis of the CBF is visualized and compared to the centralized approach in Figure 5.10.

The proposed method for the *decentralized state reconstruction* of space-time continuous physical systems can be applied to the general decomposed system (5.4). However, we restrict our attention to a specific structure where the individual estimates $\underline{x}_k^i$ depend only on estimates of adjacent nodes (see following example). Such kind of system structure naturally results from the employment of finite-difference methods to linear partial differential equations (1.2).

Example 5.8: Considered system structure in decomposed form
By applying the finite-difference method, the space-time continuous system (5.1) can always be decomposed in such a way that the local state vectors $\underline{x}_k^i$ depend only on the previous state of adjacent nodes $i-1$ and $i+1$ (see Example 5.1). In addition, the measurement matrix $\mathbf{H}_k$ can be assumed to consists only of diagonal entries. In this case, the structure of the general decomposed system (5.4) reduces to the following

$$\underline{x}_{k+1}^i = \sum_{\substack{j=i-1 \\ 1 \leq j \leq N_C}}^{i+1} \mathbf{A}_k^{ij}\,\underline{x}_k^j + \mathbf{B}_k^{ii}\left(\hat{\underline{u}}_k^i + \underline{w}_k^i\right) \;, \qquad \hat{\underline{y}}_k^i = \mathbf{H}_k^{ii}\,\underline{x}_k^i + \underline{v}_k^i \;, \tag{5.20}$$

where i is the node being considered, $i-1$ is the left neighboring node, and $i+1$ is the right neighboring node. The structure of this special type of decomposed system is visualized in Figure 5.2 **(b)**.
∎

In general, there exist both *spatial and temporal correlations* inherently affecting the space-time continuous system being observed. These correlations are usually caused by partially stochastic dependent and spatially distributed noise sources affecting more than one location, and thus more than one sensor node. In this research work, the individual components of the *global* system uncertainty $\underline{w}_k$ and the *global* measurement uncertainty $\underline{v}_k$ are assumed to be uncorrelated for simplicity reasons. Thus, the covariance matrices are given by

$$\mathbf{C}_k^w = \begin{cases} \mathbf{C}_k^{wij} & \text{for } i = j \\ 0 & \text{for } i \neq j \end{cases}, \qquad \mathbf{C}_k^v = \begin{cases} \mathbf{C}_k^{vij} & \text{for } i = j \\ 0 & \text{for } i \neq j \end{cases},$$

which means that no common source term is affecting more than one location and sensor node. In the case of spatial/temporal correlations affecting the space-time continuous system, an appropriate model is required that describes these correlations. Then, for decentralized processing the underlying noise terms $\mathbf{C}_k^w$ and $\mathbf{C}_k^v$ must be decomposed as proposed in Section 5.3 and illustrated in Figure 5.3. However, in this thesis, only the unknown correlations caused by the decentralized reconstruction process itself are considered, see (5.5). The extension to the case of imprecisely known noise terms is conceptually straightforward.

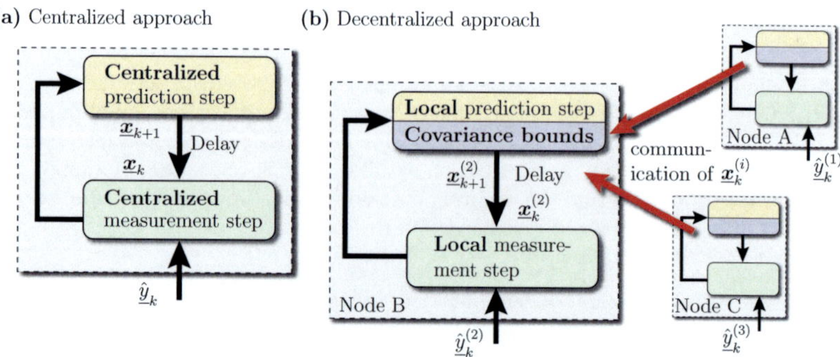

Figure 5.10: Comparison of different approaches for the reconstruction of space-time continuous physical systems using a spatially distributed measurement system, such as a sensor network. **(a)** Centralized approach (as introduced in Chapter 2), and **(b)** decentralized approach on the basis of the Covariance Bounds Filter (CBF).

5.5.1 Decentralized prediction step

The purpose of the prediction step that is locally performed on each node is to propagate the state estimate $\underline{x}_k^i$ through the system equation (5.20) to the next time step k (see Section 2.5.1 for the linear and Section 3.4.1 for the nonlinear prediction step). Here, in the case of the *decentralized prediction step* the processing can be performed on the basis of state estimates that are received from adjacent nodes. The individual mean values $\hat{\underline{x}}_k^{pi}$ are simply derived by the weighted sum of previous adjacent states and the input state according to

$$\hat{\underline{x}}_k^{pi} = \sum_{\substack{j=i-1 \\ 1 \leq j \leq N_C}}^{i+1} \mathbf{A}_{k-1}^{ij} \, \hat{\underline{x}}_{k-1}^{ej} + \mathbf{B}_{k-1}^{ii} \hat{\underline{u}}_{k-1}^i \ .$$

It is obvious that the resulting mean does not depend on the cross-correlation between the individual substates $\underline{x}_k^i$, i.e., unknown correlations can be neglected concerning the mean.

The calculation of the covariance matrix $\widetilde{\mathbf{C}}_k^{pii}$ is more involved due to the general dependency of the predicted covariance matrix on the cross-covariance matrices between the individual substates $\underline{x}_k^i$. In the uncorrelated case when the cross-covariance matrices between the system state $\underline{x}_k$ and the system input $\underline{u}_k$ are zero matrices, the diagonal entries are given by

$$\widetilde{\mathbf{C}}_k^{pii} = \sum_{\substack{j=i-1 \\ 1 \leq j \leq N_C}}^{i+1} \mathbf{A}_{k-1}^{ij} \, \widetilde{\mathbf{C}}_{k-1}^{ejj} \left(\mathbf{A}_{k-1}^{ij} \right)^{\mathrm{T}} + \underbrace{\sum_{r=i-1}^{i+1} \sum_{\substack{s=i-1 \\ s \neq r}}^{i+1} \mathbf{A}_{k-1}^{ir} \, \widetilde{\mathbf{C}}_{k-1}^{ers} \left(\mathbf{A}_{k-1}^{is} \right)^{\mathrm{T}}}_{\text{error caused by neglecting cross-correlations}} + \mathbf{B}_{k-1}^{ii} \mathbf{C}_{k-1}^{wii} \left(\mathbf{B}_{k-1}^{ii} \right)^{\mathrm{T}} \ .$$

$$\tag{5.21}$$

It can be easily seen that by unknown cross-covariance matrices $\widetilde{\mathbf{C}}_k^{eij}$ for $i \neq j$ an error in the resulting covariance matrices $\widetilde{\mathbf{C}}_k^{pii}$ is caused. This results in an unjustifiable improvement of the state estimate, and thus over-optimistic estimation results. In such cases, the estimator assumes to be more accurate than it is justified and sticks in a possibly wrong estimate, as it was shown in Example 5.2. By replacing the unknown covariance matrix $\widetilde{\mathbf{C}}_k^e$ in the *decentralized prediction step* by the covariance bounds (see Section 5.4) leads to a bound for the predicted covariance matrix. It is emphasized that the resulting covariance bound $\mathbf{E}_k^{pii}(\kappa_k)$ for (5.21) depends on the parameter vector $\underline{\kappa}_k$, i.e., the predicted state consists of a parameterized set of density functions. In the following, the structure of the covariance bounds $\mathbf{E}_k^{pii}$ is discussed for the three cases of correlation constraints.

Completely unkown correlation In the case of completely unknown cross-covariances, i.e., the correlation coefficients vary in the entire natural bound $r_k^{ij} \in [-1, 1]$, the following covariance bounds of the predicted covariance matrix (5.21) can be derived

$$
\mathbf{E}_k^{pii}(\underline{\kappa}_k) = \sum_{\substack{j=i-1 \\ 1 \leq j \leq N_C}}^{i+1} \frac{1}{\kappa_k^j} \mathbf{A}_{k-1}^{ij} \widetilde{\mathbf{C}}_{k-1}^{ejj} \left(\mathbf{A}_{k-1}^{ij} \right)^{\mathrm{T}} + \mathbf{B}_{k-1}^{ii} \mathbf{C}_{k-1}^{wii} \left(\mathbf{B}_{k-1}^{ii} \right)^{\mathrm{T}} \; .
$$

The individual parameters κ_k^{i-1}, κ_k^i, and κ_k^{i+1} that parameterize the covariance bounds $\mathbf{E}_k^{pii}(\cdot)$ of the predicted covariance matrix $\widetilde{\mathbf{C}}_k^{pii}$ vary in the interval $(0,1)$ and sum up to one. Similar parameterizations of the covariance bounds for the predicted covariance matrix (5.21) can be derived in the case of constrained correlations, described in the following.

Symmetric correlation constraints In the case of symmetric constraints for the correlation between the substates $\underline{x}_k^i$, i.e., the coefficients vary in the interval $|r_k^{ij}| \leq r_{\max}^{ij} \leq 1$, the covariance bounds of the predicted covariance matrix (5.21) is obtained on the basis of the methods that are proposed in Section 5.4.2. This results in the following covariance bounds for the decentralized prediction step

$$
\mathbf{E}_k^{pii}(\underline{\kappa}_k) = \underbrace{\sum_{\substack{j=i-1 \\ 1 \leq j \leq N_C}}^{i+1} \frac{\beta_k^j}{\kappa_k^j} \mathbf{A}_{k-1}^{ij} \widetilde{\mathbf{C}}_{k-1}^{ejj} \left(\mathbf{A}_{k-1}^{ij} \right)^{\mathrm{T}}}_{\text{completely unknown correlation}} + \underbrace{\sum_{\substack{j=i-1 \\ 1 \leq j \leq N_C}}^{i+1} \left(1 - \beta_k^j \right) \mathbf{A}_{k-1}^{ij} \widetilde{\mathbf{C}}_{k-1}^{ejj} \left(\mathbf{A}_{k-1}^{ij} \right)^{\mathrm{T}}}_{\text{known component depending on constraints}} ,
$$

where the input is omitted here for brevity reasons. In the case of *three substate vectors* (i.e., own local estimate and estimate of its two adjacent nodes) the following parameters for the matrix separation can be derived

$$
\beta_k^{i-1} = \frac{r_{\max}^{i-1,i}\, r_{\max}^{i-1,i+1}}{r_{\max}^{i,i+1}} \; , \qquad \beta_k^i = \frac{r_{\max}^{i-1,i}\, r_{\max}^{i,i+1}}{r_{\max}^{i-1,i+1}} \; , \qquad \beta_k^{i+1} = \frac{r_{\max}^{i-1,i+1}\, r_{\max}^{i,i+1}}{r_{\max}^{i-1,i}} \; ,
$$

which is similar to the equation given in (5.15). The individual parameters κ_k^{i-1}, κ_k^i, and κ_k^{i+1} of the covariance bounds $\mathbf{E}_k^{pii}$ vary in the interval $(0,1)$ and sum up to one, i.e., $\sum_{j=i-1}^{i+1} \kappa_k^j = 1$.

Asymmetric correlation constraints In this section, the covariance bounds are derived that bound the predicted covariance matrix (5.21) with asymmetrically constrained cross-correlations, i.e., the correlation may vary in the interval $-1 \leq r_{\min}^{ij} \leq r_k^{ij} \leq r_{\max}^{ij} \leq 1$. Here, only the *scalar case* is considered for simplicity; the vector case is more involved and beyond the scope of this thesis. By using the methods proposed in Section 5.4.2, the following covariance bounds for the predicted covariance matrix (5.21) can be obtained

$$
E_k^{pii}(\underline{\kappa}_k) = \underbrace{\sum_{\substack{j=i-1 \\ 1 \leq j \leq N_C}}^{i+1} \frac{\beta_k^j}{\kappa_k^j} \left(A_{k-1}^{ij}\right)^2 \widetilde{C}_{k-1}^{ejj}}_{\text{completely unknown correlation}}
$$

$$
+ \underbrace{\sum_{\substack{j=i-1 \\ 1 \leq j \leq N_C}}^{i+1} \left(1 - \beta_k^j\right) \left(A_{k-1}^{ij}\right)^2 \widetilde{C}_{k-1}^{ejj} + \sum_{r=i-1}^{i+1} \sum_{\substack{s=i-1 \\ s \neq r}}^{i+1} \left(A_{k-1}^{ir}\right)^2 r_{\text{avrg}}^{rs} \sqrt{\widetilde{C}_k^{rr} \widetilde{C}_k^{ss}}}_{\text{known component depending on constraints}} ,
$$

where the input is omitted here for brevity reasons. In the case of three substates, the following parameters for the matrix separation can be derived

$$
\beta_k^{i-1} = \frac{r_{\text{d}}^{i-1,i} r_{\text{d}}^{i-1,i+1}}{r_{\text{d}}^{i,i+1}} , \qquad \beta_k^i = \frac{r_{\text{d}}^{i-1,i} r_{\text{d}}^{i,i+1}}{r_{\text{d}}^{i-1,i+1}} , \qquad \beta_k^{i+1} = \frac{r_{\text{d}}^{i-1,i+1} r_{\text{d}}^{i,i+1}}{r_{\text{d}}^{i-1,i}} ,
$$

which is similar to the equation stated in (5.19). The averaged correlation coefficients r_{avrg}^{rs} and the difference correlation coefficient r_{d}^{rs} can be derived by using (5.18) as follows

$$
r_{\text{avrg}}^{rs} = \frac{r_{\text{max}}^{rs} + r_{\text{min}}^{rs}}{2} , \qquad r_{\text{d}}^{rs} = \frac{r_{\text{max}}^{rs} - r_{\text{min}}^{rs}}{2} ,
$$

for $r, s \in \{i-1, i, i+1\}$ and $r \neq s$. The individual parameters κ_k^{i-1}, κ_k^i, and κ_k^{i+1} of the covariance bounds $\mathbf{E}_k^{pii}$ vary in the interval $(0, 1)$ and sum up to one, i.e., $\sum_{j=i-1}^{i+1} \kappa_k^j = 1$.

5.5.2 Local measurement step

For the purpose of reducing the uncertainty, measurements are locally incorporated that are related to the state via the measurement equation (5.20). Since it is assumed that there is no spatial correlation in the considered domain, the local measurement step can be performed based only on local measurements $\hat{\underline{y}}_k^i$, i.e., exhange of measurements between the nodes is not necessary in that case. Assuming the cross-covariances between substate vectors $\underline{x}_k^i$ and measurements to be zero matrices, the *local measurement step* can be performed according to

$$
\hat{\underline{x}}_k^{ei}(\underline{\kappa}_k) = \hat{\underline{x}}_k^{pi} + \mathbf{K}_k(\underline{\kappa}_k) \left(\hat{\underline{y}}_k^i - \mathbf{H}_k^{ii} \hat{\underline{x}}_k^{pi}\right) ,
$$

$$
\mathbf{E}_k^{eii}(\underline{\kappa}_k) = \mathbf{E}_k^{pii}(\underline{\kappa}_k) - \mathbf{K}_k(\underline{\kappa}_k) \mathbf{H}_k^{ii} \mathbf{E}_k^{pii}(\underline{\kappa}_k) ,
$$

where the Kalman gain $\mathbf{K}_k(\underline{\kappa}_k)$ is given by

$$
\mathbf{K}_k(\underline{\kappa}_k) = \mathbf{E}_k^{pii}(\underline{\kappa}_k)(\mathbf{H}_k^{ii})^{\mathrm{T}} \left(\mathbf{C}_k^{vii} + \mathbf{H}_k^{ii} \mathbf{E}_k^{pii}(\underline{\kappa}_k)(\mathbf{H}_k^{ii})^{\mathrm{T}}\right)^{-1} .
$$

Due to the dependency of the predicted covariance matrix $\mathbf{E}_k^{pii}(\cdot)$ on the parameter $\underline{\kappa}_k$ the estimated mean $\hat{\underline{x}}_k^{ei}(\cdot)$ and covariance matrix $\mathbf{E}_k^{eii}(\cdot)$ results in a set of bounding densities parameterized by $\underline{\kappa}_k$.

Selection of optimal bounding density The individual members of the covariance matrix are an upper bound for the union of all possible matrices with arbitrary correlations. Here, it is emphasized that the intersection is a bound for this union. In general, it is desired to keep the

(a) Numeric solution of deterministic case   (b) Correlation between individual variances of node 25

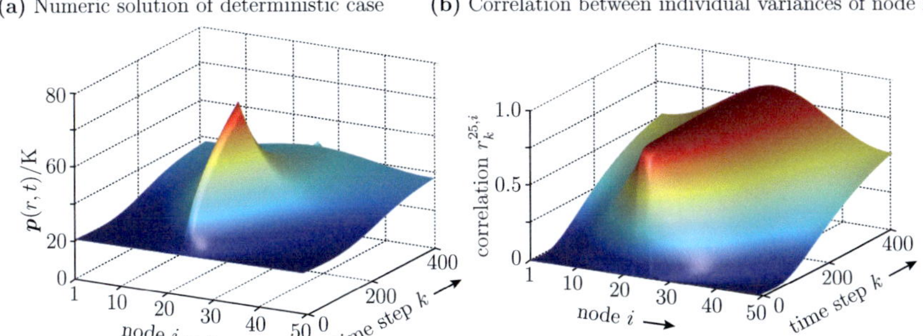

Figure 5.11: (a) Numeric solution of the considered space-time continuous physical system. (b) Correlation coefficient $r_k^{25,i}$ between the individual variances of node 25 with right and left neighboring nodes. It is obvious that the entire network becomse nearly fully correlated during the reconstruction process. The existing correlations usually cannot be neglected, and thus need to be systematically considered.

entire set of bounding densities during their further processing. However, the parameter space describing the members of bounding densities is increasing with every processing step. Hence, for practical reasons it is necessary to select an optimal parameter $\underline{\kappa}^*$ after a certain number of processing steps. The $\underline{\kappa}_k$ may be selected in some optimum way, for example by minimizing the determinant or trace of $\mathbf{E}_k^{eii}$, see [55, 53, 75]. In this thesis, the optimal parameter is selected immediately after the prediction step when there are no measurements available. In the case of a local measurement step, the optimal $\underline{\kappa}^*$ is selected after the measurement step.

5.6 Simulation Results

This section is devoted to demonstrate the performance of the proposed decentralized reconstruction of space-time continuous systems that is based on the *Covariance Bounds Filter*.

Example 5.9 In this simulation study, the one-dimensional diffusion equation (5.1) is considered subject to boundary conditions corresponding to insulation at both ends and characterized by the diffusion coefficient $\alpha(r,t) = 1\,\mathrm{m^2\,h^{-1}}$. The space-time continuous system is discretized by 50 software nodes with a spatial sampling period $\Delta t = 0.5\,\mathrm{m}$ and a sampling time $\Delta t = 0.05\,\mathrm{h}$. There exists a noisy input in the center of the considered solution domain Ω characterized by

$$\hat{u}_k^{25} = \begin{cases} 100 & \text{for } 0 \le t_k < 200 \\ 0 & \text{for } t_k \ge 200 \end{cases}.$$

The system noise term for the individual discretization nodes is assumed to be $C_k^{wii} = 0.5$. The individual initial states for the estimator are $\hat{x}_0^i = 20\,°\mathrm{C}$, whereas the true initial realization is assumed to be $\tilde{x}_0^i = 19\,°\mathrm{C}$. Furthermore, there is a sensor node at each discretization node with a measurement noise variance $C_k^{vii} = 3\,\mathrm{K^2}$. At every time step, randomly chosen nodes perform a measurement step in order to reconstruct the physical system in a decentralized fashion. $\blacksquare$

The numeric solution of the considered space-time continuous physical system is depicted in Figure 5.11 (a). Due to the propagation of state vectors, the information in the entire network

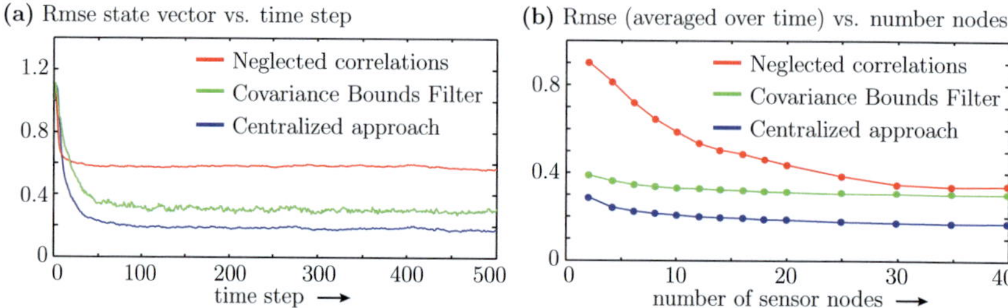

Figure 5.12: Results of 100 simulation runs of the reconstruction process based on centralized Kalman filter (blue), decentralized Kalman filter with neglected correlations (red), and Covariance Bounds Filter (green). **(a)** Root mean square error (rmse) of the state vector $\underline{x}_k$. **(b)** Rmse averaged over time versus number of randomyl chosen sensor nodes for each processing step.

becomes almost fully correlated during the reconstruction process. In Figure 5.11 **(b)**, the correlation coefficient $r^{25,i}$ between the state estimate x_k^i at discretization node 25 and all the neighboring nodes is depicted; only prediction steps are performed without measurement steps. Hence, this correlation cannot be neglected during the reconstruction process.

In Figure 5.12 **(a)**, the root mean square error (rmse) of the state vector $\underline{x}_k$ for 100 simulation runs is depicted. At every processing step, *ten randomly chosen sensor nodes* are performing a measurement update. The centralized Kalman filter (blue line) stores and consideres the entire covariance matrix at each step. This means, the estimation esult can be regarded as the reference solution. In the case of a fully decentralized reconstruction, the correlations between the individual estimates are not stored, and thus are unknown at each update step. It is obvious from Figure 5.12 **(a)** (red line) that neglecting the unknown correlations between the individual estimates causes over-optimistic and wrong results. This leads to the unjustified improvement of the estimates of the individual nodes. Therefore, the measurements have a minor influence on the estimation and reconstruction errors remain. A higher number of sensor nodes or more accurate measurements would be necessary to solve this problem, as can be seen in Figure 5.12 **(b)**. The *Covariance Bounds Filter* (CBF) provides a *systematic way* to consider the unknown correlations between the individual estimates during the estimation process. By this means, it is possible to derive conservative and consistent estimation results with a lower number of sensor nodes.

5.7   Summary and Discussion

This chapter introduces a novel methodology for the decentralized reconstruction of space-time continuous physical systems by means of a sensor network. In order to estimate the entire system state in a decentralized fashion, the system description is converted and decomposed. This results in a network consisting of *software nodes* allocated to *hardware nodes*. For the efficient reconstruction of physical systems that are distributed over a wide area, local information has to be propagated through the sensor network in a fully decentralized fashion. This automatically causes unknown stochastic correlations between the individual estimates. Since the joint probability density function with its information about the correlation is required for fusing local estimates, the joint density needs to be reconstructed or an appropriate so-called bounding density needs to be derived.

The proposed estimator — *Covariance Bounds Filter (CBF)* — allows the systematic consideration of imprecisely known correlation during the estimation process in order to derived conservative and consistent results. The novelty of this decentralized estimator is the exploitation of prior knowledge about correlation constraints, such as *symmetric* and *asymmetric* constraints. By this means tighter bounding densities can be obtained compared to simply using the natural correlation bound. Another novelty is the universal applicability of the proposed estimator. The method of covariance bounds allow to cope with imprecisely known correlations not only in the measurement step but also in the prediction step. Moreover, uncertainties in the model description may be systematically considered by using the proposed covariance bounds. The CBF is restricted to random vectors that are described by Gaussian probability density functions. A prospective way toward the generalization to non-Gaussian densities is given in Chapter 6; there, parameterizations of joint density functions for given marginal Gaussian mixture densities are derived.

The *Covariance Bounds Filter (CBF)* can be applied to a wide variety of applications, such as the simultaneous localization and map building *(SLAM)*, similar to [57]. In this chapter, however, the *CBF* is applied to the decentralized reconstruction of space-time continuous physical systems in order to demonstrate its performance. By this means, a decentralized reconstruction process can be derived that is robust against imprecisely known correlation both in the *decentralized prediction step* and the *local measurement step*. This makes it possible to *locally* reconstruct large-area physica systems and exchange local estimates only with adjacent nodes (without storing information about correlations). For the considered one-dimensional partial differential equation, the decentralized solution may seem unnecessarily involved. However, the same principles can easily be extended to the multi-dimensional case.

CHAPTER 6

Towards Non-Gaussian and Nonlinear Decentralized Estimation

This chapter is devoted to the challenge of processing random vectors represented by non-Gaussian densities with imprecisely known stochastic dependencies. This problem mainly occurs in decentralized estimation[1] where the stochastic dependencies between the individual states are not stored. In the previous chapter, a method was proposed for the decentralized estimation of system states that are characterized by a Gaussian density. The exploitation of parameterized joint densities with Gaussian mixture marginals are proposed to cope with such problems. Under structural assumptions these so-called *parameterized joint densities* contain all information about the stochastic dependencies between their marginal densities in terms of a *generalized correlation parameter vector* $\underline{\xi}$. The parameterized joint densities are applied to the prediction step and the measurement step under imprecisely known stochastic dependencies leading to a set of possible and valid estimation results. The resulting density functions are characterized by the parameter vector $\underline{\xi}$. Once this structure and the bounds of these parameters are known, it may be possible to find bounding densities representing all possible density functions, i.e., conservative and consistent estimation results. The proposed joint densities parameterized by the generalized correlation parameter vector are based on [174, 175].

6.1 Parameterized Joint Densities with Gaussian Marginals

This section is devoted to a description of three different types of prospective parameterizations of joint densities for given *Gaussian marginal densities*. The first two types mainly serve for didactic purposes for understanding the problem of imprecisely known stochastic dependencies between two random variables. The third type, however, may be useful for robust decentralized linear estimation, and thus is of practical relevance.

Piecewise Gaussian densities with different weighting factors This section consists of a description for the simplest non-Gaussian joint density with Gaussian marginals. This type frequently appears in informal discussions on the internet. Basically, a jointly Gaussian density is "sliced" into different pieces that are raised or lowered, respectively. This simple parameterized joint density is depicted in Figure 6.1 **(a)**.

---

[1] e.g., space-time continuous physical systems as shown in the previous chapter

Example 6.1: Gaussian density sliced into *four pieces*

Given two Gaussian marginal densities $f_x(x) := \mathcal{N}(\hat{x}, C_x)$ and $f_y(y) := \mathcal{N}(\hat{y}, C_y)$, a set of possible joint densities $f(x, y)$ can be parameterized by

$$f(x, y) = \begin{cases} \xi_1 \, \widetilde{f}(x, y) & \text{for} \quad x \cdot y \geq 0 \\ \xi_2 \, \widetilde{f}(x, y) & \text{for} \quad x \cdot y < 0 \end{cases} , \tag{6.1}$$

where $\xi_1 = 2(1 - \xi)$ and $\xi_2 = 2\xi$. The free parameter $\xi \in [0, 1]$ can be regarded as a generalized correlation parameter that specifies the individual member of the set. To assure that the parameterized joint density $f(x, y)$ is a valid joint density for the given marginals $f_x(x)$ and $f_y(y)$, the density $\widetilde{f}(x, y)$ must be defined according to

$$\widetilde{f}(x, y) = \mathcal{N}(x - \hat{x}, C_x) \, \mathcal{N}(y - \hat{y}, C_y) .$$

To prove this, it must be shown that the marginal densities of $f(x, y)$ in (6.1) are represented by $f_x(x) = \mathcal{N}(\hat{x}, C_x)$ and $f_y(y) = \mathcal{N}(\hat{y}, C_y)$, respectively. The marginal density $f_x(x)$ can be derived by direct integration over y. Assuming $x > 0$, it follows

$$f_x(x) = \int_0^\infty \xi_1 \widetilde{f}(x, y) \mathrm{d}y + \int_{-\infty}^0 \xi_2 \widetilde{f}(x, y) \mathrm{d}y = 2(1 - \xi) \int_0^\infty \widetilde{f}(x, y) \mathrm{d}y + 2\xi \int_{-\infty}^0 \widetilde{f}(x, y) \mathrm{d}y$$

$$= 2 \int_0^\infty \widetilde{f}(x, y) \mathrm{d}y - 2\xi \int_0^\infty \widetilde{f}(x, y) \mathrm{d}y + 2\xi \int_{-\infty}^0 \widetilde{f}(x, y) \mathrm{d}y .$$

Due to the symmetry of the Gaussian density this integral can be simplified, which yields

$$f_x(x) = \int_{-\infty}^\infty \widetilde{f}(x, y) \mathrm{d}y = \mathcal{N}(\hat{x}, C_x) . \tag{6.2}$$

Similar calculations for $x \leq 0$ justify the choices for ξ_1 and ξ_2. ∎

Sum of positive and negative Gaussians A second type of non-Gaussian joint density with Gaussian marginals could be constructed by the sum of *positive* and *negative* jointly Gaussian densities. The mean values, variances, and weighting coefficients of the individual joint densities need to be chosen appropriately, i.e., in such way that the joint density is both a valid density function and the marginals are Gaussian densities. For the sake of simplicity only the case of three components is considered in the following example.

Example 6.2: Sum of positive/negative Gaussians (*three components*)

Given two Gaussian marginal densities $f_x(x) = \mathcal{N}(\hat{x}, C_x)$ and $f_y(y) = \mathcal{N}(\hat{y}, C_y)$, the unknown joint density $f(x, y)$ may be defined by the sum of positive and negative Gaussians according to

$$f(x, y) = f_1(x, y) + f_2(x, y) - f_3(x, y) ,$$

where the individual densities $f_1(\cdot)$, $f_2(\cdot)$, and $f_3(\cdot)$ are given by

$$f_1(x, y) = \mathcal{N}(x - \hat{x}^*, C_y) \, \mathcal{N}(y - \hat{y}, C_y)$$
$$f_2(x, y) = \mathcal{N}(x - \hat{x}, C_x) \, \mathcal{N}(y - \hat{y}^*, C_x)$$
$$f_3(x, y) = \mathcal{N}(x - \hat{x}^*, C_y) \, \mathcal{N}(y - \hat{y}^*, C_x) ,$$

To assure that the parameterized joint density $f(\cdot)$ is a valid joint density, the mean values and variances of the individual joint densities need to be chosen so that $f(x, y) \geq 0$ holds. This simple case is visualized in Figure 6.1 **(b)**. The marginal density $f_x(x)$ can be derived by direct integration over y according to

$$f_x(x) = \int_{\mathbb{R}} f(x,y)\,dy$$
$$= \mathcal{N}(x - \hat{x}^*, C_y) + \mathcal{N}(x - \hat{x}^*, C_x) - \mathcal{N}(x - \hat{x}^*, C_y)$$
$$= \mathcal{N}(x - \hat{x}^*, C_y)$$

Similar calculations for the marginal density $f_y(y)$ justify the choices for the individual mean values and variances of the parameterized joint density. It is possible to extend this type to joint densities with more components, for example with eight components as shown in Figure 6.1 **(b)**. ∎

Infinite mixture of correlated jointly Gaussian densities   In the following, a parameterized joint density with practical relevance is introduced that is based on the integral of jointly Gaussian densities with different *classical correlation coefficients*. The weighting factors of the individual joint densities need to be chosen in such a way that the marginals are represented by the given Gaussian marginal densities.

Theorem 6.1 *Given two Gaussian marginal densities $f_x(x) = \mathcal{N}(\hat{x}, C_x)$ and $f_y(y) = \mathcal{N}(\hat{y}, C_y)$, a set of possible joint densities that depends on the generalized correlation function $\xi(r)$ can be parameterized by*

$$f(x,y) = \int_{-1}^{1} \xi(r)\,\mathcal{N}\left(\begin{bmatrix} x - \hat{x} \\ y - \hat{y} \end{bmatrix}, \mathbf{C}(r) \right) dr \ , \tag{6.3}$$

where $\xi(r)$ is defined on $r \in [-1, 1]$. The parameterized continuous Gaussian mixture $f(x,y)$ is a valid normalized density function for

$$\xi(r) \geq 0 \ , \qquad \int_{-1}^{1} \xi(r)dr = 1 \ .$$

PROOF. The results directly follow from the integration of the joint density $f(x,y)$ over y and x, respectively. Hence, the marginal density $f_x(x)$ can be derived by direct integration of the joint density $f(x,y)$ over y according to

$$f_x(x) = \int_{\mathbb{R}} \int_{-1}^{1} \xi(r)\,\mathcal{N}\left(\begin{bmatrix} x - \hat{x} \\ y - \hat{y} \end{bmatrix}, \mathbf{C}(r) \right) dr\,dy = \int_{-1}^{1} \xi(r) \int_{\mathbb{R}} \mathcal{N}\left(\begin{bmatrix} x - \hat{x} \\ y - \hat{y} \end{bmatrix}, \mathbf{C}(r) \right) dy\,dr \ .$$

With reference to [109] it can be shown that the solution of the integral does *not depend* on the correlation coefficient r at all. Thus, it can easily be obtained

$$f_x(x) = \int_{-1}^{1} \xi(r)\,\mathcal{N}\left(x - \hat{x}, C_x \right) dr = \mathcal{N}\left(x - \hat{x}, C_x \right) \ ,$$

which justifies the condition $\int_{-1}^{1} \xi(r)dr = 1$. Similar calculations for the marginal density $f_y(y)$ leads to the same condition and eventually concludes the proof. Two examples for this type of parameterized joint density that are based on mixtures of correlated jointly Gaussian densities are depicted in Figure 6.1 **(c)**. □

In the following, a rough idea is shown on how this type of parameterized joint density may be used for the development of a novel estimator for an *imprecisely known correlation coefficient*.

Consider two marginal densities $f_x(x)$ and $f_y(y)$. Assuming that just the mean value $\hat{r}$ and variance C_r of their *classical correlation coefficient* r is known, then a density function $\xi(r)$ for the correlation coefficient can be defined according to

$$\xi(r) = c_n \mathcal{N}\left(r - \hat{r}, C_r\right) \qquad r \in [-1, 1] \ ,$$

with normalization constant c_n

$$(c_n)^{-1} = \int_{-1}^{1} \mathcal{N}\left(r - \hat{r}, C_r\right) dr \ .$$

The density function $\xi(r)$ depicted in the right column of Figure 6.1 **(c)**, can be regarded as a generalized correlation function. This means, this function contains all information about the correlation structure. Using this information, the joint density $f(x, y)$ can be parameterized by

$$f(x, y) = \int_{-1}^{1} c_n \mathcal{N}\left(r - \hat{r}, C_r\right) \mathcal{N}\left(\underline{z}, \mathbf{C}(r)\right) dr \ . \tag{6.4}$$

It is possible to use this parameterized joint density as the predicted joint density $f_k^p(x_k, u_k)$ that is required in order to perform Bayes' law (3.12). Based on the processing of the parameterized joint density, the estimated density $f_{k+1}^e(x_{k+1})$ that depends on the parameters of the generalized correlation function $\xi(r)$ can then be derived. This idea could lay the foundation for a novel filtering technique taking into account the imprecisely known classical correlation coefficient r and gives a parameterization of the estimation result.

6.2 Gaussian Mixture Marginals

So far, parameterized joint densities only with Gaussian marginals were considered. In this section, these ideas are generalized to the parameterization of joint densities with *Gaussian mixture marginals*. Gaussian mixtures consist of the convex sum of weighted Gaussian densities, similar to (1.3). Due to the fact that Gaussian mixture densities are universal approximators, they are well-suited for nonlinear estimation problems [56]. Thus, by finding a parameterization for the imprecisely known joint density with Gaussian mixture marginals, it is possible to develop a novel filtering technique that could possibly cope with both nonlinear systems and unknown stochastic dependencies in a systematic manner.

As it was mentioned in the introduction of this chapter, the first challenge of a robust decentralized estimation for Gaussian mixture densities is that the classical correlation coefficient r is not a sufficient measure for describing stochastic dependencies. Therefore, in this section a so-called *generalized correlation parameter vector* ξ for Gaussian mixtures is introduced. Finding bounding densities that are compatible with all stochastic dependency structures in terms of ξ, it may be possible to arrive at a robust decentralized estimator for non-Gaussian/nonlinear systems. For the sake of simplicity, two scalar Gaussian mixture marginals are considered according to

$$f_x(x) = \sum_{i=1}^{m} w_{x,i} \mathcal{N}\left(x - \hat{x}_i, C_{x,i}\right) \ , \qquad f_y(y) = \sum_{i=1}^{n} w_{y,i} \mathcal{N}\left(y - \hat{y}_i, C_{y,i}\right) \ , \tag{6.5}$$

where $\hat{x}_i$ and $\hat{y}_i$ are the individual means, $C_{x,i}$ and $C_{y,i}$ are the individual variances, and $w_{x,i}$ and $w_{y,i}$ are the individual weighting factors, which must be positive and sum to one.

(a) Piecewise Gaussian with different weighting factors

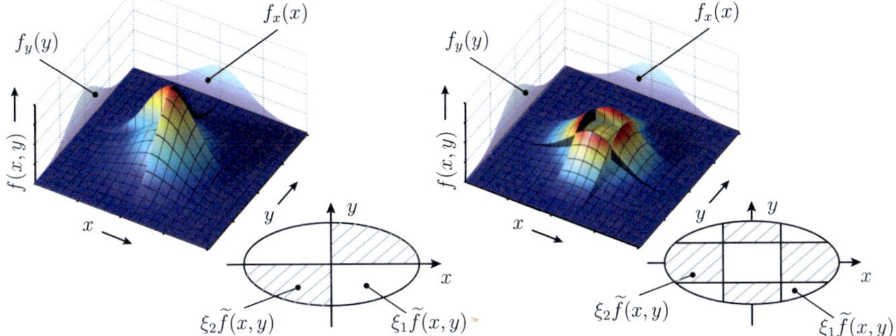

(b) Sum of positive and negative Gaussians

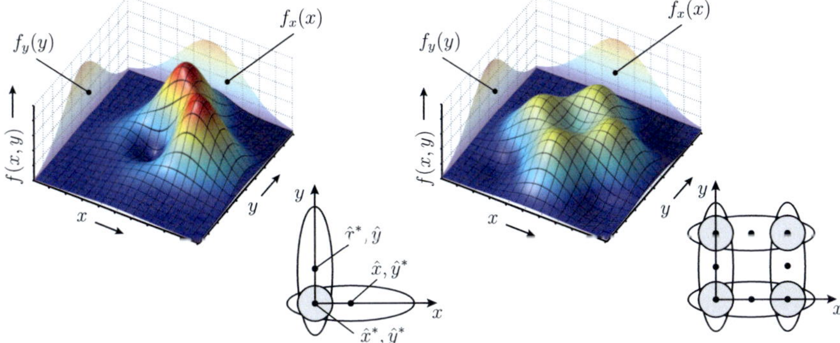

(c) Mixtures of correlated jointly Gaussian densities

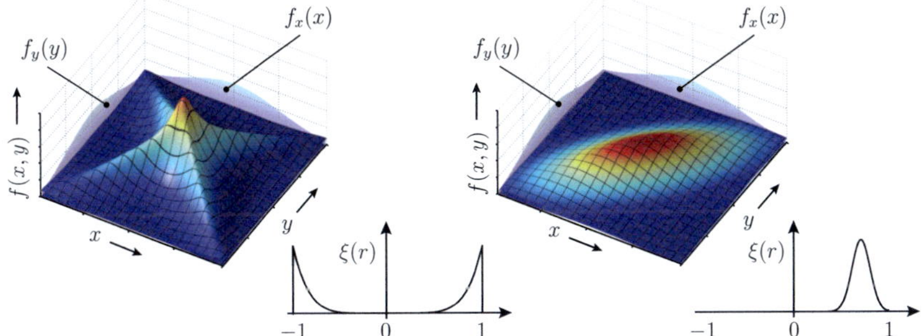

Figure 6.1: Visualization of different types of parameterizations of non-Gaussian joint densities with Gaussian marginals. **(a)** Piecewise Gaussian density with different weighting factors. The joint density is sliced into several symmetricly located pieces with different weighting coefficients, while the marginals remain Gaussian densities. **(b)** Sum of positive and negative Gaussian densities with three components and eight components. **(c)** Sum of correlated Gaussian densities for different correlation function, e.g., $\xi(r) = \frac{7}{2}r^6$ and $\xi(r) = \mathcal{N}(r - \hat{r}, C_r)$.

Theorem 6.2 *Given two Gaussian mixture marginal densities $f_x(x)$ and $f_y(y)$, a set of possible joint densities $f(x,y)$ depending on the weighting factors w_{ij} is defined by*

$$f(x,y) = \sum_{i=1}^{m} \sum_{j=1}^{n} w_{ij} \, \mathcal{N}\left(\begin{bmatrix} x - \hat{x}_i \\ y - \hat{y}_j \end{bmatrix}, \mathbf{C}_{ij}(r_{ij}) \right) \ . \tag{6.6}$$

To assure that the parameterized Gaussian mixture $f(x,y)$ is a valid normalized density function, the weighting factors w_{ij} must be positive and sum to one

$$w_{ij} \geq 0 \ , \qquad \sum_{i=1}^{m} \sum_{j=1}^{n} w_{ij} = 1 \ . \tag{6.7}$$

In addition, the weighting factors must satisfy

$$\sum_{j=1}^{n} w_{ij} = w_{x,i} \ , \qquad \sum_{i=1}^{m} w_{ij} = w_{y,j} \ , \tag{6.8}$$

to ensure that the parameterized joint density $f(x,y)$ is a valid joint density for the given marginal density functions $f_x(x)$ and $f_y(y)$.

PROOF. These properties and conditions can be proven by showing that the marginal densities of $f(x,y)$ are represented by $f_x(x)$ and $f_y(y)$, given by (6.5). The marginal density $f_x(x)$ can be derived by direct integration over y according to

$$f_x(x) = \int_{\mathbb{R}} \sum_{i=1}^{m} \sum_{j=1}^{n} w_{ij} \mathcal{N}\left(\begin{bmatrix} x - \hat{x}_i \\ y - \hat{y}_j \end{bmatrix}, \mathbf{C}_{ij}(r_{ij}) \right) dy = \sum_{i=1}^{m} \sum_{j=1}^{n} w_{ij} \int_{\mathbb{R}} \mathcal{N}\left(\begin{bmatrix} x - \hat{x}_i \\ y - \hat{y}_j \end{bmatrix}, \mathbf{C}_{ij}(r_{ij}) \right) dy$$

Refering to [109] it can be shown that the integral solution does *not depend* on the correlation coefficient r_{ij} at all. Thus,

$$f_x(x) = \sum_{i=1}^{m} \sum_{j=1}^{n} w_{ij} \, \mathcal{N}\left(x - \hat{x}_i, C_{x,i} \right)$$

can easily be obtained. Now, it is obvious that for the condition $\sum_{j=1}^{n} w_{ij} = w_{x,i}$ this leads to the desired Gaussian mixture marginals

$$f_x(x) = \sum_{i=1}^{m} w_{x,i} \, \mathcal{N}\left(x - \hat{x}_i, C_{x,i} \right) \ .$$

Similar calculations for marginal density function $f_y(y)$ leads to the desired condition $\sum_{i=1}^{m} w_{ij} = w_{y,j}$. This concludes the proof. $\qquad\qquad\Box$

For the following calculations it is more convenient to rearrange the weighting factors of the joint Gaussian mixture density w_{ij} from matrix form to vector form according to

$$\underline{w} = \begin{bmatrix} w_{11} & \cdots & w_{1n}, & w_{21} & \cdots & w_{2n}, & \cdots & w_{mn} \end{bmatrix}^{\mathrm{T}} \ .$$

The weighting factors of marginals are given by

$$\underline{w}_x = \begin{bmatrix} w_{x,1} & \cdots & w_{x,m} \end{bmatrix}^{\mathrm{T}} \ , \qquad \underline{w}_y = \begin{bmatrix} w_{y,1} & \cdots & w_{y,n} \end{bmatrix}^{\mathrm{T}} \ .$$

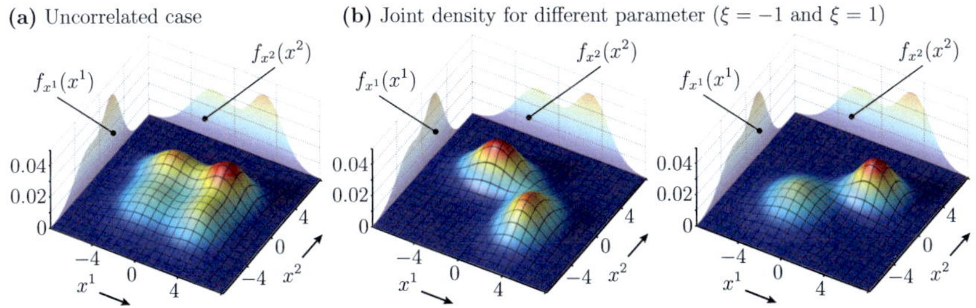

Figure 6.2: Visualization of different joint densities with the same *Gaussian mixture marginal densities*. The marginal densities consists of two components, $f_{x^1}(x^1)$ with mean $\hat{x}^1 = [-2, -3]^{\mathrm{T}}$, standard deviation $\sigma^1 = [2, 1.6]^{\mathrm{T}}$ and $f_{x^2}(c^2)$ with mean $\hat{x}^2 = [-2, 2]^{\mathrm{T}}$, standard deviation $\sigma^2 = [2.1, 1.4]^{\mathrm{T}}$. **(a)** uncorrelated case, i.e., $\xi = 0$, and **(b)** correlated case with $\xi = 1$ and $\xi = -1$, respectively.

The conditions (6.8) for a valid joint density $f(x, y)$ with marginals $f_x(x)$ and $f_y(y)$ can be expressed by a linear equation, which transforms weighting factors of joint density to weighting factors of marginals. This linear transformation is given by

$$\mathbf{T}\,\underline{w} = \begin{bmatrix} \underline{w}_x \\ \underline{w}_y \end{bmatrix} \ .$$

Due to the fact that the matrix $\mathbf{T} \in \mathbb{R}^{(n+m)\times nm}$ in general is not a square matrix and does *not* have full rank, there exists a null space (kernel) $\ker \mathbf{T}$, which is given by

$$(\ker \mathbf{T})\,\underline{w} = \underline{\xi} \ .$$

The null space $\ker \mathbf{T}$ is spanned by the free parameter vector $\underline{\xi}$. Thus, for the calculation of valid weighting factors $\underline{w}$ the following Lemma is proposed.

Lemma 6.1 *The weighting factors $\underline{w}$ of the joint density $f(x, y)$ can be derived according to*

$$\underline{w} = \mathbf{T}_e^{\dagger} \begin{bmatrix} \underline{w}_x \\ \underline{w}_y \\ \underline{\xi} \end{bmatrix} \ , \qquad \mathbf{T}_e = \begin{bmatrix} \mathbf{T} \\ \ker \mathbf{T} \end{bmatrix} \ ,$$

where $\mathbf{T}_e$ describes a unique transformation of weighting factors for valid joint densities to weighting factors of given marginal densities. The pseudo-inverse is denoted by $\mathbf{T}_e^{\dagger}$. Similar to the other types of parameterized joint densities the free parameter vector ξ can be regarded as a kind of generalized correlation parameter for Gaussian mixtures. This parameter vector needs to be specified in order to define the joint density $f(x, y)$ uniquely.

Example 6.3 In this example possible joint densities $f(x, y)$ for two given Gaussian mixture marginals $f_x(x)$ and $f_y(y)$ are considered; see Figure 6.2. The weighting factors for components of the joint density are obtained by

$$\begin{bmatrix} w_{11} \\ w_{12} \\ w_{21} \\ w_{22} \end{bmatrix} = \frac{1}{8} \begin{bmatrix} 3 & -1 & 3 & -1 & -2 \\ -1 & 3 & 3 & -1 & 2 \\ -1 & 3 & -1 & 3 & 2 \\ 3 & -1 & -1 & 3 & -2 \end{bmatrix} \cdot \begin{bmatrix} w_{x,1} \\ w_{x,2} \\ w_{y,1} \\ w_{y,2} \\ \xi \end{bmatrix} \ ,$$

where ξ is the free parameter. Possible joint densities for different parameters are shown in Figure 6.2. ∎

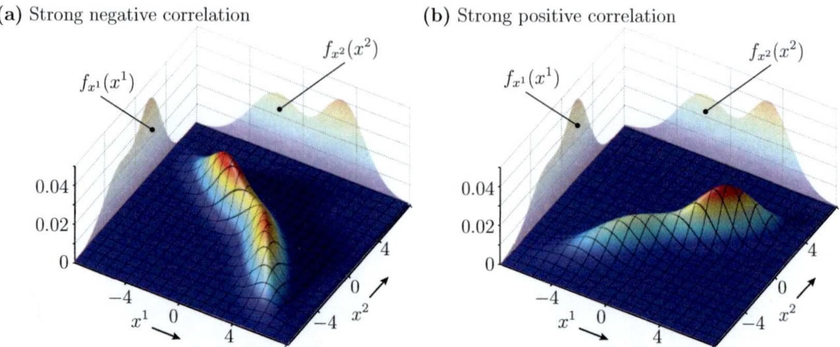

Figure 6.3: Combination of two types of parameterized joint densities with the same marginal densities. **(a)** Strong negative correlation (i.e., $\xi = -1$, $\alpha = -1$), and **(b)** strong positive correlation (i.e., $\xi = 1$, $\alpha = 1$).

Here, the individual components of the Gaussian mixture are assumed to be uncorrelated, i.e., $r_{ij} = 0$. That's why the resulting generalized correlation vector $\underline{\xi}$ is derived only by the weighting factors $\underline{w}$; and not the correlation coefficients r_{ij}. In general, it is possible to combine all the types of parameterized joint densities introduced in this chapter. The most relevant combination is applying the mixtures of correlated jointly Gaussian to the individual components of a Gaussian mixture. For simplicity the previous example is considered and the *generalized correlation function* $\xi_{ij}(r)$ for the ij-th component is assumed to be given by

$$\xi_{ij}(r) = \delta(r - \alpha) \ ,$$

where δ is the Dirac delta distribution and α denotes the *classical correlation coefficient*. In Figure 6.3 the parameterized joint density is depicted for different α and ξ. It turns out that in the case of $\alpha = -1$ and $\xi = -1$ the two considered random variables that are described by Gaussian mixtures, are fully correlated, i.e., similar to the Gaussian case $r \Rightarrow -1$.

6.3 Processing of Parameterized Joint Densities

In this section, it is demonstrated how the parameterized joint densities introduced in the previous section can be possibly used for a novel filtering technique. This is achieved both for (a) the prediction step and (b) the measurement step.

Prediction step (time update) For the sake of simplicity, a simple discrete-time dynamic model is considered with the system state $\boldsymbol{x}_k \in \mathbb{R}$, and the system input $\boldsymbol{u}_k \in \mathbb{R}$ according to

$$\boldsymbol{x}_{k+1} = a_k(\boldsymbol{x}_k, \boldsymbol{u}_k) \ ,$$

where $\boldsymbol{x}_k$ and $\boldsymbol{u}_k$ are random variables represented by the density functions $f_x(x_k)$ and $f_u(u_k)$, respectively. In the case of precisely known joint density $f_k^e(x_k, u_k)$, the predicted density can be obtained using the well-known Chapman-Kolmogorov equation [109] (see Section 3.4.1)

$$f_{k+1}^p(x_{k+1}) = \int_{\mathbb{R}^2} \delta\left(x_{k+1} - a_k(x_k, u_k)\right) f_k^e\left(x_k, u_k\right) \, \mathrm{d}x_k \, \mathrm{d}u_k \ , \tag{6.9}$$

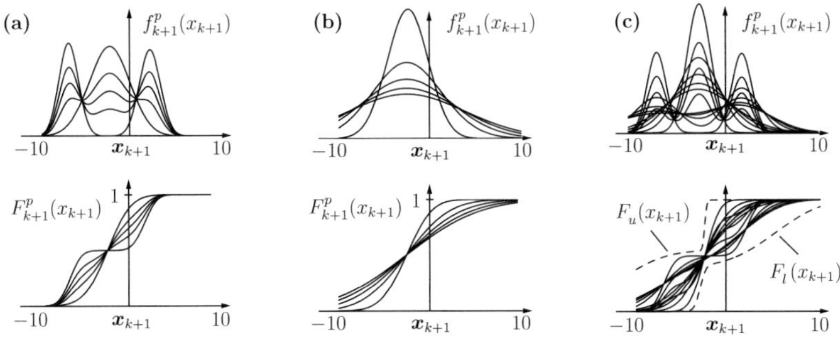

Figure 6.4: Predicted density $f^p_{k+1}(x_{k+1})$ and its cumulative distribution function $F^p_{k+1}(x_{k+1})$ for variation of the generalized correlation parameter ξ of the prior density $f^e_k(x_k, u_k)$. **(a)** $\alpha_{ij} = -1$, $\xi = -1 \ldots 1$. **(b)** $\xi = 1$, $\alpha_{ij} = -1 \ldots 1$. **(c)** Various members of the set of possible predicted densities and their bounding densities, $F_l(x_{k+1})$ and $F_u(x_{k+1})$.

where $\delta(\cdot)$ denotes the Dirac delta distribution. However, it is assumed that the state estimate x_k and the system input u_k are stochastically dependent with a *not precisely known* structure. This means, although the marginal density functions $f^e_x(x_k)$ and $f^e_u(u_k)$ are known, the joint density function $f^e_k(x_k, u_k)$ with all its information about the stochastic dependency is unknown. As it can be seen in (6.9), the knowledge of the joint density $f^e_k(x_k, u_k)$ or at least its parameterization in terms of a correlation paramter is required for deriving prediction results.

The goal is to find a bounding density for the prediction result f^p_{k+1} of all possible joint densities $f^e_k(x_k, u_k)$ for the given marginal densities. Thus, based on structural assumptions concerning the stochastic dependency the unknown prior density $f^e_k(x_k, u_k)$ can be paramterized by

$$f^e_k(x_k, u_k) = \sum_{i=1}^{m} \sum_{j=1}^{n} w_{ij} \int_{-1}^{1} \xi_{ij}(r)\, \mathcal{N}\left(\begin{bmatrix} x_k - \hat{x}^e_{k,i} \\ u_k - \hat{u}^e_{k,j} \end{bmatrix}, \mathbf{C}^e_{ij}(r) \right) \mathrm{d}r \ ,$$

where $\xi_{ij}(r)$ and $\underline{\xi}$ (affecting the calculation of w_{ij} are the generalized correlation function and the generalized correlation parameter vector, respectively. The individual joint covariance matrices between the i-th component $f^e_x(x_k)$ and j-th component of $f^e_u(u_k)$ are given by

$$\mathbf{C}^e_{ij}(r) = \begin{bmatrix} C_{x,i} & r\,\sqrt{C_{x,i}\,C_{u,j}} \\ r\,\sqrt{C_{x,i}\,C_{u,j}} & C_{u,j} \end{bmatrix} \ ,$$

where r denotes the classical correlation parameter. By means of the parameterized prior joint density $f^e_k(x_k, u_k)$ the resulting predicted density $f^p_{k+1}(x_{k+1})$ can be described in terms of a generalized correlation parameter $\underline{\xi}$ and a generalized correlation function $\xi(r)$. This parameterized density function $f^p_{k+1}(x_{k+1})$ describes a whole set of possible prediction results. This is clarified in more detail in the following example.

Example 6.4 For the sake of simplicity and brevity only a linear state-space model is considered according to

$$x_{k+1} = A_k\, x_k + B_k\, u_k \ ,$$

where the two random variables x_k and u_k are represented by Gaussian mixtures with two components, visualized in Figure 6.2. Although more complex correlation functions $\xi_{ij}(r)$ for the

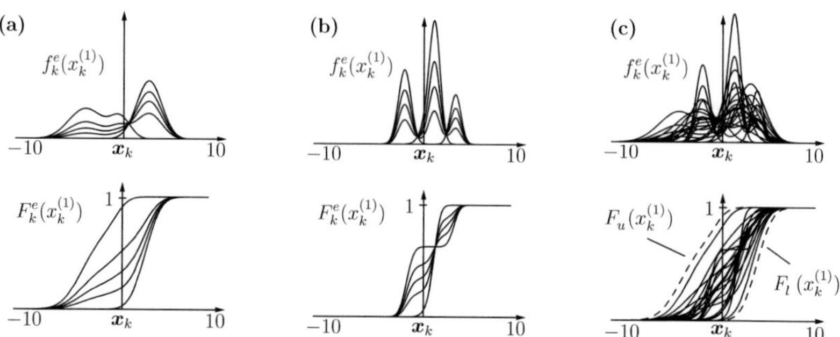

Figure 6.5: Estimated density $f_k^e(x_k^{(1)})$ and its cumulative distribution function $F_k^e(x_k^{(1)})$ for variation of the generalized correlation parameters of $f_k^p(x_k^{(1)}, x_k^{(2)})$. **(a)** $\alpha_{ij} = -1$, $\xi = -1 \ldots 1$. **(b)** $\alpha_{ij} = 1$, $\xi = -1 \ldots 1$. **(c)** Various members of possible estimated densities and their bounding densities, $F_l(x_k^{(1)})$ and $F_u(x_k^{(1)})$.

parameterization of the prior density $f_k^e(\cdot)$ can be chosen, for simplicity this function is given by

$$\xi_{ij}(r) = \delta(r - \alpha_{ij}) \; ,$$

where α_{ij} denotes a specific *classical* correlation coefficient. The predicted density f_{k+1}^p for various generalized correlation parameter vectors ξ and α_{ij} is visualized in Figure 6.4. These figures clearly show that the prediction result f_{k+1}^p strongly depends on the stochastic dependency, however can be described by a generalized correlation parameter. It is obvious that the parameterized predicted distribution functions F_k^p may be bound by so-called bounding distribution functions $F_u(x_{k+1})$ (upper bound) and $F_l(x_{k+1})$ (lower bound), depicted in Figure 6.4 **(c)**. In addition, it can be said that once a representation of such bounding densities is found, a filtering technique may be derived that can cope with *nonlinear models* and is robust against imprecisely known stochastic dependencies.

■

Filter step (measurement update)　In this section, the example mentioned in the introduction (i.e., decentralized self-localization of a sensor network) is taken up. For illustration purposes, we consider just two sensor nodes and assume that the relative distance measurement $\hat{y}_k$ is related nonlinearly to their positions. The measurement equation is given by

$$\hat{y}_k = h_k(\underline{x}_k) + \underline{v}_k \; ,$$

where $\underline{x}_k = \left[x_k^{(1)}, x_k^{(2)}\right]^{\mathrm{T}}$ are the estimated sensor positions and $\underline{v}_k$ represents the measurement uncertainty. In the case of precisely known joint density $f_k^p(x_k^{(1)}, x_k^{(2)})$, the posterior density f_k^e can be easily calculated by using Bayes' formula

$$f_k^e(\underline{x}_k) = c_k^e \, f^L\left(\hat{y}_k - h_k(\underline{x}_k)\right) f_k^p(x_k^{(1)}, x_k^{(2)}) \; , \tag{6.10}$$

where c_k^e is a normalization constant. However, the stochastic dependency between the individual estimated positions is assumed to be imprecisely known. This means, although the marginal density function $f_k^p(x_k^{(1)})$ and $f_k^p(x_k^{(2)})$ are known, their corresponding joint density $f_k^p(x_k^{(1)}, x_k^{(2)})$ with its information about the stochastic dependency is unknown. Unfortunately, the knowledge of the joint density or at least its parameterization in terms of a correlation parameter is essential for deriving estimated densities f_k^e using (6.10).

Similar to the time update, the *imprecisely known* joint density $f_k^p(x_k^{(1)}, x_k^{(2)})$ can be parameterized by a joint density according to

$$f_k^p(\underline{x}_k) = \sum_{i=1}^{m} \sum_{j=1}^{n} w_{ij} \int_{-1}^{1} \xi_{ij}(r)\, \mathcal{N}\left(\begin{bmatrix} x_k^{(1)} - \hat{x}_{k,i}^{e,(1)} \\ x_k^{(2)} - \hat{x}_{k,i}^{e,(2)} \end{bmatrix}, \mathbf{C}_{ij}^p(r) \right)\, dr \ ,$$

where $\xi_{ij}(r)$ and $\underline{\xi}$ (affecting the calculation of w_{ij}) are the generalized correlation function and the generalized correlation vector, respectively. The following example illustrates the results.

Example 6.5 For the sake of simplicity, a linear measurement equation is given as follows

$$\hat{y} = \boldsymbol{x}_k^{(1)} + \boldsymbol{x}_k^{(2)} + \boldsymbol{v}_k \ ,$$

where the two random variables $\boldsymbol{x}_k^{(1)}$ and $\boldsymbol{x}^{(2)}$ are represented by Gaussian mixtures with two components, visualized in Figure 6.2. The estimated density $f_k^e(x^{(1)})$ for various generalized correlation parameter vectors $\underline{\xi}$ and α_{ij} is depicted in Figure 6.5. These figures clearly show that the estimation result strongly depends on the stochastic dependency, however can be parameterized in terms of a generalized correlation parameter $\underline{\xi}$ and a generalized correlation function $\xi(r)$. It is obvious that the parameterized estimated distribution function $F_k^e(x^{(1)})$ can be bounded by means of bounding distribution functions $F_u(\cdot)$ (upper bound) and $F_k(\cdot)$ (lower bound), depicted in Figure 6.5 **(c)**. ∎

6.4 Summary and Discussion

This chapter focuses on the parameterization of different types of joint densities with both Gaussian marginals and Gaussian mixture marginals. It is shown that by assuming a specific stochastic dependency structure, these joint densities contain all information about this dependency in terms of a *generalized correlation parameter* $\underline{\xi}$ and/or a *generalized correlation function* $\xi(r)$. Unlike the classical correlation coefficient r, the generalized correlation parameter and function is a sufficient measure for the stochastic dependency between two random variables represented by Gaussian mixtures.

Depending on these correlation parameters, detailed prediction results and measurement results are presented. In addition, it is shown that there could exist bounding densities containing all possible joint densities characterized by the generalized correlation parameter vector $\underline{\xi}$ and the generalized correlation function $\xi(r)$. To find such bounding densities representing the stochastic dependency constraints is left for future research. A possible direction for finding bound densities can be found in [82]. Once such a bounding density is found, the derivation of a filtering technique that can cope with *nonlinear models* and is robust against imprecisely known stochastic dependencies is possible.

CHAPTER 7

Conclusion and Future Research

This research work was devoted to the development of efficient probabilistic methods for the model-based state estimation and parameter identification of space-time continuous systems. The main applications for the derived methods are the observation, monitoring, and exploration of dynamic and spatially distributed physical phenomena, such as temperature distributions or biochemical concentrations. The main goals are the systematic interpolation of space-time discrete, spatially distributed measurements and the estimation of non-measureable quantities. The challenge is that the estimation and identification results in a high-dimensional and nonlinear problem to be solved; however, with a linear substructure that can be exploited. Moreover, for physical systems widely distributed and for measurement systems consisting of a large number of measurement points, decentralized estimation approaches are required that are scalable. For coping with these challenges, efficient methods were developed within this research work.

In order to assure smooth, precise, and physically correct estimation results, physical background knowledge (in terms of a system model) were rigorously exploited. The space-time continuous physical systems that were considered can be modelled by *stochastic partial differential equations*. The description and explanations of the developed methods were restricted to the convection-diffusion equation for simplicity and brevity reasons; however, the application to any (linear) partial differential equation is straightforward. Besides the rigorous model-based approach, the novelties are the systematic consideration and the integrated treatment of uncertainties. The following *uncertainty models* are considered, (a) stochastic uncertainties for system states and unknown model parameters, and (b) set-valued uncertainties for imprecisely known stochastic dependencies between individual estimates. On the basis of these model descriptions, two different methods were developed for the nonlinear and decentralized estimation of space-time continuous systems; separately described in the following.

Sliced Gaussian Mixture Filter (SGMF)   For the estimation of nonlinear systems approximation methods are necessary due to its high computational demand and the resulting non-parametric density representation. The SGMF exploits linear substructures in mixed linear/nonlinear systems, and thus is well-suited for the estimation of space-time continuous systems. In the following, its properties and contributions are shortly stated:

- The estimator is based on a novel general-purpose density representation (the sliced Gaussian mixture) for the decomposition of the estimation problem. The proposed probability density function consists of a Dirac mixture and a Gaussian mixture in different subspaces.

- The density approximation necessary within the proposed framework is based on *minimizing a certain distance measure*. The systematic approximation technique (nonrandom, deterministic) yields close to optimal estimation results.

- The individual slices of the proposed density representation are jointly considered during the approximation process. Thus, a kind of interaction between them is enforced in an almost natural way and leads to better approximation results.

- Thanks to the systematic positioning of the density slices while minimizing a distance measure, the underlying density function can be usually represented with less parameters. This results in a lower number of Kalman filter updates that are required.

- Here, for simplicity the density approximation were restricted to the consideration of the subspace that is represented by the Dirac mixture. However, the *systematic approach* introduced in this work allows the consideration of the *joint space*, i.e., the subspaces represented by the Dirac mixture and the Gaussian mixture.

The SGMF was applied to the high-dimensional and nonlinear lumped-parameter system model that results from the conversion of a space-time continuous system. By this means, the state and the parameters of physical phenomena can be simultaneously estimated in a very efficient manner. The proposed estimator provides novel prospects not only for the estimation of space-time continuous systems but also for sensor network applications in general. The performance was demonstrated using various extensive simulation studies: (a) identification of process parameters, (b) localization of sensor nodes based on local observations of a space-time continuous physical system, and (c) localization of spatially distributed sources and leakages. It was shown that thanks to the simultaneous approach and the SGMF, the network is able to estimate the entire distributed state of the physical system, identify non-measurable quantities, and would be able to adapt its algorithms and behavior in an autonomous fashion.

Future directions for the extension of the SGMF could consist in the consideration of the entire joint density (i.e., both in the direction represented by Dirac mixture and Gaussian mixture density) for the density approximation. By this means, the accuracy of the approximation could be further improved and less density slices would be necessary for a precise estimation result. In addition, the system equation (transition density) as well as the measurement equation (likelihood) could be exploited for the determination of optimal positions and additionaly reducing the number of density slices. Moreover, by the direct processing of the individual density slices, the expensive reapproximation of the density function may be avoided.

Covariance Bounds Filter (CBF)   For the estimation of physical systems that are spatially distributed over a wide area, decentralized approaches are required in order to assure a scalable processing of the information. The main problem is that such approaches leads to stochastic dependencies, e.g., correlations, between the individual estimates that may either be too expensive to maintain or are simply not available for several reasons. In the case of Gaussian probability densities, the CBF provides a technique for coping with imprecisely known correlations. The properties and contributions are shortly stated in the following:

- The CBF is a general-purpose and systematic estimator for processing individual random variables with cross-covariances that possesses set-valued uncertainties. This is, for example, the case of unknown cross-correlations caused by a fully decentralized processing.

- The robust estimator assures conservative and consistent (an upper bound in the positive definite sense) estimation results when the correlations between the individual estimates to be processed are imprecisely known.

- For sensor network applications, the CBF is not restricted to certain types of topologies, e.g., fully-connected or tree-connected topology. Rather can be employd on any kind of topology, since the method is not based on tracking stochastic dependencies between each individual node in the network.

- It allows the systematic consideration of prior knowledge in terms of correlation constraints (symmetric and asymmetric constraints). By this means tighter bounding densities, and thus more precise estimation results can be derived.

- The decomposition of the system model into several subsystems and the consideration of prior knowledge with the CBF provides a continuous scaling between a fully centralized and a fully decentralized estimation of physical systems distributed over a wide area.

- Unlike other estimators that are robust against unknown correlations, the CBF can be applied not only to the measurement step, but in particular to the prediction step. This property is essential for the decentralized reconstruction of space-time continuous systems.

- Since the CBF is based on bounding ellipses (representing covariance matrices), it can be applied to a wide variety of applications. For example, conservative results can be obtained for systems with uncertain parameters represented by set-valued uncertainty models.

The CBF can be applied to a wide variety of applications, such as the simultaneous localization and map building (SLAM). However, in this research work, the novel estimator was applied to the decentralized state estimation of space-time continuous systems observed by a sensor network. By this means, a processing can be derived that is robust against imprecisely known correlations caused by the fully decentralized approach or a common source of uncertainties affecting more than one sensor node. The individual sensor nodes in the network locally reconstruct widely distributed physical systems and exchange local estimates only with adjacent nodes, i.e., storing expensive information about correlations is not required.

The CBF is restricted to random variables that are uniquely characterized by covariance matrices, such as Gaussian probability density functions, and cannot be readily extended to non-Gaussian densities. For example, by applying the CBF directly to the individual components of a Gaussian mixture density function does not assure consistent, and thus correct estimation results anymore. As a consequence more involved methods are required for the generalization of the CBF to arbitrary density functions. The first challenge is to find a method for the parameterization of the imprecisely known joint probability density function. The parameterized joint density proposed in this research work contains all information, under structural assumptions, about the stochastic dependencies between their marginal densities. A parameterization of all valid jointly Gaussian mixture densities were derived for given Gaussian mixture marginals; parameterized by a so-called generalized correlation parameter vector. Future direction for the application of the proposed parameterized joint densities is the derivation of bounding densities that sufficiently represent the entire set of valid joint densities, and thus yields conservative and consistent estimation results. A promising approach would be the derivation of a bounding density in terms of a dispersive order, which is a stochastic order applicable to arbitrary density functions. Based on the proposed parameterization of joint densities and an efficient method for finding bounding densities, the CBF may be generalized to arbitrary probability density functions, such as Gaussian mixtures.

List of Figures

List of Examples

Bibliography

[1] Perfect Ice Conditions Ensure Faster Speed Skating Times (url: http://www.zigbee.org/imwp/download.asp?ContentID=12588). *ZigBee Alliance*, 2008.

[2] Mohammad N. Almasri and Jagath J. Kaluarachchi. Modeling Nitrate Contamination of Groundwater in Agricultural Watersheds. *Journal of Hydrology*, 343:211–229, 2007.

[3] M. E. Alpay and M. H. Shor. Model-based Solution Techniques for the Source Localization Problem. *IEEE Transactions on Control Systems Technology*, 8(6):895–904, 2000.

[4] Daniel L. Alspach and Harold W. Sorenson. Nonlinear Bayesian Estimation Using Gaussian Sum Approximations. *IEEE Transactions on Automatic Control*, AC-17(4):439–448, August 1972.

[5] Mary P. Anderson and William W. Woessner. *Applied Groundwater Modeling: Simulation of Flow and Advective Transport*. Academic Press, 1992.

[6] Christophe Andrieu and Arnaud Doucet. Particle Filtering for Partially Observed Gaussian State Space Models. *Journal of the Royal Statistical Society: Series B (Statistical Methodology)*, 64(4):827–836, October 2002.

[7] Pablo O. Arambel, Constantino Rago, and Raman K. Mehra. Covariance Intersection Algorithm for Distributed Spacecraft State Estimation. In *Proceedings of the American Control Conference (ACC 2001)*, Arlington, June 2001.

[8] M. S. Arulampalam, S. Maskell, N. Gordon, and T. Clapp. A Tutorial on Particle Filters for Online Nonlinear/Non-Gaussian Bayesian Tracking. *IEEE Transactions on Signal Processing*, 50(2):174–188, February 2002.

[9] Peter M. Atkinson and C. D. Lloyd. Non-stationary Variogram Models for Geostatistical Sampling Optimisation: An Empirical Investigation Using Elevation Data. *Computers and Geosciences*, 33:1285–1300, 2007.

[10] Thomas Bader, Alexander Wiedemann, Kathrin Roberts, and Uwe D. Hanebeck. Model–based Motion Estimation of Elastic Surfaces for Minimally Invasive Cardiac Surgery. In *Proceedings of the 2007 IEEE International Conference on Robotics and Automation (ICRA 2007)*, pages 2261–2266, Rome, Italy, April 2007.

[11] A. J. Baker. *Finite Element Computational Fluid Mechanics*. Taylor and Francis, 1983.

[12] P. Bartelt and M. Lehning. A Physical SNOWPACK Model for the Swiss Avalanche Warning, Part I: Numerical Model. *Cold Regions Science and Technology*, 35:123–145, 2002.

[13] E. T. Baumgartner, H. Aghazarian, A. Trebi-Ollennu, T. L. Huntsberger, and M. S. Garrett. State Estimation and Vehicle Localization for the FIDO Rover. In *Proceedings of SPIE - The International Society for Optical Engineering*, volume 4196, pages 329–336, Bellingham, WA, USA, 2000.

[14] Randal Beard, Jacob Gunther, Jonathan Lawton, and Wynn Stirling. The Nonlinear Projection Filter. *AIAA Journal of Guidance, Control and Dynamics*, 1998.

[15] T. Belytschko, Y. Krongauz, D. Organ, M. Fleming, and P. Krysl. Meshless Methods: An Overview and Recent Developments. *Computer Methods in Applied Mechanics and Engineering*, 139:3–47, 1996.

[16] T. Belytschko, D. Organ, and Y. Krongauz. A Coupled Finite Element-Element-Free Galerkin Method. In *Computational Mechanics*, volume 17, pages 186–195. Springer, May 1995.

[17] D. Blatt, A. O. Hero, and H. Guachman. A Convergent Incremental Gradient Method with Constant Stepsize. *SIAM Journal of Optimization*, 18, 2007.

[18] Patrick Bogaert and Dimitri D'Or. Estimating Soil Properties from Thematic Soil Maps. *Soil Science Society of America Journal*, 66:1492–1500, 2002.

[19] E. Bolviken, P. J. Acklam, N. Christophersen, and J.-M. Stordal. Monte Carlo Filters for Non-Linear State Estimation. *Automatica*, 37:177–183, 2001.

[20] Dietrich Braess. *Finite Elemente*. Springer, 2003.

[21] Damiano Brigo, Bernard Hanzon, and Francois LeGland. A Differential Geometric Approach to Nonlinear Filtering: The Projection Filter. *IEEE Transactions on Automatic Control*, 42(2):247–252, 1998.

[22] Dietrich Brunn and Uwe D. Hanebeck. A Model-Based Framework for Optimal Measurements in Machine Tool Calibration. In *Proceedings of the 2005 IEEE International Conference on Robotics and Automation (ICRA 2005)*, Barcelona, Spain, 2005.

[23] Laurent Buisson and Gerald Giraud. Two Examples of Expert Knowledge Based System for Avalanche Forecasting and Protection. *Surveys in Geophysics*, 16:603–619, 1995.

[24] Claudio Canuto, M. Yousuff Hussaini, Alfio Quarteroni, and Thmas A. Zang. *Spectral Methods: Fundamentals in Single Domains*. Springer Verlag, 2006.

[25] George Casella and Christian P. Robert. Rao-Blackwellisation of Sampling Schemes. *Biometrika*, 83(1):81–94, 1996.

[26] J. A. Castellanos, J. D. Tardos, and G. Schmidt. Building a Global Map of the Environment of a Mobile Robot: The Importance of Correlations. In *IEEE International Conference on Robotics and Automation (ICRA 1997)*, Albuquerque, New Mexico, 1997.

[27] J.-C. Chai, S.-L. Shen, H.-H. Zhu, and X.-L. Zhang. Land Subsidence due to Groundwater Drawdown in Shanghai. *Géotechnique*, 54(2):143–147, 2004.

[28] Rahul Chattery, Vassilis L. Syrmos, and Pradeep Misra. Finite Modeling of Parabolic Equations Using Galerkin Methods and Inverse Matrix Approximations. *Circuits Systems Signal Processing*, 15:631 – 648, 1996.

[29] Lingji Chen, Pablo O. Arambel, and Raman K. Mehra. Fusion under Unknown Correlation - Covariance Intersection as a Special Case.

[30] Lingji Chen, Pablo O. Arambel, and Raman K. Mehra. Estimation under Unknown Correlation: Covariance Intersection Revisited. *IEEE Transaction on Automatic Control*, 47(11):1879 – 1882, November 2002.

[31] Rong Chen and Jun S. Liu. Mixture Kalman Filters. *Journal of the Royal Statistical Society*, 62(3):493–508, 2000.

[32] C. Y. Chong and S. Mori. Convex Combination and Covariance Intersection Alorithms in Distributed Fusion. In *The 4th International Conference on Information Fusion (Fusion 2001)*, Montreal, Canada, 2001.

[33] George Christakos. A Bayesian/Maximum-Entropy View to the Spatial Estimation Problem. *Mathematical Geology*, 22(7):763–777, 1990.

[34] George Christakos, Patrick Bogaert, and Marc Laurent Serre. *Temporal GIS – Advanced Functions for Field-Based Applications*. Springer, 2001.

[35] Timothy H. Chung, Vijay Gupta, Joel W. Burdick, and Richard M. Murray. On a Decentralized Active Sensing Strategy using Mobile Sensor Platforms in a Network. In *43rd IEEE Conference on Decision and Control*, volume 2, pages 1914–1919, December 2004.

[36] T.J. Chung. *Computational Fluid Dynamics*. Cambridge University Press, 2002.

[37] Vlatko Cingoski, Naoki Miyamoto, and Hideo Yamashita. Element-free Galerkin Method for Electromagnetic Field Computations. *IEEE Transactions on Magnetics*, 34(5):3236–3239, 1998.

[38] Noel A. C. Cressie. *Statistics for Spatial Data*. John Wiley & Sons, 1993.

[39] David Culler, Deborah Estrin, and Mani Srivastava. Overview of Sensor Networks. *IEEE Computer*, 37(8):41–49, 2004.

[40] Paul J. Curran and Peter M. Atkinson. Geostatistics and Remote Sensing. *Progress in Physical Geography*, 22:61–78, 1998.

[41] Dimitri D'Or. *Spatial Prediction of Soil Properties*. Phd thesis, Université catholique de Louvain, 2003.

[42] A. Fournier, H.-P. Bunge, R. Hollerbach, and J.-P. Vilotte. Application of the Spectral-Element Method to the Axisymmetric Navier-Stokes Equation. In *Geophysical Journal International*, number 156, pages 682–700, 2004.

[43] Zhi-Fang Fu and Jimin He. *Modal Analysis*. Butterworth Heinemann, September 2001.

[44] Roger G. Ghanem and Pol D. Spanos. *Stochastic Finite Elements: A Spectral Approach*. Dover Pubn Inc, December 2003.

[45] Gerald Giraud, Eric Martin, Eric Brun, and Jean-Pierre Navarre. CrocusMepraPC Software: A Tool for Local Simulations of Snow Cover Stratigraphy and Avalanche Risks. In *International Snow Science Workshop*, Penticton, B.C., 2002.

[46] Robert M. Gray and Lee D. Davisson. *Random Processes: A Mathematical Approach for Engineers*. Prentice Hall, 1985.

[47] Marian Grigoras, Olga Feiermann, and Uwe D. Hanebeck. Data–Driven Modeling of Signal Strength Distributions for Localization in Cellular Radio Networks (Datengetriebene Modellierung von Feldstärkeverteilungen für die Ortung in zellulären Funknetzen). *at - Automatisierungstechnik, Sonderheft: Datenfusion in der Automatisierungstechnik*, 53(7):314–321, July 2005.

[48] Ben Grocholsky, Alexei Makarenko, and Hugh Durrant-Whyte. Information-Theoretic Coordinated Control of Multiple Sensor Platforms. In *International Conference on Robotics and Automation*, volume 1, pages 1521–1526, Taipei, Taiwan, September 2003.

[49] Fredrik Gustafsson, Fredrik Gunnarsson, Niclas Bergman, Urban Forssell, Jonas Jansson, Rickard Karlsson, and Per-Johan Nordlund. Particle Filters for Positioning, Navigation, and Tracking. *IEEE Transactions on Signal Processing*, 50(2):425–437, 2002.

[50] Fredrik Gustafsson, Thomas B. Schön, Rickard Karlsson, and Per-Johan Nordlund. State-of-the-Art for the Marginalized Particle Filter. *IEEE Nonlinear Statistical Signal Processing Workshop*, pages 172–174, September 2006.

[51] Heiko Hamann and Heinz Wörn. A Space- and Time-Continuous Model of Self-Organizing Robot Swarms for Design Support. In *First IEEE International Conference on Self-Adaptive and Self-Organizing Systems, Boston, USA*, pages 23–31, Jul 2007.

[52] Heiko Hamann and Heinz Wörn. An Analytical and Spatial Model of Foraging in a Swarm of Robots. In A. F. T. Winfield E. Sahin, W. M. Spears, editor, *Swarm Robotics - 2nd SAB 2006 International Workshop, Rome, Italy*, volume 4433 of *LNCS*, pages 43–55. Springer, 2007.

[53] Uwe D. Hanebeck and Kai Briechle. New Results for Stochastic Prediction and Filtering with Unknown Correlations. In *Proeceedings of the IEEE Conference on Multisensor Fusion and Integration for Intelligent Systems (MFI 2001)*, pages 147–152, 2001.

[54] Uwe D. Hanebeck, Kai Briechle, and Joachim Horn. Fusing Information Simultaneously Corrupted by Uncertainties with Known Bounds and Random Noise with Known Distribution. *Information Fusion, Elsevier Science*, 1(1):55–63, 2000.

[55] Uwe D. Hanebeck, Kai Briechle, and Joachim Horn. A Tight Bound for the Joint Covariance of Two Random Vectors with Unknown but Constrained Cross-Correlation. In *International Conference on Multisensor Fusion and Integration for Intelligent Systems (MFI 2001)*, number 11, pages 85 – 90, Baden-Baden, Germany, August 2001.

[56] Uwe D. Hanebeck, Kai Briechle, and Andreas Rauh. Progressive Bayes: A New Framework for Nonlinear State Estimation. In *Proceedings of SPIE, AeroSense Symposium*, volume 5099, pages 256 – 267, Orlando, Florida, May 2003.

[57] Uwe D. Hanebeck and Joachim Horn. An Efficient Method for Simultaneous Map Building and Localization. In *Proceedings of SPIE, AeroSense Symposium*, Orlando, Florida, 2001.

[58] Uwe D. Hanebeck and Vesa Klumpp. Localized Cumulative Distributions and a Multivariate Generalization of the Cramér-von Mises Distance. In *Proceedings of the 2008 IEEE International Conference on Multisensor Fusion and Integration for Intelligent Systems (MFI 2008)*, Seoul, Republic of Korea, August 2008.

[59] Uwe D. Hanebeck and Oliver C. Schrempf. Greedy Algorithms for Dirac Mixture Approximation of Arbitrary Probability Density Functions. In *IEEE Conference on Decision and Control (CDC 2007)*, December 2007.

[60] Richard D. Hedger, Nils R. B. Olsen, Tim J. Malthus, and Peter M. Atkinson. Coupling Remote Sensing with Computational Fluid Dynamics Modelling to Estimate Lake Chlorophyll-a Concentration. *Remote Sensing of Environment*, 79:116–122, 2002.

[61] Thomas C. Henderson, Christopher Sikorski, Edwart Grant, and Kyle Luthy. Computational Sensor Networks. In *Proceedings of the 2007 IEEE/RSJ International Conference on Intelligent Robots and Systems (IROS 2007)*, San Diego, USA, 2007.

[62] Jeffrey Hightower and Gaetano Borriello. Location Systems for Ubiquitous Computing. *IEEE Computer*, 2001.

[63] Nico Hübel, Sandra Hirche, A. Gusrialdi, T. Hatanaka, M. Fujita, and O. Sawodny. Coverage Control with Information Decay in Dynamic Environments. In *Proceedings of the 17th IFAC World Congress (IFAC 2008)*, Seoul, Korea, July 2008.

[64] Marco F. Huber and Uwe D. Hanebeck. Gaussian Filter based on Deterministic Sampling for High Quality Nonlinear Estimation. In *Proceedings of the 17th IFAC World Congress (IFAC 2008)*, Seoul, Korea, July 2008.

[65] Marco F. Huber and Uwe D. Hanebeck. Progressive Gaussian Mixture Reduction. In *Proceedings of the 11th International Conference on Information Fusion (Fusion 2008)*, Cologne, Germany, July 2008.

[66] Michael B. Hurley. An Information Theoretic Justification for Covariance Intersection and Its Generlization.

[67] Aleksandar Jeremic and Arye Nehorai. Design of Chemical Sensor Arrays for Monitoring Disposal Sites on the Ocean Floor. *IEEE Journal of Oceanic Engineering*, 23:334–343, 1998.

[68] Aleksandar Jeremic and Arye Nehorai. Landmine Detection and Localization Using Chemcial Sensor Array Processing. *IEEE Transactions on Signal Processing*, 48:1295–1305, 2000.

[69] Don H. Johnson and Sinan Sinanovic. Symmetrizing the Kullback-Leibler Distance. Technical report, Rice University, March 2001.

[70] Simon J. Julier. An Empirical Study into the Use of Chernoff Information for Robust, Distributed Fusion of Gaussian Mixture Models. In *Fusion*, 2006.

[71] Simon J. Julier, Tim Bailey, and Jeffrey K. Uhlmann. Using Exponential Mixture Densities for Suboptimal Distributed Data Fusion. In *The 1st IEEE Nonlinear Statistical Signal Processing Workshop (NSSPW 2007)*, 2007.

[72] Simon J. Julier and Jeffrey K. Uhlmann. A New Extension of the Kalman Filter to Nonlinear Systems. 1997.

[73] Simon J. Julier and Jeffrey K. Uhlmann. A Non-divergent Estimation Algorithm in the Presence of Unknown Correlations. In *Proceedings of the American Control Conference (ACC 1997)*, Albuquerque, New Mexico, June 1997.

[74] Simon J. Julier and Jeffrey K. Uhlmann. Unscented Filtering and Nonlinear Estimation. In *Proceedings of the IEEE*, volume 92, pages 401–422, 2004.

[75] Simon J. Julier and Jeffrey K. Uhlmann. Using Covariance Intersection for SLAM. *Robotics and Autonomous Systems*, 55:3–20, 2007.

[76] Thomas Kailath, Ali H. Sayed, and Babak Hassibi. *Linear Estimation*. Prentice Hall, March 2000.

[77] R. E. Kalman. A New Approach to Linear Filtering and Prediction Problems. *Transactions of the ASME - Journal of Basic Engineering*, 1960.

[78] Rickard Karlsson, Thomas Schön, and Fredrik Gustafsson. Complexity Analysis of the Marginalized Particle Filter. *IEEE Transactions on Signal Processing*, 53(11):4408–4411, 2005.

[79] G. E. Karniadakis and S. Sherwin. *Spectral/hp Element Methods for Computational Fluid Dynamics*. Oxford University Press, 2005.

[80] Andreas Keese. A Review of Recent Developments in the Numerical Solution of Stochastic Partial Differential Equations (Stochastic Finite Elements). Informatikbericht 2003-06, Institute of Scientific Computing, Technical University of Braunschweig, October 2003.

[81] John Kenney and Wynn Stirling. Nonlinear Filtering of Convex Sets of Probability Distributions. *Journal of statistical planning and inference*, 105(1):123–147, 2002.

[82] Vesa Klumpp, Dietrich Brunn, and Uwe D. Hanebeck. Approximate Nonlinear Bayesian Estimation Based on Lower and Upper Densities. In *Proceedings of the 9th Internation Conference on Information Fusion (Fusion 2006)*, Florence, Italy, 2006.

[83] Vesa Klumpp and Uwe D. Hanebeck. Dirac Mixture Trees for Fast Suboptimal Multi-Dimensional Density Approximation. In *Proceedings of the 2008 IEEE International Conference on Multisensor Fusion and Integration for Intelligent Systems (MFI 2008)*, Seoul, Republic of Korea, August 2008.

[84] Vesa Klumpp and Uwe D. Hanebeck. Direct Fusion of Dirac Mixture Densities using an Efficient Approximate Solution in Joint State Space. In *Proceedings of the 2008 IEEE International Conference on Multisensor Fusion and Integration for Intelligent Systems (MFI 2008)*, Seoul, Republic of Korea, August 2008.

[85] Dimitri Komatitsch, Jean-Pierre Vilotte, Rossana Vai, Jose M. Castillo-Covarrubias, and Francisco J. Sanchez-Sesma. The Spectral Element Method for Elastic Wave Equations - Application to 2-D and 3-D Seismic Problems. In *International Journal for Numerical Methods in Engineering*, volume 45, pages 1139–1164, 1999.

[86] J. Kondo and T. Yamazaki. A Prediction Model for Snowmelt, Snow Surface Temperature and Freezing Depth Using a Heat Balance. *Journal of Applied Meteorology*, 29:375–384, 1990.

[87] J. Korbicz, M. Z. Zgurovsky, and A. N. Novikov. Suboptimal Sensors Location in the State Estimation Problem for Stochastic Non-Linear Distributed Parameter Systems. *International Journal of Systems Science*, 19(9):1871–1882, 1988.

[88] Andrew M. Ladd, Kostas E. Bekris, Algis Rudys, Guillaume Marceau, and Lydia E. Kavraki. Robotics-Based Location Sensing using Wireless Ethernet. In *Proceedings of the 8th annual international conference on mobile computing and networking*, pages 227–238. ACM Press, 2002.

[89] Michael Lehning, Perry Bartelt, Bob Brown, and Charles Fierz. A Physical SNOW-PACK Model for the Swiss Avalanche Warning Part III: Meterological Forcing, Thin Layer Formation and Evaluation. *Cold Regions Science and Technology*, 35:169–184, 2002.

[90] Michael Lehning, Perry Bartelt, Bob Brown, Charles Fierz, and Pramod Satyawali. A Physical SNOWPACK Model for the Swiss Avalanche Warning Part II: Snow Microstructure. *Cold Regions Science and Technology*, pages 147–167, 2002.

[91] Jörg C. Lemm. Econophysics WS 1999/2000: Notizen zur Vorelsung über Econophysics. Technical report, Institut für Theoretische Physik I, Universität Münster, Wilhelm-Klemm Str. 9, D-48149 Münster, Germany, 2000.

[92] P. Li, R. Goodall, and V. Kadirkamanathan. Estimation of parameters in a linear state space model using a Rao-Blackwellised particle filter. *IEE Proceedings Control Theory and Applications*, 151(6):727–738, November 2004.

[93] Shaofan Li and Wing Kam Liu. *Meshfree Particle Methods*. Springer, 2007.

[94] Gui-Rong Liu. *Mesh Free Methods : Moving beyond the Finite Element Method*. CRC Press LLC, 2003.

[95] C. D. Lloyd and Peter M. Atkinson. Assesing Uncertainty in Estimates with Ordinary and Indicator Kriging. *Computers and Geosciences*, 27:929–937, 2001.

[96] Cassio G. Lopes and Ali H. Sayed. Incremental Adaptive Strategies Over Distributed Networks. *IEEE Transactions on Signal Processing*, 55:4064–4077, 2007.

[97] H. Malebranche. Simultaneous State and Parameter Estimation and Location of Sensors for Distributed Systems. *International Journal of Systems Science*, 19(8):1387–1405, 1988.

[98] Jörg Matthes. *Eine neue Method zur Quellenlokalisierung auf der Basis räumlich verteilter, punktweiser Konzentrationsmessungen*. PhD thesis, Universität Karlsruhe (TH), Fakultät für Maschinenbau, 2004.

[99] Peter S. Maybeck and Brian D. Smith. Multiple Model Tracker based on Gaussian Mixture Reduction for Maneuvering Targets in Clutter. *8th International Conference on Information Fusion (Fusion 2005)*, 1:40–47, July 2005.

[100] Cleve Moler and Charles Van Loan. Nineteen Dubious Ways to Compute the Exponential of a Matrix, Twenty-Five Years Later. *SIAM Review*, 45(1):3–49, January 2003.

[101] J. J. Monaghan. An Introduction to SPH. *Computer Physics Communications*, 48:89–96, 1988.

[102] Arthur G. Mutambara. *Decentralized Estimation and Control for Multisensor Systems*. CRC Press Inc, 1998.

[103] Wolfgang Niehsen. Information Fusion Based on Fast Covariance Intersection Filtering. In *Proceedings of the Fifth International Conference on Information Fusion (Fusion'02)*, volume 2, pages 901 – 904, July 2002 2002.

[104] Petter Ögren, Edward Fiorelli, and Naomi Ehrich Leonard. Cooperative Control of Mobile Sensor Networks: Adaptive Gradient Climbing in a Distributed Environment. *IEEE Transactions on Automatic Control*, 49(8):1292–1302, August 2004.

[105] Lee-Ling Ong, Matthew Ridley, Ben Upcroft, Suresh Kumar, and Tim Bailey. A Comparison of Probabilistic Representations for Decentralised Data Fusion. In *Intelligent Sensors, Sensor Networks and Information Processing Conference*, pages 187–192, December 2005.

[106] Lee-Ling Ong, Ben Upcroft, Matthew Ridley, Tim Bailey, Salah Sukkarieh, and Hugh Durrant-Whyte. Decentralised Data Fusion with Particles. In Claude Sammut, editor, *Proceedings of the Australasian Conference on Robotics and Automation*, December 2004.

[107] Tobias Johannes Ortmaier. *Motion Compensation in Minimally Invasive Robotic Surgery*. PhD thesis, Lehrstuhl für Realzeit-Computersysteme, Technische Universität München, 2003.

[108] Mathias Ortner, Arye Nehorai, and Aleksandar Jeremic. Biochemical Transport Modeling and Bayesian Source Estimation in Realistic Environments. *IEEE Transactions on Signal Processing*, 55(6):2520–2532, June 2007.

[109] Athanasios Papoulis and S. Unnikrishna Pillai. *Probability, Random Variables and Stochastic Processes*. McGraw Hill, 2002.

[110] Bruno Betoni Parodi, Andrei Szabo, Joachim Bamberger, and Joachim Horn. SPLL: Simultaneous Probabilistic Localization and Learning. In *Proceedings of the 17th IFAC World Congress (IFAC 2008)*, Seoul, Korea, 2008.

[111] R. F. Pawula. Generalizations and Extensions of the Fokker-Planck-Kolmogorov Equations. *IEEE Transactions on Information Theory*, 13(1):33–41, 1967.

[112] Friedrich Pukelsheim. *Optimal Design of Experiments*. John Wiley & Sons, New York, 1993.

[113] M. Rabbat and R. Nowak. Distributed Optimization in Sensor Networks. 2004.

[114] K. Rankinen, T. Karvonen, and D. Butterfield. A Simple Model for Predicting Soil Temperature in Snow-covered and Seasonally Frozen Soil: Model Description and Testing. *Hydrology and Earth System Sciences*, 8:706–716, 2004.

[115] Andreas Rauh, Kai Briechle, Uwe D. Hanebeck, Joachim Bamberger, Clemens Hoffmann, and Marian Grigoras. Localization of DECT Mobile Phones Based on a New Nonlinear Filtering Technique. In *Proceedings of SPIE, Vol. 5084, AeroSense Symposium*, pages 39–50, Orlando, Florida, May 2003.

[116] Kathrin Roberts and Uwe D. Hanebeck. Prediction and Reconstruction of Distributed Dynamic Phenomena Characterized by Linear Partial Differential Equations. In *Proceedings of the 8th International Conference on Information Fusion (Fusion 2005)*, Philadelphia, Pennsylvania, July 2005.

[117] T. Ross, P. Myllymaki, H. Tirri, P. Misikangas, and J. Sievanen. A Probabilistic Approach to WLAN User Location Estimation. *International Journal of Wireless Information Networks*, 9(3), July 2002.

[118] L. A. Rossi, B. Krishnamachari, and C.-C.J. Kuo. Distributed Parameter Estimation for Monitoring Diffusion Phenomena using Physical Models. In *Sensor and Ad Hoc Communications and Networks, 2004. IEEE SECON 2004. 2004 First Annual IEEE Communications Society Conference on*, pages 460–469, Los Angeles, USA, 2004.

[119] Lorenzo A. Rossi, Bhaskar Krishnamachari, and C.-C. Jay Kuo. Monitoring of Diffusion Processes with PDE Models in Wireless Sensor Networks. In *Proceedings of the SPIE*, volume 5417, pages 324–335, 2004.

[120] Patrick Rößler, Uwe D. Hanebeck, Marian Grigoras, Paul T. Pilgram, Joachim Bamberger, and Clemens Hoffmann. Automatische Kartographierung der Signalcharakteristik in Funknetzwerken. October 2003.

[121] Andrew R. Runnalls. Kullback-Leibler Approach to Gaussian Mixture Reduction. *IEEE Transactions on Aerospace and Electronic Systems*, 43(3):989–999, July 2007.

[122] D. J. Salmond. Mixture Reduction Algorithms for Target Tracking in Clutter. In O. E. Drummond, editor, *Proc. SPIE Vol. 1305, p. 434-445, Signal and Data Processing of Small Targets 1990*, volume 1305 of *Presented at the Society of Photo-Optical Instrumentation Engineers (SPIE) Conference*, pages 434–445, October 1990.

[123] Thomas B. Schön and Fredrik Gustafsson. Particle Filters for System Identification of State-Space Models Linear in either Parameters or States. In *Proceedings of the 13th IFAC Symposium on System Identification*, 2003.

[124] Thomas B. Schön, Rickard Karlsson, and Fredrik Gustafsson. The Marginalized Particle Filter in Practice. In *IEEE Aerospace Conference*, March 2006.

[125] Oliver C. Schrempf, Dietrich Brunn, and Uwe D. Hanebeck. Density Approximation Based on Dirac Mixtures with Regard to Nonlinear Estimation and Filtering. In *Proceedings of the 2006 IEEE Conference on Decision and Control (CDC 2006)*, San Diego, California, December 2006.

[126] Oliver C. Schrempf and Uwe D. Hanebeck. A State Estimator for Nonlinear Stochastic Systems Based on Dirac Mixture Approximations. In *Proceedings of the 4th International Conference on Informatics in Control, Automation and Robotics (ICINCO 2007)*, volume SPSMC, pages 54–61, Angers, France, May 2007.

[127] Oliver C. Schrempf and Uwe D. Hanebeck. Recursive Prediction of Stochastic Nonlinear Systems Based on Dirac Mixture Approximations. In *Proceedings of the 2007 American Control Conference (ACC 2007)*, pages 1768–1774, New York, New York, July 2007.

[128] Frank Schweitzer. Brownian Agent Models for Swarm and Chemotactic Interaction. In *Fifth German Workshop on Artificial Life 2002. Abstracting and synthesizing the principles of living systems*, pages 181–190, Lübeck, May 2002.

[129] Frank Schweitzer. *Brownian Agents and Active Particles. On the Emergence of Complex Behavior in the Natural and Social Sciences*. Springer-Verlag, Berlin, Germany, 2003.

[130] F. C. Schweppe. *Uncertain Dynamic Systems*. Prentice-Hall, Englewood Cliffs, NJ, 1973.

[131] Marc Laurent Serre. *Environmental Spatiotemporal Mapping and Ground Water Flow Modelling Using the BME and ST Methods*. Phd thesis, University of North Carolina at Chapel Hill, North Carolina, 1999.

[132] Dan Simon. *Optimal State Estimation: Kalman, H Infinity, and Nonlinear Approaches*. John Wilay and Sons, 2006.

[133] H. W. Sorenson. *Kalman Filtering: Theory and Application*. Piscataway, NJ: IEEE, 1985.

[134] M. Stoffel. *Numerical Modelling of Snow Using Finite Elements*. PhD thesis, Swiss Federal Institute of Technology Zürich, May 2005.

[135] Michael C. Sukop and Daniel T. Thorne. *Lattice Boltzmann Modeling*. Springer, 2007.

[136] John C. Tannehill, Dale A. Anderson, and Richard H. Pletcher. *Computational Fluid Mechanics and Heat Transfer*. Taylor & Francis, 1997.

[137] Ping Tao, Algis Rudys, Andrew M. Ladd, and Dan S. Wallach. Wireless LAN Location-sensing for Security Applications. In *Proceedings of the 2nd ACM workshop on wireless security*, pages 11–20, 2003.

[138] Dariusz Ucinski. *Measurement Optimization for Parameter Estimation in Distributed Systems*. Technical University Press, Zielona Gora, Poland, 1999.

[139] Dariusz Ucinski and J. Korbicz. Parameter Identification of Two-Dimensional Distributed Systems. *International Journal of Systems Science*, 21(12):2441–2456, 1990.

[140] Jeffrey K. Uhlmann, Simon Julier, and Michael Csorba. Nondivergent Simultaneous Map Building and Localization using Covariance Intersection. 1997.

[141] Ben Upcroft, Lee-Ling Ong, Suresh Kumar, Matthew Ridley, Tim Bailey, Salah Sukkarieh, and Hugh Durrant-Whyte. Rich Probabilistic Representations for Bearing Only Decentralised Data Fusion. In *7th International Conference on Information Fusion (Fusion 2005)*, Philadelphia, PA, USA, 2005.

[142] Rudolph van der Merwe, Eric A. Wan, and Simon Julier. Sigma-Point Kalman Filters for Nonlinear Estimation and Sensor-Fusion – Applications to Integrated Navigation –. In *AIAA Guidance, Navigation, and Control Conference and Exhibit*, Providence, Rhode Island, 2004.

[143] Jaco Vermaak, Arnaud Doucet, and Patrick Perez. Maintaining Multi-Modality through Mixture Tracking. In *Nineth IEEE International Conference on Computer Vision*, volume 2, pages 1110–1116, 2003.

[144] Hans Wackernagel. *Multivariate Geostatistics*. Springer, 1998.

[145] Herbert F. Wang and Mary P. Anderson. *Introduction to Groundwater Modeling – Finite Difference and Finite Element Methods*. Academic Press, 1995.

[146] Hui Wang, Henning Lenz, Andrei Szabo, Joachim Bamberger, and Uwe D. Hanebeck. Enhancing the Map Usage for Indoor Location-Aware Systems. In *International Conference on Human-Computer Interaction (HCI 2007)*, Peking, China, July 2007.

[147] Hui Wang, Henning Lenz, Andrei Szabo, and Uwe D. Hanebeck. Fusion of Barometric Sensors, WLAN Signals and Building Information for 3–D Indoor/Campus Localization. In *Proceedings of the 2006 IEEE International Conference on Multisensor Fusion and Integration for Intelligent Systems (MFI 2006)*, pages 426–432, Heidelberg, Germany, September 2006.

[148] Jan-Philipp Weiß. *Numerical Analysis of Lattice Boltzmann Methods for the Heat Equation on a Bounded Interval*. PhD thesis, Universität Karlsruhe (TH), 2006.

[149] Greg Welch, B. Danette Allen, Adrian Ilie, and Gary Bishop. Measurement Sample Time Optimization for Human Motion Tracking/Capture Systems. In *Proceedings of Trends and Issues in Tracking for Virtual Environments, Workshop at the IEEE Virtual Reality 2007 Conference*, 2007.

[150] Mike West. Approximating Posterior Distributions by Mixtures. *Journal of the Royal Statistical Society: Series B*, 55(2):409–422, 1993.

[151] Christopher K. I. Williams. Prediction with Gaussian Processes: from Linear Regression to Linear Prediction and Beyond. *Learning in graphical models*, pages 599–621, 1999.

[152] Christopher K. I. Williams and Carl Edward Rasmussen. Gaussian Processes for Regression. In David S. Touretzky, Michael C. Mozer, and Michael E. Hasselmo, editors, *Proc. Conf. Advances in Neural Information Processing Systems (NIPS 1995)*, volume 8. MIT Press, 1995.

[153] X. Xu and S. Negahdaripour. Application of Extended Covariance Intersection Principle for Masaic-based Optical Positioning and Navigation of Underwater Vehicles. In *Proceedings of IEEE International Conference on Robotics and Automation*, pages 2759–2766, Seoul, Korea, May 2001.

[154] J. Yin, V. L. Syrmos, and D. Y. Y. Yun. System Identification using the Extended Kalman Filter with Applications to Medical Imaging. In *Proceedings of the American Control Conference (ACC 2000)*, 2000.

[155] Tong Zhao and Arye Nehorai. Detecting and Estimating Biochemical Dispersion of a Moving Source in a Semi-Infinite Medium. *IEEE Transactions on Signal Processing*, 54(6):2213–2225, June 2006.

Supervised Student Works

[156] Rene Gröne. Modellbasierte Rekonstruktion verteilter Phänomene aus punktuellen Messungen am Beispiel der Luftfeuchte (Model-based Reconstruction of Spatially Distributed Phenomena with Focus on Humidity Applications). Diploma Thesis, Intelligent-Sensor-Actuator Systems Laboratory, Universität Karlsruhe (TH), 2007.

[157] Christian Herdtweck. Rekonstruktion und Parameteridentifikation verteilter Phänomene mittels Sensornetzwerken (Reconstruction and Parameter Identification of Distributed Phenomena using Sensor Networks). Diploma Thesis, Intelligent-Sensor-Actuator Systems Laboratory, Universität Karlsruhe (TH), 2007.

[158] Christian Hirsch. Räumliche und zeitliche Interpolationsverfahren zur Überwachung der Grundwasserqualität (Spatial and Temporal Interpolation Methods for Groundwater Monitoring). Diploma Thesis, Intelligent-Sensor-Actuator Systems Laboratory, Universität Karlsruhe (TH), 2008.

[159] Julian Hörst. Extension of the Sliced Gaussian Mixture Filter with Application to Cooperative Passive Target Tracking. Diploma Thesis, Intelligent-Sensor-Actuator Systems Laboratory, Universität Karlsruhe (TH), 2008.

[160] Julian Hörst. Suboptimale Approximation von mehrdimensionalen Gaussian–Mixtures durch Sliced Gaussian–Mixtures (Suboptimal Approximation of Multi-dimensional Gaussian–Mixtures with Sliced Gaussian–Mixtures). Student Research Project, Intelligent-Sensor-Actuator Systems Laboratory, Universität Karlsruhe (TH), 2008.

[161] Achim Kuwertz. Verteilte Sensoreinsatzplanung zur modellbasierten Rekonstruktion räumlich ausgedehnter Phänomene (Distributed Sensor Scheduling for Model-based Reconstruction of Spatially Distributed Phenomena). Student Research Project, Intelligent-Sensor-Actuator Systems Laboratory, Universität Karlsruhe (TH), 2008.

[162] Achim Kuwertz. Nichtlineare Sensoreinsatzplanung zur modellbasierten Quellenverfolgung bei räumlich ausgedehnten Phänomenen (Nonlinear Sensor Management for Model-based Source Detection in Spatially Distributed Phenomena). Diploma Thesis, Intelligent-Sensor-Actuator Systems Laboratory, Universität Karlsruhe (TH), 2009.

[163] Daniel Ota. Dichterepräsentationen für Mengen von Dirac-Mixture-Dichten basierend auf der dispersiven Ordnung (Density Representations of Set of Dirac-Mixture Densities based on Dispersive Orders). Diploma Thesis, Intelligent-Sensor-Actuator Systems Laboratory, Universitüt Karlsruhe (TH), 2008.

[164] Daniel Seth. Verfahren zur dezentralen Informationsfusion von nicht-gaußschen Wahrscheinlichkeitsdichtefunktionen (Methods for Decentralized Information Fusion of Non-Gaussian Probability Density Functions). Diploma Thesis, Intelligent-Sensor-Actuator Systems Laboratory, Universität Karlsruhe (TH), 2007.

[165] Eric Stiegeler. Prädiktions- und Einsatzplanungsverfahren zur effizienten Zustandsschätzung von Prozessketten (Prediction and Scheduling Methods for Efficient State Estimation of Supply Chains). Diploma Thesis, Intelligent-Sensor-Actuator Systems Laboratory, Universität Karlsruhe (TH), 2007.

Own Publications

[166] Dietrich Brunn, Felix Sawo, and Uwe D. Hanebeck. Efficient Nonlinear Bayesian Estimation based on Fourier Densities. In *Proceedings of the 2006 IEEE International Conference on Multisensor Fusion and Integration for Intelligent Systems (MFI 2006)*, pages 312–322, Heidelberg, Germany, September 2006.

[167] Dietrich Brunn, Felix Sawo, and Uwe D. Hanebeck. Informationsfusion für verteilte Systeme. In Jürgen Beyerer, Fernando Puente Leon, and Klaus-Dieter Sommer, editors, *Informationsfusion in der Mess- und Sensortechnik*, pages 75–90. Universitätsverlag Karlsruhe, September 2006.

[168] Dietrich Brunn, Felix Sawo, and Uwe D. Hanebeck. Nonlinear Multidimensional Bayesian Estimation with Fourier Densities. In *Proceedings of the 2006 IEEE Conference on Decision and Control (CDC 2006)*, pages 1303–1308, San Diego, California, December 2006.

[169] Dietrich Brunn, Felix Sawo, and Uwe D. Hanebeck. Modellbasierte Vermessung verteilter Phänomene und Generierung optimaler Messsequenzen — Model-based Reconstruction of Distributed Phenomena and Optimal Sensor Placement. *tm - Technisches Messen, Oldenbourg Verlag*, 3:75–90, March 2007.

[170] Julian Hörst, Felix Sawo, Vesa Klumpp, Uwe D. Hanebeck, and Dietrich Fränken. Extension of the Sliced Gaussian Mixture Filter with Application to Cooperative Passive Target Tracking. In *Proceedings of the 11th International Conference on Information Fusion (Fusion 2009)*, Seatle, Washington, July 2009.

[171] Marco F. Huber, Achim Kuwertz, Felix Sawo, and Uwe D. Hanbeck. Distributed Greedy Sensor Scheduling for Model-based Reconstruction of Space-Time Continuous Physical Phenomena. In *Proceedings of the 11th International Conference on Information Fusion (Fusion 2009)*, Seatle, Washington, July 2009.

[172] Vesa Klumpp, Felix Sawo, Uwe D. Hanebeck, and Dietrich Fränken. The Sliced Gaussian Mixture Filter for Efficient Nonlinear Estimation. In *Proceedings of the 11th International Conference on Information Fusion (Fusion 2008)*, Cologne, Germany, July 2008.

[173] Felix Sawo, Frederik Beutler, and Uwe D. Hanebeck. Decentralized State Estimation of Distributed Phenomena based on Covariance Bounds. In *Proceedings of the 17th IFAC World Congress (IFAC 2008)*, Seoul, Korea, July 2008.

[174] Felix Sawo, Dietrich Brunn, and Uwe D. Hanebeck. Parameterized Joint Densities with Gaussian and Gaussian Mixture Marginals. In *Proceedings of the 9th International Conference on Information Fusion (Fusion 2006)*, Florence, Italy, July 2006.

[175] Felix Sawo, Dietrich Brunn, and Uwe D. Hanebeck. Parameterized Joint Densities with Gaussian Mixture Marginals and their Potential Use in Nonlinear Robust Estimation. In *Proceedings of the 2006 IEEE International Conference on Control Applications (CCA 2006)*, Munich, Germany, October 2006.

[176] Felix Sawo, Masayuki Fujita, and Oliver Sawodny. Passivity–Based Dynamic Visual Feedback Control of Manipulators with Kinematic Redundancy. In *Proceedings of the 2005 IEEE Conference on Control Applications (CCA 2005)*, pages 1200–1205, 2005.

[177] Felix Sawo and Uwe D. Hanebeck. Bayesian Estimation of Distributed Phenomena. In Thomas C. Henderson, editor, *Computational Sensor Network*, chapter 9, pages 167–196. Springer-Verlag, May 2009.

[178] Felix Sawo, Thomas C. Henderson, Christopher Sikorski, , and Uwe D. Hanebeck. Sensor Node Localization Methods based on Local Observations of Distributed Natural Phenomena. In *Proceedings of the 2008 IEEE International Conference on Multisensor Fusion and Integration for Intelligent Systems (MFI 2008)*, Seoul, Republic of Korea, August 2008, (**Winner Best Paper Award**).

[179] Felix Sawo, Thomas C. Henderson, Christopher Sikorski, and Uwe D. Hanebeck. Passive Localization Methods exploiting Models of Distributed Natural Phenomena. In *Lecture Notes in Electrical Engineering (Collection of best papers from MFI 2008)*. Springer-Verlag, 2009 (to appear).

[180] Felix Sawo, Marco F. Huber, and Uwe D. Hanebeck. Parameter Identification and Reconstruction Based on Hybrid Density Filter for Distributed Phenomena. In *Proceedings of the 10th International Conference on Information Fusion (Fusion 2007)*, Quebec, Canada, July 2007.

[181] Felix Sawo, Vesa Klumpp, and Uwe D. Hanebeck. Simultaneous State and Parameter Estimation of Distributed-Parameter Physical Systems based on Sliced Gaussian Mixture Filter. In *Proceedings of the 11th International Conference on Information Fusion (Fusion 2008)*, Cologne, Germany, July 2008.

[182] Felix Sawo, Kathrin Roberts, and Uwe D. Hanebeck. Bayesian Estimation of Distributed Phenomena using Discretized Representations of Partial Differential Equations. In *Proceedings of the 3rd International Conference on Informatics in Control, Automation and Robotics (ICINCO 2006)*, pages 16–23, Setubal, Portugal, August 2006.

[183] Felix Sawo, Kathrin Roberts, and Uwe D. Hanebeck. Model-Based Reconstruction of Distributed Phenomena Using Discretized Representations of Partial Differential Equations. In *Lecture Notes in Electrical Engineering (Collection of best papers from ICINCO 2006)*. Springer-Verlag, 2008.